Badiou and Plato

An Education by Truths

A. J. Bartlett

EDINBURGH UNIVERSITY PRESS

Edinburgh University Press Ltd
22 George Square, Edinburgh

www.euppublishing.com

Typeset in 11/13 Sabon
by Servis Filmsetting Ltd, Stockport, Cheshire, and
printed and bound in Great Britain by
CPI Antony Rowe, Chippenham and Eastbourne

A CIP record for this book is available from the British Library

ISBN 978 0 7486 4375 2 (hardback)

Contents

Acknowledgments

This book is the result of several 'summers of Platonic love'. It owes everything to Angela Cullip and to Che, Strummer, Sunday and Jezebel: Plato awaits you just as he awaits us all! I cannot thank my friend Justin Clemens enough, not only for his support and intelligence but also for sharing with me the absolute conviction that 'the world never offers you anything other than the temptation to yield'. My greatest appreciation goes to Ray Brassier and Mladen Dolar for their generous critiques of an earlier version of this work. Merci, chaleureusement, Alain Badiou. Many thanks to Alex Ling, Jon Roffe, Jessica Whyte and Geraldine Kelder. This work is dedicated to the very much-missed Tristam Claremont: a true philosopher.

Abbreviations

PLATO

Apology	Ap.
Charmides	Chrm.
Cratylus	Crt.
Crito	Cri.
Euthydemus	Euthd.
Euthyphro	Euthphr.
Gorgias	Grg.
Hippias Major	Hp. Ma.
Laches	La.
Laws	L.
Lysius	Lys.
Meno	Men.
Parmenides	Prm.
Phaedo	Phd.
Phaedrus	Phdr.
Philebus	Phlb.
Protagoras	Prt.
Republic	R.
Sophist	Sph.
Statesman	Stm.
Symposium	Smp.
Theaeteus	Tht.
Timaeus	Ti.

BADIOU

BE	*Being and Event/L'Être et l'événement*
C	*Conditions*
CM	*The Concept of Model*
CT	*Court traité d'ontologie transitoire*

D	*Deleuze: The Clamor of Being*
E	*Ethics: An Essay on the Understanding of Evil*
HB	*Handbook of Inaesthetics*
IT	*Infinite Thought: Truth and the Return to Philosophy*
LM	*Logiques des mondes: l'être et l'événement, 2*
M	*Metapolitics*
MP	*Manifeste pour la philosophie*
OB	*On Beckett*
P	*Polemics*
SP	*Saint Paul: The Foundation of Universalism*
TC	*The Century*
TS	*Théorie du sujet*
TW	*Theoretical Writings*

'My friends, we must "chance our arm" as the saying is. If we are prepared to stake the whole constitution on a throw of 'three sixes" or "three ones", then, that is what we'll have to do, and I'll shoulder my part of the risk by giving a full explanation of my views on training and education, which we've now started to discuss all over again. However, the risk is enormous and unique.'

Plato, *Laws* (969a)

'Whatever is thought truly is immediately shared . . . whatever is understood is radically undivided. To know is to be absolutely and universally convinced.'

Alain Badiou, 'Mathematics and Philosophy'

'Why do you laugh? The name changed, the tale is told of you!'

Horace, *Satires*, Book I, Satire 1

Introduction: Trajectory

'And so not here only but in the journey of a thousand years of which I have told you, we shall fare well.' (R. 621d)[1]

'*C'est la vielle.*' (TS, 346)

'. . . you are already committed.' (Pascal, *Pensées*)

In a short meditation concerning the pedagogical relation between art and philosophy, Alain Badiou makes the claim that 'the only education is an education by truths' (HB, 15).[2] There are at least three key assumptions supporting this claim: the existence of truths; the existence of education; and the link between the two, a link that in fact requires that education be thought as something other than an adjunct to any institutional form. What we seek to do in this work is to enquire into the possibility of 'an education by truths'. If, as is the case for Badiou, truths are what force 'holes in knowledge', which interrupt, subvert and are subtracted from the circulating rule of opinion or the 'encyclopaedia' – for Badiou, the order, rule and currency of the 'state' – then what we are seeking has to be a non-state education. What we present here, through a new reading of the Platonic corpus, is an elaboration of what might constitute such an 'education', an education that, as by truths, has done with the state.

Badiou: Intervention and dialectic

Two 'methodological injunctions' bookend Alain Badiou's *Being and Event*. The first:

> The categories that this book deploys, from the pure multiple to the subject, constitute the general order of a thought such that it can be *practised* across the entirety of the contemporary system of reference. These categories are available for the service of scientific procedures just as they are for those of politics or art. They attempt

> to organise an abstract vision of the requirements of the epoch. (BE, 4/10)[3]

The second:

> It is possible to reinterrogate the entire history of philosophy, from its Greek origins on, according to the hypothesis of a mathematical regulation of the ontological question. [. . .] In particular, the genealogy of the doctrine of truth will lead to a signposting, through singular interpretations, of how the categories of the event and the indiscernible, unnamed, were at work throughout the metaphysical text. (BE, 435/475)

These injunctions serve to authorise our analysis and determine that the following enquiry is both dialectical and interventionist. It is interventionist because we are addressing the Platonic corpus with categories formally created outside of the Platonic text itself. We are putting these categories into practice in the Platonic corpus in order to produce a new conception of the import of these dialogues for thought, and particularly for the mode of thought of education. Or, more precisely, we are seeking to 'produce' from this intervention a *thinking of* education. One aspect of our argument is that this *thinking of* education subtends, and yet is foreclosed by, what comes to pass as educational discourse within any 'state' configuration. This disjunctive relation between *thought* and the *state* is recognisable in the dialogues – the suppression of Socrates' impious and corruptive discourse is the extant symbol of this – and it is entirely because it is that we address our investigation there. In a real sense, the Platonic corpus founds the history of western education, what education might be thought as, and at its heart is this disjunction between sophistry (education by opinion) and what is not sophistry (education by truths). This is what makes an analysis of Plato contemporary rather than anachronistic or historical. To intervene in the Platonic dialogues is to expose something of the contemporary situation, both for Plato and for us.

Our enquiry is dialectical because Badiou duly identifies his own project as a 'contemporary Platonism' (albeit heavily indebted to a variety of conditional figures from Mallarmé to Lacan, Cantor to Mao), at once faithful to the mathematical conditioning of thought, whereby the most rigorous thinking of being passes through the most contemporary discoveries in mathematics, and to the 'Platonic gesture' that declares 'there are truths', that there is more than opinion and that there will have been a body subject to this truth.

The attempt to produce a discourse on truth 'coincident' with – and yet not determined by – the most exacting thinking of being qua being – in Badiou's case, set and category theory – is what Badiou regards as his 'Platonism'. Plato thus provides Badiou with extensive resources for his own project. This is explicit in the Platonic institution of the founding divisions between opinion and truth, sophistry and wisdom. It is also implicit in that Plato's structural definition regarding what constitutes philosophical discourse – that it is *subtracted* from all forms of sophistic knowledge and is as such a practice of separation, division *and* invention – forms the basis for Badiou's contemporary project. Moreover, that Plato pursues this effort in dialogues concerned with the thinking of being, art, love and politics, which are, for Badiou, the four conditions for the existence of philosophy, the discourses wherein truths are played out, confirms the immanence of Badiou's work to Platonic discourse.

To reinsert Badiou's concepts and categories back into Plato is, in a certain sense, to return them anew to whence they came: a return, moreover, whose form is dialogical rather than repetitious, productive rather than comparative, whereby, in speaking to the Platonic corpus, it once again speaks back. In this way the Platonic corpus avoids the fate Plato describes for what is written down – the inability to answer back – and instead resumes again as dialogue, as *subject*. Nevertheless, this project is not without a certain Platonic resistance and we will see that the corpus is not simply transitive to the philosophy of Alain Badiou. However, Plato's extensive (in both senses) fidelity to Socrates requires that he associates with the Socratic figure certain conceptions that are not fully formed in the discourse of Socrates himself and so, in a similarly faithful fashion, we discern in Plato some consequences he was himself yet to draw.

What we hope to articulate by exploring the dialogues in this way, that is by deploying Badiou's 'platonic' categories back into the Platonic corpus, is the logical and implicative link between our primary axiomatic statement: that 'the only education is an education by truths' *and* what we might call its consequent yet coincident axiomatic statement that 'thought is nothing other than the desire to finish with the exorbitant excess of the state' (BE, 282/312). In conformity to Badiou's 'methodological injunctions', we will have articulated within the metaphysical text the concepts and categories that existed there unnamed.[4] In doing so, we will have also revivified, without corruption, the foundational trajectory that established the discourse which became the paradigm, however neglected or betrayed, of an 'education for all'. Again, crucially, we will see that education, as established in and by the Platonic corpus, cannot be in accord with the state. We will see that it follows an interventionist, radically subtractive trajectory, one that displaces and a-voids the mere transmission of established knowledge and the repetitious meanderings of the state, and the brutal yet arbitrary determinations its (lack of) knowledge prescribes, supporting instead the invention of a new form of thought.

Methodological considerations

When Badiou says 'by truths' he is referring explicitly to the 'concepts and categories' he has developed to support the programme of education. These concepts and categories have been developed most particularly in his second major work *Being and Event* and it is with these categories and concepts we work. While it is true that the subsequent publication of *Logiques des mondes: l'être et l'événement, 2*, has introduced a certain re-articulation of several of Badiou's important categories, it is still the case that, insofar as commentary, exegesis, critique and, most importantly, deployment of these categories is concerned, the implications of *Being and Event* are still far from being properly drawn. For this reason *Being and Event*, what Badiou calls his 'foundational' text, will remain our focus.

For the purposes of our enquiry we have abstracted from Badiou's *philosophical* project six categories that serve as the framework for discerning the form and trajectory of Plato's 'staging' of an education by truths. These are: state, site, event/intervention, fidelity, subject and the generic or indiscernible. Each of these six categories marks a link in what Badiou calls a 'truth process'. We devote a chapter to each category, establishing first its meaning and place within Badiou's schema and, secondly, demonstrating the form by which it can be seen to operate within the Platonic corpus in the service of Plato's subjective, 'Socratic' and non-state education. Working with these categories allows us to sidestep the three dominant approaches to Plato's corpus: the analytic, the hermeneutic and the critical. We are not engaged in a search for ultimate meaning, nor an exercise in definition, comparison and contrast, and we do not set out to offer an immanent or transcendental critique of the Platonic position set against some other assumption or philosophical enterprise – whether productive or reductive, announced or denied. Instead, we present the points, movements, spaces, breaks and aporias of the actual subjective trajectory demonstrated in the dialogues which, in Badiou's terms, manifest what is true for any situation. In short, we seek to affirm that which is there, central to the corpus but has hitherto remained at best at the margins of scholarship – whether hermeneutic, analytic, critical or categorical. To put it in terms of Badiou's earlier work, *Théorie du sujet*, what we seek to do is unfold a trajectory or establish a gesture *while at the same time* establishing the place of its displacement. As such, and under the direction of these categories, we ask a series of questions concerning the situation the Platonic corpus presents to us. Working backwards, we see that these questions implicate each other:

- What is the generic or indiscernible set that the corpus seeks to establish? In other words, what is the truth of the Platonic corpus?
- What is the state that must be avoided by this generic procedure, a procedure that is a step-by-step subtraction from this state?
- What is the subject body that supports the former and sustains the interruption of, or break with, the latter?
- By what prescriptions, what declarations of principle, does the subject proceed in order to constitute itself as the support of the new? In other words, what does the subject declare 'here and now'?
- On what basis does it make these declarations and institute the intervention into 'state knowledge', and in whose name? Thus, what is the name for the event or encounter that the subject decides for and declares itself 'faithful to'?
- What *is* the event of the encounter?
- What is the site within the dialogues which harbours the possibility for the transformation signalled by the very movement sketched in these questions, from the event to the indiscernible?

Immanent trajectory

By elaborating this immanent trajectory – from state to site to event to name to fidelity to subject to the generic – and by establishing the link between these concepts across the dialogues we subvert rather than avoid the incessant debates surrounding both the order of the dialogues and the 'problem of Socrates'. To trace this singular movement across the entirety of the corpus is to re-interrogate the Platonic corpus in a way that re-establishes the importance of the link between truth and education. In this way we can show that for

Plato the former is the fundamental condition of the very possibility of the latter.

Badiou's work offers the chance to link several aspects of the corpus – sophistry, education, the figure of Socrates, the claim to ignorance, the relation of Plato to the Socratic figure, and the status of the Republic as the '(void) *place* of philosophy', in an entirely new and, in regard to the sophistic state, 'incommensurable' way. In establishing the links between these aspects under the condition of Badiou's categories, we are able to see an education by truths actually *taking place*. Our analysis allows us to see that the Platonic corpus stages 'an education by truths' and that it does so under the injunction that this is the *only* education. In Platonic terms, education is only education if it is rigorously non-sophistic: or in Badiou's words, if it is 'something other than opinion' (HB, 15). To this end, we argue that Plato's corpus unfolds from within itself an education by truths, a radical transformation, and that the corpus entire, the 'subtractive inventive institution' of a non-sophistic discourse, provides this thought with its form. What makes this work distinct is precisely that we elaborate the trajectory of this thought in terms of its very invention. That is to say, we read the corpus in terms of its operation rather than coming to it as a fully formed sovereign set of concepts and categories. Indeed, the latter approach already betrays a certain historicism and more often than not a certain unavowed ideological taint.

Plato's lifelong task

In his last dialogue, the *Laws*, Plato makes a remark that directly expresses what we contend is at stake for Plato across the entirety of his corpus. He claims that what usually passes for education in any state, the teaching of skills for commercial prowess, technical skills which serve the whims of interest and power, or a training in debate which might ensure the subject a reputable place within the polis, does not 'deserve the name' of education. These 'teachings',[5] as Plato cynically refers to them in *Protagoras* (Prt. 313d), are a training which lacks wisdom or truth. It is not to say these skills have no use in the maintenance of the polis, constituted as it is, but that these teachings establish habit at the expense of decision, and rule at the expense of reason (cf. R. 492–4). Plato in no way considers this sophistic education nothing. Indeed, within the confines of the state it is practically everything. Sophistry, for Plato, and especially insofar as it sometimes realises what he calls 'right opinion', is an obstacle to truth that cannot simply be dispensed with, but must be worked through. In this regard we might say that for Plato education is the formal lack of inconsistency (Men. 97c). What we will see is that the lack of truth Plato identifies in 'state education' is not a *consequence* of these teachings, but is constitutive. In his exemplary, non-cynical fashion, Plato continues that whenever we see education traduced in such a manner and reduced to functioning as a servant of state interests, interests for whom truth is an irrelevance to the practicalities of power and pleasure, we must do all we can to (re-)establish education's proper form. In other words, we must establish education's fundamental constitution. Consequently, Plato continues, education should nowhere 'be despised, for when combined with great virtue, it is an asset of incalculable value. If it ever becomes corrupt, but can be put right again, this is a lifelong task which everyone should undertake to the limit of his strength' (L. 644a–b).

For Plato, if what the situation presents is not education, even though it dominates the use of this name, we should thereby extend all efforts to realising the (unknown) truth of this name. Consistent with the Socratic claim to ignorance – to not know what the sophist knows – we can say that, with this statement, Plato recognises that in the 'state of the Athenian situation' *there is* the *lack of a non-sophistic education*. This, for Plato, is the universal condition *for* education in the Athenian situation. As we will see, education is therefore axiomatically universal in its address and is, as such, founded on an equal yet, within the sophistic Athenian state, *unknown* capacity for reason. This alone makes it singular and Ideally *other* to what the state and its sophists profess. For the sophist, and this is what Plato calls his 'conceit', there is no lack of knowledge. Ultimately, this is because, for the state, true knowledge is predicated on interest. All knowledge is therefore in one form or another adequate to one's interest and – so the great sophistic maxim of relative interests contends – one is never not interested in interest.[6] We will demonstrate that it is Socrates, the only 'non-sophist' in the state of Athens (which is to say, for Athens itself, the singular figure of corruption) which marks the point of this 'lack'. To go a little further, the immanent lack of which Socrates, for 'sophistic-Athens', is the name becomes, under the force of the Platonic trajectory, the very 'local' mark of the transformative and universal capacity inherent in a 'non-sophistic education'. It is in this way that the name *and* the figure of Socrates is the key to Plato's education and to why the latter holds it must be by truths.

That Plato's declaration concerning what is true of education comes at the end of a series of dialogues whose singular goal has been 'to have the world turned upside down' – to use Callicles' accusation *against* the sophists as Plato intended – we take it as a sign of two things: that indeed a non-sophistic education is the central goal pursued by Plato across the corpus, and secondly, that this goal is *still* to be pursued today. After all the *Laws* ends with the 'Athenian' proposing to return to the question of education all over again should it be required (L. 969a). The implication is clear: it *is* and *will be* required. To this end, we will show that the Platonic corpus demonstrates the form and trajectory of such an education by truths and that only this education – or rather an education that takes the existence of truths as its constitutive and subjective basis – is worthy of the name. In this sense Plato is the first word *on* education and it is to this *we* must return.

Footnotes to Plato part 1: one divides into two

If we trace the history of Platonic scholarship, as distinct from the history of philosophy, from the nineteenth century we note that it has wrestled with a series of 'relations' prevalent in the dialogues: those between Plato and Socrates; between the Athens that condemned Socrates and the Athens he fought for and whose laws he dutifully followed; between the Republic as ideal city and as blueprint for a Platonic politics; between the sophist and philosopher; between forms and appearance; between the discursive and the poetic; between mathematics and debate; and so on. These relations and their variations have been staples of the last century or so of Plato studies and, as part of the tradition of 'footnotes to Plato', have influenced the history of philosophy itself.[7]

In this vein, the contemporary Plato scholar Terence Irwin has noted that the problems generated by these relations are difficult to track because Plato's work, Irwin claims, is 'unsystematic'.[8] He considers the dialogues to present a series of questions that go mostly unanswered. He argues that Plato deals only with discrete philosophical problems in one-off conversations: while the same problem may return in another dialogue, it will not necessarily be treated the same way; indeed, if some are to be believed, the orientation to the problem will change entirely. For Irwin, somewhat despairingly, yet at the same time in line with a notion cherished by some, the dialogues are read as questions that provoke only more questions. Irwin claims that, as the dialogues do not constitute a system, they are not philosophy in the sense that one might understand the work of Kant, Hegel and Aristotle. Putting aside the 'prejudice' against the dialogue form (and the concept of Form itself) that many Aristotelian-inflected Platonists appear to have, one wonders if perhaps a viable way of reading the dialogues that demonstrates their systematicity may not have yet been found.[9]

As we will see, for Plato, as he never tires of arguing, what is at stake in (his) Socratic discourse is not 'an academic quibble' (HB, 15 and P, 8) but a 'way of life'. As such, education is fundamental, constitutive and ongoing. However, if it is not by truths, that is to say 'tied down' such that it is in place *and* for all time, it is like the statues of Daedalus forever shifting position the better to accommodate the demands of perspective (Euthphr. 11b+; Men. 97e+). In other words, where the history of Platonic scholarship – as distinct from the history of philosophy – has seen the problems posed in the dialogues in terms of the category of relations and, as such, ultimately irreconcilable without recourse to transcendence, Plato conceives of these problems in terms of division: divisions whose non-relation must be traversed. This is the essence of his concept of participation – the rigorous and formal procedure of establishing the truth of non-relation subject to the conditions of its emergence. In Plato, in philosophy, to think the situation is to 'stage an impossible relation' and establish it affirmatively 'as the negation of all relations' (P, 9). As such 'the only education, an education by truths' is that which proceeds, step by step and formally, from the *point* of the immanent, existing division or non-relation between that which is and that which is not – the latter, as Plato attests in the *Sophist*, being no less *real* than the former.

This is contrary to sophistry, which both Plato and Badiou argue is predicated on relations that are linguistically constructed, whose presence is poetically attested and that accords ultimately with particular interests and that therefore *cannot* constitute a *way* of life (R. 600b). What is lacking in sophistry – a lack certain aspects of Platonic scholarship *reproduce* – is precisely the decision *for* such a 'way of life'. Significantly, sophistry, at all times, prides itself on this very lack and insofar as sophistry, rhetorically, establishes itself as in dissent from traditional authority, it has the appearance or semblance of a radical virtue. This *appearance*, which signifies precisely its lack of truth and thus, ultimately, its coincidence with the 'state' (Plato is explicit about this), is exactly what prompts Badiou to say – and in the context of education – that 'when one abdicates universality, one obtains universal horror' (TS, 197). It is on the presumption of the former, a presumption which is constitutive, that the state works its 'inclusive' pedagogical regimes, training the youth in an interest in interest. The clash, to put it at its most basic, is between universalism or the rigorous formalisation of that which is unbound from such pedagogical regimes, and a false universalism which is predicated precisely on the prohibition of unbinding (BE, 109/125–6). As we will see, this can be said as the *Republic* against the Homeric or, if you like, of the evental 'unfolding' against the fold – the break against the return. The entire problem, then, is not so much an opposition between a non-sophistic and a sophistic education but in establishing the real break between an education for all as the immanent realisation of that which a collective is capable, and the determination, by default, of its impossibility. Conceptually speaking, the radical imposture of sophistry is predicated on the conservative conceit regarding the inexistence of incommensurability; for the non-sophistic discourse of Plato, incommensurability, as he demonstrates in *Meno*, is the sole criterion for thought. From a Platonic point of view, then, it is necessary to break with sophistry *and* with those aspects of Platonic scholarship which are themselves coincident with such sophistry. Plato's fundamental claim, *a claim that links the entirety of the dialogues*, is that 'non-sophistry is possible'.

Platonists and/or anti-Platonists

In his book on Deleuze, Badiou quotes the old proverb 'tell me what you think of Plato and I will tell you who you are' (D, 101). The history of philosophy could be duly divided into Platonists and anti-Platonists. Philosophies could even be divided into their 'Platonic' and 'anti-Platonic' parts. Avowed Platonists might in fact be, on examination, un-Platonic[10] and avowed anti-Platonists might in fact be more Platonic than they know. In truth, these divisions are themselves extensions of the type of divisions the history of philosophy has discerned within Plato. Our enquiry naturally brings us into contact with this history. On the one hand, then, we take our lead from what we can conceive of as the immanent Platonism of every philosophy. This amounts to the fact that every major philosopher has been constrained to deal with education and to do so in a way that ties their philosophical project to education, and how, in each case, what they conceive of as education is consistently at a distance from the state of (their own particular) situation. On the other hand, and in order to rethink the Platonic corpus in the way we do below, we have to separate ourselves from the contemporary anti-Platonism – and this includes those Platonists who, on reflection, are less Platonist than they presume.

Footnotes to Plato part 2: Immanent Platonism

If we look to some exemplary figures of the philosophical tradition post-Plato – Aristotle, Augustine, Descartes, Spinoza, Leibniz, Hobbes, Marx, Nietzsche, Lacan, for example[11] – we can see in each the very Platonic desire to establish education's proper form (L. 644a). As it is from this trajectory that we can claim some legitimacy for our project, it is worth highlighting, albeit in a very reductive form. What matters, however, is the principled division each figure addresses to their situation and, as such, our reduction should be taken as exemplary. We will take them in the order given above.

Aristotle, despite his rejection of Plato's concept of Form – a rejection whose influence on scholasticism Descartes will in turn reject – recognises nevertheless that truths are in 'immanent rivalry' to the state. Any state, that is, where truth has no place. Aristotle argues that, even as education is known to be what supports the perseverance of any regime, correct or incorrect, good or bad (i.e. in accord or discord with 'nature'),[12] any education by truths, in Aristotle's sense, requires a state which accords truth (happiness)[13] its highest achievement, and any such state is the realisation of a truthful procedure – the realisation through practical reason of the truth of one's nature.[14]

Augustine's own re-education is predicated on a break with the education that led him to a position in the state. After his 'event style' awakening,[15] he formally articulates the division as between 'rhetorical splendour' and 'what is actually said'.[16] In this way education presented itself to Augustine as a philosophical problem in its own right. It became a question of transformation and not merely of transmission – from belief *to* understanding. Augustine not only comes to think education non-sophistically, he embodies its movement – literally and textually.

Descartes, not dissimilarly, establishes a deductive and meditative method whose consequences demonstrate that a real break with Aristotelian logicism – *disputatio*, 'the schoolmen' – has taken place.

The 'logic of the schools', for Descartes, is 'nothing but a dialectic which teaches ways of expounding to others what one already knows or even of holding forth without judgement about things one does not know'.[17] In rejecting all forms of the *authority* of the senses, all that one already presumes to know (and pretends to) –adequately, experientially – Descartes also rejects all that he has learned hitherto. To doubt again the entirety of what one is taught is to break with the 'dubiousness of the whole superstructure' and begin again 'from the very foundations'.[18]

Even Hobbes, steeped as he is in the dominant form of education of his day (he is a pedagogue and teacher of rhetoric to rich youth), nevertheless contends that the Socratic-cum-Pauline ideal of subtractive, subjective enquiry ('a free education freely given and freely taken') *is* education. As such, an education predicated on the immanent distinction between free enquiry – something unseen in the contemporary university, he claimed, controlled as it was by 'the heathen politician and the deceiving priests alike' – and common opinion. That is, free enquiry *into* common opinion. Thus, if opinion is the discourse on what is common, it is not the 'truth of commonality'. The latter is the critical factor in Hobbes' 'social contract'.[19]

For Spinoza, joy is the word for right education and is to be understood in terms of a movement of a body from a lesser to a greater activity – from imagination to intellect. This 'transformation' is not predicated on a particular knowledge. On the contrary, for Spinoza, there is no knowledge a priori of that which a body is capable. Its capabilities will have been realised in regard to what such a body *encounters*.[20] What is lacking in any individual is not *capacity* but precisely the *encounter* that breaks with the established limits of knowledge and that offers the real possibility of transformation, a transformation whereby the fictive currency of day-to-day living is stripped of its representational power.[21]

Leibniz is paradigmatic for this debate, for in a real sense he embodies the sophist/non-sophist division. On the one hand, he is 'faithful' to the Platonic notion of the intelligible, its link to the universal and its dialectical relation to the apparent or 'manifest particular', thus rationally comprehending the distinction between two educative regimes. On the other, he is a courtier par excellence, assuming the political state of things as they are, attempting with all his skill to make his way within this state, and, as an educator himself, seeking to bring enlightenment to those who rule rather than to have rule itself subject to enlightenment.[22] Nevertheless,

Leibniz philosophically – and this is where his true educational effect lay – understood that the truth of the subject lay in its capacity for thought. For Leibniz, the subject is the site of the dialectical passage between politics (the state and its functions), on the one hand, and *caritas* on the other. Education is what circulates between them, via this subject who comes into being as such through this dialectic. The truly educated subject is enlightened by reason, Leibniz claims, only insofar as the expression of this reason takes the form of *caritas* – or giving without 'interest' (Grace, in Pauline terms). For Leibniz (despite his personal interests of course), education, after the Platonic fashion, was only 'by truths' and thus '*for* all'.

On the face of it, Nietzsche is no disciple of Plato. Nevertheless, he situates an education by truths in the division of the philosophical act. For Nietzsche, what a true educator does is to liberate. Rather than this being revealed as some form of narcissistic self-realisation, for Nietzsche it was something one came to, something set higher over and above the situation which one inhabited at the day-to-day level – the self *as* subject we might say. Nietzsche explicitly affirms *education* against what he sees passing for education under direction of the state. The state, he says, is 'a mystagogue of culture, and while it advances its purposes, it compels each of its servants to appear before it only with the torch of universal state education in their hands: in whose restless light they are supposed to recognise again it itself as the highest goal, as the reward of all their educational exertions.' What the state requires is 'a speedy education so that one may quickly become a money earning being'.[23] By contrast, Nietzsche contends, 'your true educators and formative teachers reveal to you that the true, original meaning and basic stuff of your nature is something completely incapable of being educated or formed and is in any case difficult of access, bound and paralysed'.[24] Thus education is the realisation of an immanent and unknown capacity. For Nietzsche (who on this point is gladly a sophist), this pertains to the individual against the state, while for Plato, for whom, constitutionally, the individual and the collective coincide in the Idea, what is unbound from the state is 'for all'.[25]

Concerning Lacan, an avowed 'anti-philosopher' and, as such, for Badiou, the 'educator to every philosophy to come', it suffices for our purposes to note his contention that the 'university discourse' is the contemporary pretender to the 'discourse of the master'. In Lacan's articulation of the 'four discourses' – Master, University, Hysteric and Analyst – the University discourse dominates when 'knowledge' occupies the place of power or when knowledge, its 'construction' and 'transmission' determine the form of the social bond. Whereas in the Master's discourse the master struggles to appropriate the surplus (value and/or jouissance) inherent to the work of the slave – the slave having been put to work as slave by the master – in the University discourse 'neutral' or 'objective' knowledge signifies both the direction of the subject – subject to this social bond (the subject of such knowledge is divided between the knower and the 'student') – and, in turn, the necessity of appropriating all *new* knowledge to its 'hegemonic' discursive control.[26] Its field is the 'encyclopaedia', the *rationalisation* of all knowledge. Ultimately, this is done for the sake of the master.[27] In classical (and dare we say) *philosophical* form, Lacan reaffirms and reinvigorates, the constitutive division between truth – impotent, yet *existent*, as that which will have interrupted the 'social bond' – and knowledge. Knowledge, as such, is *not all* there is.[28]

What we see, then, in all of the aforementioned thinkers is, despite their extraordinary differences, a just as extraordinary conviction that a true education must go beyond what is good for the state. It is precisely this conviction which we not only wish to identify as centrally at work in philosophy from Plato to Lacan, but to show, by means of Badiou's categories, how and under what pressures Plato himself establishes and exemplifies it in his Dialogues. In order to do this, however, it will first be necessary to 'deconstruct' the opinions that currently encase the Platonic corpus.

Part 3: Contemporary anti-Platonist Platonism

Even as we draw a certain Platonic form from within this philosophical history it is obvious that the history of philosophy has maintained an ambiguous relationship to Plato, both internally and externally. This ambiguity leaves a complex mark on the contemporary philosophical scene such that, for Badiou, philosophy since Nietzsche can be summarised under the term 'anti-Platonist'. It is precisely from this anti-Platonism, whose condition is 'Platonic', that 'Plato must be restored'.

In his most recent seminars entitled 'Plato *for* Today', Badiou repeats and extends the six categories of anti-Platonism he identified in 1989's *Manifesto for Philosophy*: the vitalist (Nietzsche, Bergson, Deleuze), the analytic (Russell, Wittgenstein, Carnap), the Marxist, the existentialist (Kierkegaard, Sartre), the Heideggerian, and that of the 'political philosophers' (Arendt and Popper).[29] He says, 'ultimately the 20th century reveals a constellation of multiple and heteroclite anti-Platonisms'. Taken together 'their anti-Platonism is incoherent' but what unites them is that each ostensibly accuses Plato of being ignorant of something essential to philosophy and 'this something is identified with the real itself' (change for the vitalists, language for the analytics, concrete social relations for the Marxists, negation for the existentialists, thought in as much as it is other than understanding for Heidegger, democracy for the political philosophers). In his most succinct presentation of contemporary anti-Platonism, Badiou not only outlines its general thread but notes that it is itself constitutive of what is understood by 'Platonism'.

This 'Platonism' is:

> that common figure, the contemporary montage of opinion, or configuration that circulates from Heidegger to Deleuze, from Nietzsche to Bergson, but also from Marxists to positivists, and which is still used by the counterrevolutionary new philosophers ('Plato as the first of the totalitarian master thinkers'), as well as by neo-Kantian moralists. 'Platonism' is the great fallacious construction of modernity and post-modernity alike. It serves as a type of general negative prop: it only exists to legitimate the new under the heading of anti-Platonism. (D, 101–2)[30]

As in Plato's Athens, the influence of contemporary anti-Platonism extends across the contemporary 'system of reference' into the fields of politics, love, mathematics, art and of course today's 'state education' (SP, 12 and LM, 72–8). In *Conditions* and in *Infinite Thought*, Badiou elaborates three predominant 'philosophical' tendencies derived from this anti-Platonist collective: (1) the hermeneutic tendency, whose central concept is interpretation; (2) the analytic, whose concept is the 'rule'; and (3) the postmodern, concerned with the deconstruction of totalities in favour of the diverse and the multiple. Badiou shows that what they have in common is a commitment to language, its capacities, rules and diversity such that language is the 'great transcendental of our times' (IT, 46). The obvious consequence is a commitment to the end of metaphysics and thus philosophy since Plato (IT, 45–6). Plato thus marks the point of an inception that must be reversed. Contemporary 'philosophy' or anti-Platonism, he says, effectively 'puts the category of truth on trial' (IT, 46).

Badiou's position here is to invert this accusation and argue that it is precisely Plato's conception of what *there is* that matters and what there is are truths. Badiou agrees with two claims that arise from the contemporary critiques: that Being is essentially multiple (MP, 85) and that Plato does mark a singular and decisive point in the history of thought. Here Heidegger as much as Deleuze is a central figure of reference. However, concerning the first point of agreement, to say being is multiple today is to say it falls under the regime of mathematics qua ontology and not 'language'. In regard to the second point, Plato is to be understood as the *incitement to thought*, through whom thought is given 'the means to refer to itself as philosophical' and thus 'independently of any total contemplation of the universe or any intuition of the virtual' (D, 102). Plato is decidedly not the moment at which thought turns to despair. For Badiou, the rejection of the linguistic (re)turn is predicated on the existence 'of a regime of the thinkable that is inaccessible to this total jurisdiction of language'. What is required therefore is a 'Platonic gesture' whose condition is a 'Platonism of the multiple'.

Anti anti-Platonism

In this work what we in effect do is combine the Platonic trajectory noted above as current to the history of philosophy with a commitment to anti-anti-Platonism – in all its above forms. This is not to say we do not have to pass through them. Without going into the specifics of each tendency, we will directly confront various instances of each. For example, we will contend with Derrida's Heideggerian-influenced interpretation of Plato's 'logos', showing not that Derrida is wrong per se but that the concept of exchange he deploys is already sophistic. Indirectly, we will demonstrate the invalidity of Deleuze's contention that philosophy, under the injunction of the reversal of Platonism, 'means to make the simulacra rise and to affirm their rights among icons and copies.'[31] Indeed, the entire problem for Plato and thus of an education by truths is that the simulacrum *is* risen and gives the state its rule. Plato's discourse is not a sovereign discourse in the sense that it denies being to what exists. Instead, firstly, it is a discourse that precisely has no place in the contemporary polis and, as such, seeks only to delineate its place as the place of all. What falls outside such a place does so by consequence of its passion for interest – the simulacrum of truth.

While Badiou's declaration that 'the only education is an education by truths' is immediately comparable to Heidegger's claim that 'truth is the essence of education,'[32] the two are ultimately incompatible in that for Heidegger, Plato, within a 'single train of thought' and via a certain treatment of the idea, moves 'the' definition of truth to one in which truth is established as adequatory power; truth is established, he says, as 'correct gaze'. Speaking from his own present Heidegger says, 'for a long time now in Western thinking, "truth" has meant the agreement of the representation in thought with the thing itself: *adaequatio intellectus et rei.*'[33] For Badiou, the Platonic concept par excellence is 'participation' and most decidedly not representation, which, for Badiou is the form par excellence of the state (BE, 36).[34] In this context, Platonism, as Badiou conceives it, is both the 'knowledge of ideality' and 'the knowledge that access to ideality is only through that which participates in ideality' (CM, 92).[35] Or: 'the Idea is the occurrence in beings of the thinkable' (BE, 36). In this sense, Plato, maintaining the 'co-belonging' or 'ontological commensurability' of 'the knowing mind and the known' is heir to Parmenides' injunction 'that it is the same to think as to be' (TW, 49). In a move foreign to Heidegger and the hermeneutic method *tout court*, Badiou reinvigorates a theory of the subject as generic participation and it is in this manner that we will track the Platonic invention of an avowedly non-representative education (representation being 'a long way from reality') (R. 598b). For both Badiou and Plato mathematics provides the discursive model for the rigorous and thoughtful delimiting of representation, adequation and interpretation and thus for the productive refusal to submit thought itself to the rule of grammar, the charms of rhetoric, the pluralities of meaning and the pleasures of sense or the comforts of majority. It is with regard to this that Badiou himself quotes Plato from the *Cratylus*: 'we philosophers begin not with words but with things'.

Among contemporary Plato scholars Gregory Vlastos continues to hold a pre-eminent position. As Alexander Nehamas and Debra Nails contend, whether contemporary analytic scholars agree or disagree with Vlasto's findings, they are in a real sense all conditioned by his formulation of what is called the problem of Socrates.[36] Two points coalesce in Vlastos' work to give his Platonism an ultimately anti-Platonic force. He resolutely separates a 'Socratic' from a 'Platonic' discourse. Linked to this determination is an equally resolute, though not necessarily conceptually consistent, chronological or developmental ordering of the dialogues such that we have 'early', 'middle' and 'late' works of Plato. The distinguishing measure for Vlastos is, in essence, 'how much' Plato is in each, which is to say, what is the discernible influence of the 'geometric paradigm'? For Vlastos, the good Plato is the Plato who wrote Socratic dialogues wherein the voice of the master is clearly heard; the bad Plato, the one who ushers in a political tyranny, à la Karl Popper (among many others), is the Plato who succumbs, as Vlastos puts it, to the seductions of mathematics. As we will argue, this link between the effect of mathematical discourse and political tyranny, as much as anything else, demonstrates how little Vlastos understands mathematics, by which we mean that 'mathematics thinks' (TW, 50), and, moreover, the philosophy established on the basis of its existence as a discourse which is not bound by opinion. Indeed, that mathematics is not opinion (and in a related context, not subject to the a priori laws of logic) is the crux of the problem for Vlastos – as we will see.

Our argument is consistent with the history of philosophy insofar as it is inextricably linked to education. This is the fundamental Platonic motif present in all philosophies: this, whether these philosophies are ultimately exposed as sophistry or anti-philosophy by virtue of Badiou's delimitation of the field. At the same time, by tracking the educational theme in the dialogues under the direction of Badiou's categories, we demonstrate, against the trajectory of anti-Platonism, explicitly denominated as such since Nietzsche (but really since Aristotle), a new form of the link between the divisions already mentioned – being and appearing, truth and knowledge, model and copy, education and sophistry – and across the dialogues themselves, such that, as a consequence of the formal axiom that an education be *by truths*, a (non-state) system of sorts emerges. It becomes possible to suggest that education is the foundational theme of the corpus, in that every problem tackled in the dialogues, each conversation, each intervention by Plato in the predominantly sophistic terrain of politics, art, being or love is directed towards the problem of an education by truths. We can then demonstrate that despite the variations of Plato's approach in the different dialogues – variations that give rise to anti-Platonic hopes – the goal is always the same: to undo the sophistic matrix which the Athenian state presents of itself and to insist on the primacy of truth over victory, of knowledge over opinion and of the courage to go on in pursuit of these aims rather than subordinate oneself to a way of life ruled by the sophistic character of the state.

BADIOU'S *DECISION*

This seems a good point to say what we are *not* doing and why. By now it is a staple of all secondary literature on Badiou's work to mention the fundamental decision which lies at its heart: the decision that 'mathematics is ontology', that set theory inscribes what can be presented of being qua being, and that, in doing so, it shows that being qua being is infinite multiplicity, pure inconsistency and that any philosophy today must be conditioned by the rigorous 'paradox' that 'the one is not' and that '*the* nothing is'. The properly philosophical question that results is: 'how is something new possible if every situation is circumscribed by nothing on the one hand and by its state on the other?' What we will not be doing here is rehearsing either the ontology itself or Badiou's metaontological justifications for his 'decision'. That set theory *is* ontology is a fundamental assumption. It alone thinks the being of this situation, whose state we propose to examine and whose 'interruption' we expose. What we *are* assuming is simply that Badiou is right to (Platonically) conceive of the relation between philosophy and ontology and mathematics in the way he does.

However, a few remarks are in order because, for Badiou, this is not an assumption: it is a *decision*. Not unlike Sartre's notion of the choice, for Badiou, to decide is to think, to become 'subject', and what Badiou's philosophy constitutes is the elaboration of the consequences of *this* decision regarding contemporary mathematics. In a certain sense, this decision frees philosophy to re-begin its task of discerning that which becomes true for any situation and under various conditions, separated from the temptation to produce a knowledge of these truths in their essence. Badiou determines that his project, by properly subjecting itself to contemporary mathematics – a discourse that thinks 'essence' *as* existence – avoids the problems associated with the 'great modern sophistry' of the past century or so (C, 76): the hermeneutic, the analytic and the 'post-modern' (IT, 42). These, to recap, share two things in common: they all in some form declare 'the end of philosophy', the end of 'the classical conception of truth', and they each in their way declare language to be 'the fundamental site of thought' and, as such, 'meaning replaces the classical conception of truth' (IT, 46–7). Thus the decision that 'mathematics is ontology' allows Badiou to rethink the links between the classical categories of being, truth and subject in an entirely new way, one attentive to not just how mathematics thinks but also to *what it is* thinking. This 'new way' is itself subtracted from 'great modern sophistry' whose links to 'great ancient sophistry' are obvious enough.

Whether Badiou ultimately proves his case (if such proof is at all possible, being strictly speaking 'undecidable') regarding set theory being ontology or not, Badiou systematically and rigorously lays down the rationale which this decision demands and for which *his* philosophy provides the trace (TW, 82). Thus what *we* assume as the starting point of our enquiry is, on Badiou's part (as, perhaps, with Plato and Descartes before him), no assumption at all.

Let's explore this a little. For Badiou, as for Plato, mathematics is 'foundational'. It is *the* singular discourse which 'in one and the same gesture, breaks with the sensible and posits the intelligible.' Critically, it exists already as *the* discourse which is not subject to *doxa* or opinion, which precisely denies, *by* its formal existence, the right of *doxa* to elevate its form into the 'truth of that era' (TW, 29). Mathematics does this because its statements are non-linguistic, formal and apodictic. Whether this is 'really' the case, or even, 'if it is', what this 'means', is irrelevant here: the point for Badiou is that philosophy must break with opinion and this is the most powerful way to do it, by relying on a crucial discourse that exceeds philosophy itself. For Badiou, philosophy, which thinks truths, truths not being opinion (meaning, language games, the site of the ineffable, etc.), must submit itself to such a discourse. Badiou's decision amounts to accepting that a discourse exists not subject to *doxa* in any form, and that does therefore, rationally and consistently, think the being of situations and the truths that 'found' them. Philosophy, the thinking of truths, must be *conditioned* by such 'thinking' which means simply that its role is to elaborate, in a discourse specific to this elaboration, the implications for all thought of the possibility of a discourse, and even perhaps a 'way of life', which is not, fundamentally at least, subject to opinion or *doxa* alone. Such 'knowledge', he says,

> with its moderated rule, its policed immanence to situations and its transmissibility, is the ordinary regime for the relation to being under circumstances in which it is not the time for a new temporal foundation, and in which the diagonals of fidelity are somewhat deteriorated for lack of complete belief in the event they prophesise. (BE, 294/325)

For Badiou, the establishment that 'there are truths' is at the same time the disestablishment of the very doxa, opinion, knowledge, the 'encyclopaedia' which give the state its 'present' 'pattern' (to use Plato' terms). What we propose is that, for Plato, given the sophistic conditions that pertained in the Athenian state, it was time for a new 'temporal foundation' and Socrates was the figure whose 'diagonal' – which is to say 'incommensurable' – trajectory within the city state signals the re-constitution of that time.

Establishing the effects of an encounter as a transformation

Whether Badiou's philosophical concepts are verified by set theory or not and whether his concepts are legitimated in terms of set theory is not our concern. This may seem evasive, but in order to carry out our investigation of the dialogues as a situation in which an education by truths takes place we will simply take Badiou's ontological condition at face value. However, in exploring the dialogues in this way, we are examining whether the conceptual elaboration grounded in Badiou's decision is indeed consistent and operable and so we do, indirectly, offer a check on their veracity. We will have occasion to explain certain philosophical conceptualisations by recourse to Badiou's articulation of this ontology, and we will direct the reader to Badiou's ontological explanations as a matter of course; however, as we said, we will not seek to justify the initial decision.

Treating Badiou's categories heuristically allows us to intervene in the Platonic corpus in order to 'see *what is* there', to see *how* what is there is there. For Plato, clearly, there is no category called the 'site', articulated and defined as such, no category of the 'event' or the 'generic'. Rather, what Badiou's particular and formal conceptions allow us to do is recognise that which is at work in the dialogues *as* a site, *as* the event and so on, and it allows us to forge a new link between the Platonic site, its event and its subject. Something that is there in Plato – indeed, central to Plato – may only be illuminated through such a method. Thus we achieve a new or renewed understanding of the dialogues but, more importantly, we can now see an 'education by truths' at work, and understand why for Plato it is the only form education takes. In sum, our deployment of the categories in the Platonic 'metaphysical text' is an exercise in exposing their very existence there. In other words, and to reiterate, our claim is that at the very heart of western education is the injunction that an education *is only* by truths which *cannot* be that which is a priori set to serve the particularities and vagaries of contemporary forms of power, of interest, consensual or majority opinion – neither of the individual nor the state – nor that which provides for the knowledge of the link between the two. In short, for Plato the question of education remains as that which *forcefully* avoids the sophistic limit and yet *is* for all.

Finally, it is then possible to re-interrogate the conditions of this division, what is constitutive of and supported by the dialogues, with categories and concepts that can re-open this foundational division to our times. In this way it might force a rethinking of the centrality of education to Plato's corpus and force a rethinking of education along the lines of a Platonic question: what is education? This is not to say that education has gone un-thought in relation to Plato, but rather that it has been over-thought. The predominant mode of thinking education in relation to Plato's work has been contained within a pseudo-Aristotelian logic of categorisation and utility wherein the curricular prescriptions have, Daedalus-like, been excised from the *body* for redeployment, and the figure of Socrates has been rendered the exemplary pedagogue for this curriculum with a Rorty-style ironic twist producing an endless variety of 'imitators' who make up what we might call the 'history of the classroom'. For us, on the contrary, the Platonic corpus is nothing less than 'an education by truths', and as a body of thought conditioned by its Socratic event, the encounter with 'sophistics'[37] in all its imitative manifestations, it reflects the immanent trajectory of 'thought' established singularly and over again in each dialogue. This is our contention and it is our position that, given the contemporary conjuncture, such a thinking of the dialogues, wherein education can only be *by truths* and consequently cannot be the support of the state, can only be established by thinking through the philosophical inventions of Alain Badiou. In doing so we realise an essentially Platonic definition: 'Education consists in establishing the effects of an encounter as a transformation'. We will see that education is the site *for* this *encounter*; its *effects* are *established* via the Platonic intervention at this site; and the *transformation* of the situation in its 'entirety' is registered in the generic construction of the ideal non-state, the Republic.

Notes

1. Plato usually begins his Epistles with the salutation 'welfare'. This, he says, is how he begins letters to friends. However, in Letter III (whose authenticity is in doubt), addressed to Dionysius, Plato uses the word χαιρειν (from χαιρω) which is here translated as 'Greetings'. Plato then

meditates on this greeting form saying it is a salutation concerning the senses – pleasure and pain. More literally, it means to 'rejoice' or 'be glad' or 'joyful'. Plato says that he has heard that Dionysius addressed this 'fawning' greeting to the god at Delphi. He remarks on the folly of this as gods are far removed from such concerns and adds that, it is a greeting not fit for men either, as measuring life by the dictates of pleasure and pain does more harm than good. Plato says, 'Greetings to you! May you continue the pleasant life of a tyrant!' The obvious implication is that he and Dionysius are not friends (L. II. 315bc). For Plato, this is not personal per se. Rather, Dionysius proves over and again that he is no friend of reason or of the concept. *This* makes it impossible for him to be Plato's 'friend'. This is the theme of the entire corpus. As we will argue, the *Republic* is founded on the egalitarian maxim that 'friends have all things in common' and this is what Plato means by 'welfare'. Unless otherwise stated all translations of Plato are from Plato, *Complete Works*. The standard abbreviations are used throughout.

2. This is Alberto Toscano's translation of Badiou's 'il n'y a d'éducation que par les vérités' from *Petit manuel d'inesthétique*, p. 29. The word 'by' could be substituted with 'through' but conceptually it would make no difference. For a different opinion, see Alex Ling, *Badiou and Cinema*.
3. The page numbers of the French edition appear second inside the brackets.
4. Related to the terms of Plato's unequal line we can see there is the impasse of belief (*pistis*) founded on the imagination (*eikasia*); a decision at the point of this impasse of undecideability which engenders its thought (*dianoia*) and whose trajectory the subject invents as it undertakes doing so *in its name* and then there is the generic extension, the Republic, which marks the veracity of the truth inherent to the procedure. In other words it is the insistence of its understanding or *noēsis* (see R. 509de.)
5. The Greek word is μαθήμασιν, referring to 'that which is learnt' or a 'lesson'. In the text Socrates is replying to Hippocrates, who in reply to Socrates' claim that the sophist is a 'merchant who peddles provisions upon which the soul is nourished' asks, 'But what is the soul nourished on?' Guthrie's translation is: 'what it learns'.
6. This is the maxim of Protagoras: 'Of all things the measure is Man, of the things that are, that they are and of the thing that are not, that they are not' (quoted in Jacqueline De Romilly, *The Great Sophists of Periclean Athens*, p. 98).
7. 'The safest general characterization of the European philosophical tradition is that it consists of a series of footnotes to Plato. I do not mean the systematic scheme of thought which scholars have doubtfully

extracted from his writings. I allude to the wealth of general ideas scattered through them' (A. N. Whitehead, *Process and Reality*, p. 39).

8. Terence Irwin, *Plato's Moral Theory*, ch. 1.
9. In the notes to *Logiques des Mondes* Badiou asserts that all contemporary anti-Platonists, those 'doctrinaires of sense' who oppose 'mathematicsastion', be they hermeneuticists or sophists, are all, at base 'Aristotelians' (LM, 548/522). Debra Nails makes the point that many contemporary 'Platonists' read Plato through Aristotelian eyes (*Agora, Academy, and the Conduct of Philosophy*, p. 224).
10. See TA, especially pp. 49–58.
11. Given the ubiquity of this division in the history of philosophy, these names are essentially arbitrary. We know, for example, that Kant, with his concern for the faculties, was constrained by this; Schopenhauer was explicit in his contention that the modern academician was a sophistic character chastened to pursue reward – victory in Plato's sense – over truth; Hegel argued that the very possibility of speculative philosophy was at stake in such division. The same refrain runs through the history of philosophical enquiry, German, French and English, continental and analytic. The difference for us is that Plato founds his philosophical institution, the *Republic*, by this division. Since Kant perhaps, this division has been reproduced *within* the Academy but only for the purposes of avowing its lack. Secondly, we should note that, as philosophy already had no place within the Athenian sophistic state, Plato founded the Academy *outside* the city walls. Again, the post-Academy Academy has hitherto found itself well within the state walls even as it carries within it this foundational division. For an excellent summary overview of the institution since Kant see Justin Clemens, *The Romanticism of Contemporary Theory*.
12. Aristotle, 'Politics', Book VII 1337a10–30, in *The Complete Works of Aristotle*, p. 2121.
13. Aristotle, 'Politics', Book VII 1338a4.
14. It is of course no coincidence that Aristotle's influence on what we know as scholasticism was so profound. That, for Aristotle, the ideal is the proper realisation of that which is eternally present (rather than the mark of subjective participation as it is for Plato) accords more readily with the post-Augustinian Christian telos albeit one whose idealist intensity was modified to suit the temper of the time by Aquinas' rationalist and particularistic appropriation (see Pierre Pellegrin, 'The Aristotelian way', in Sara Ahbel-Rappe and Rachana Kamtekar (eds), *A Companion to Socrates*, p. 242). The problem in Aristotle's conception, as distinct from Plato, is the very conception of the form of the originary relation that organises the 'inhabitants of a situation'. The true nature of this relation, inherently hierarchical for Aristotle and his Christian adjuncts, whose unfolding was already inscribed in its origin,

is opposed by those we would regard as Platonist in their conception of the 'properly human capacity' – as Badiou has called it – the 'capacity for thought'. Reductively stated, for the Aristotelian, inequality is the generic or just state of man ((as with Protagoras) one is never *transformed* in Aristotle – it is his greatest fear – one is only improved) while for the Platonist, justice or generic equality is the axiomatic *starting* point. For Aristotle, the free man realises his perfection as a free man, becoming all that it means to be free. The slave realises his perfection in becoming, essentially, the best slave he can be. Aristotle seems to consider transformation, revolution, as contrary to nature, an act of *im*perfection.

15. Simon Harrison, 'Augustine on what we owe to our teachers', in Amélie Oksenberg Rorty (ed.), *Philosophers on Education: New Historical Perspectives*, p. 72.
16. Harrison, p. 69.
17. Daniel Garber, 'Descartes, or cultivation of the intellect', in Amélie Oksenberg Rorty (ed.), *Philosophers on Education: New Historical Perspectives*, p. 130. Garber quotes from the French preface to the *Principles of Philosophy*.
18. Descartes, 'Meditations on first philosophy', Meditation 1, *Descartes Philosophical Writings*, p. 61. In the next paragraph to the one quoted here, Descartes, after telling of the initiation of his method and its first principles, says 'when the foundation is undermined, the superstructure will collapse of itself'. Obviously, Descartes lived in 'pre-ideological' times.
19. Richard Tuck, 'Hobbes on education', in Amélie Oksenberg Rorty (ed.), *Philosophers on Education: New Historical Perspectives*, pp. 148–50. Hobbes manages to combine Aristotle's claim that common opinion, freely held and consistent over time be considered as true, and Plato's determination that such opinion is what must be worked through in order to discern that which is true. The difference is subtle yet decisive.
20. Genevieve Lloyd, 'Spinoza and the education of the imagination', in Amélie Oksenberg Rorty (ed.), *Philosophers on Education: New Historical Perspectives*, pp. 157–8.
21. Lloyd, p. 170.
22. Leibniz, *Selections*, esp. Ch. III 'Knowledge and Metaphysics' XXVI. One shouldn't overlook the inverted 'sovereignty' of this presumption, nor the fact that Leibniz's many efforts to enlighten royalty royally failed.
23. Nietzsche, *On the Future of Our Educational Institutions*, Lecture III, pp. 175–6.
24. Nietzsche, 'Schopenhauer as educator', *Untimely Meditations*, p. 151.

25. Nietzsche, for once echoing Rousseau, is explicit in saying that it is not only the manufactured desire of individuals but also the greed of the state that demands that all energies be directed toward serving the interests of the existing institutions.
26. Jacques Lacan, *The Seminar of Jacques Lacan, Book XVII: The Other Side of Psychoanalysis.*
27. Bruce Fink, *The Lacanian Subject: Between Language and Jouissance*, pp. 132–3.
28. Lacan says, 'for centuries knowledge has been pursued as a defence against truth' (quoted in Fink, *The Lacanian Subject: Between Language and Jouissance*, p. 132).
29. 'Pour aujourd'hui: Platon!' These seminars are part of an ongoing series given at the Collège de France over three years 2007–8, 2008–9 and 2009–10. The 2007–8 seminars and Badiou's seminar on the *Republic* given in 1989–90 (just after the publication of *Manifeste pour la philosophie*) are reproduced in full on François Nicolas' brilliant website. The notes which reproduce the seminars are by Daniel Fischer (http://www.entretemps.asso.fr/Badiou/07-08.htm). All translations are my own.
30. After praising Deleuze as 'the most generous' anti-Platonist, 'the most open to contemporary creations', Badiou concludes: 'All that Deleuze lacked was to finish with anti-Platonism itself.' See also 'Plato, our Dear Plato!', pp. 39–41.
31. Gilles Deleuze, *Logic of Sense*, p. 262.
32. Heidegger, *Pathmarks*, p. 167. 'If we are not satisfied with merely translating the words παιδεία and ἀλήθεια "literally", if instead we attempt to think through the issue according to the Greek way of knowing and to ponder the essential matter that is at stake in these translations, then straightaway "education" and "truth" come together into an essential unity.'
33. Heidegger, *Pathmarks*, p. 219. Cf. Quentin Meillassoux, *After Finitude*.
34. 'The in-itself of the Idea is its ek-sisting being, and its participative capacity is its "there-is", the crux of its operation. It is in the Idea itself that we find the gap between the supposition of its being (the intelligible region) and the recognition of the one-effect that it supports (participation) – pure "there is" in excess of its being – with regard to sensible presentation and worldly situations.'
35. To put this another way, *to educate* is always to re-educate and this properly consists in not only transmitting the 'intellectual, theoretical or philosophical framework but also . . . that which enabled us to think in such a way in the first place' (Alain Badiou and Bruno Bosteels, 'Can change be thought: a dialogue with Alain Badiou', p. 245; hereafter CCT).

36. Alexander Nehamas, *The Virtues of Authenticity*. Nails, *Agora, Academy, and the Conduct of Philosophy*.
37. We adopt this neologism from Barbara Cassin for whom it is 'the set of doctrines or teachings associated with the individuals known as the sophists' ('Who's afraid of the sophists? Against ethical correctness', p. 102; see also her *L'effet sophistique*).

CHAPTER 1

State

> 'Shall we go on as Aeschylus might say, to tell of "another man matched with another state" or should we keep to our plan of taking the state first?' (R. 550c)
>
> 'If you pay him sufficient to persuade him, he will make you wise too.' (Prt. 310d)
>
> 'To be on the side of virtue is not to change under an effect of law.'[1]

The enquiry into the 'state of the Athenian situation' will follow three steps: firstly, we set out the Platonic context; secondly, we elaborate the category of the state in its Badiouean framework, making use of Platonic examples where needed; thirdly, we show how this category operates within the Platonic corpus relative to this framework. The demonstration of the 'state of the Athenian situation' will set up the remainder of the enquiry for it is with the category of the state both as currently constituted (for Plato, as expressed in the dialogues) and with the distinct reality of its reconstitution that Plato is concerned. The double movement Plato makes of both staking out a position by which to conceive the character and constitution of the Athenian *state* and to subtract from it the rudiments of a new form of thought is the very model of 'an education by truths'.

Platonic context

While Platonic scholarship has not solved what it considers to be the problem of chronology in regard to the writing of the dialogues, there is a general agreement that the *Apology* is one of the first texts. However, John Sellars, following a proposal by Charles Kahn, suggests that in trying to work out a relation between the dialogues it is best to understand the *Apology* as a 'public dialogue'.[2] This is to say that what happens in this dialogue would have to ring true to Plato's fellow citizens, many of whom, like Plato, would have been at the trial or would have been well aware of the details. Sellars suggests that whatever was spoken of in the *Apology* would have to have been things known to be of central concern to Socrates and so their reappearance in other dialogues constitutes the best evidence for distinguishing the so-called Socratic dialogues from their so-called Platonic counterparts. In this chapter, we are not concerned with the chronology of the dialogues or the more vexed (and perhaps distracting) question of the distinction between what is 'Socratic' and what is 'Platonic' in the corpus. However, the notion that what is established in the *Apology* is the key to following the conceptual elaborations that take place across the corpus is of primary concern. Therefore, if we take Kahn's suggestion conceptually rather than historically, what the *Apology* represents is something like the foundation of the corpus insofar as what happens at the trial sets the conditions for what unfolds as a consequence. For example, from the first lines of the dialogue we are told by Socrates (in the form of a reply) that his accusers are adept at persuasion and he is 'worried' about their affect and yet, he notes, 'hardly anything they said was true'. In contradistinction, he himself lacks the persuasive power they accuse him of possessing unless, he says, they mean an accomplished speaker is one who tells the truth. He says that if this is what these 'accomplished orators' mean (and it is clear that for Plato it is not) then 'yes, he is an orator, though not after their pattern'.[3] This is because 'all they will hear from him is the truth'. He will not embroider or embellish, for he puts his trust 'in the justice of his words' (Ap. 17a–c).

From the first lines Plato establishes a clear division between the type of his accusers and the figure of Socrates. We should note two things: that the division is constituted at a particular point in the relation (which we will see is a particular form of non-relation) between these orator-sophists and this Socratic figure; and secondly, that at this point the division is minimal – he *is* an orator *but not* after their pattern. Plato will insist on this point, draw from it and establish its extensive consequences. These consequences, made manifest, will ultimately return us to the *Republic*. Over the coming chapters we will see how Plato again and again returns to these conditions, the fundamental division which supports them and the logic that understands the Socratic position of being present to sophistry but not itself sophistic.[4]

Let's note one point more: one of the central motifs of Socratic praxis is the demand he makes that those he speaks to speak in their own name. There are only two occasions in the entire corpus where Plato appears. He appears at the trial twice: as one who would bear witness to Socrates – to his method of discourse and to his commitment to enquiry – and as one who might pay a penalty on his behalf (Ap. 34a and 38b).[5] The other occasion is the *Phaedo*. In this dialogue he makes mention of his absence from the prison on the day of the execution – he was ill (Phd. 59b). Below we will draw another lesson from these self- mentionings and especially the present/absent dialectic but here we might understand that the appearance of Plato relates to Socrates' demand that one speak in one's own name. As such, his appearance in the *Apology* is a mark of fidelity to this prescription and one that in turn authorises a certain fidelity to the 'accuracy' – historical or conceptual – of the dialogue. In this way Plato's appearance need only take place this one time confirming as it does the foundational form of the dialogue. We will address the subjective consequences of Plato's absences below.

With regard to the concern of this chapter, the 'state' of the Athenian situation, it suffices at this stage to note two points. In arguing his defence in the *Apology*, Socrates first notes that the charges against him are nothing new. Even though his accusers now, Meletus, Anytus and Lycon, have formalised them in a charge, he has been accused of similar things his whole life, ever since Chaerephon brought back from Delphi the declaration of the oracle that there was no one wiser than Socrates (Ap. 21c). Socrates answers the history of these charges first. What we should take note of here is that the history of the charges is precisely what constitutes the entirety of the corpus. Each dialogue, portraying as it does scenes from the pre-trial life of the Socratic figure, is another step *toward* Socrates' execution on the one hand, while on the other, each dialogue is also part of Plato's re-trial of Socrates wherein what is exposed is that yes, Socrates is a corruptor, but what he corrupts is in reality a corrupt state of affairs. This state of affairs is one in which those who profess to know in fact do not know what it is they profess too. All enquiries attest to this. It is on the basis of these, Socrates says, that a 'great deal of hostility' rose against him. The result has been 'various malicious suggestions, including the description of me as a professor of wisdom' (Ap. 22a). For Plato, this retrial does not end in the execution of Socrates but in the *Republic* – a place where this corrupt state cannot be.

The second critical point is that when he does turn to the specific charges against him the telling moment comes when he prompts Meletus to declare that it is Socrates, alone in all Athens, who does not educate (Ap. 25a). This is most precise for it is directly in relation to education that Socrates is condemned to be singular and, as such, *not of the state*. Quite simply, for the state, he is the only figure present to Athens who does not educate or improve the youth of the state. He is nothing to education.[6] The obverse of this is that every Athenian citizen apart from Socrates (whose citizen credentials are certainly at stake here) does educate: as every Athenian citizen is constitutive of the state, the claim amounts to the fact the state educates while Socrates alone does not.[7] In the *Meno* this idea of the state as educator is confirmed by Anytus who, again under questioning from Socrates, says that if Meno was seeking instruction, then 'any decent Athenian gentleman whom he happens to meet, if he is willing to be persuaded, will make him a better man than the sophists would' (Men. 93e). That Anytus distinguishes the Athenian gentleman, the man of the jury, from the sophist gives us pause:[8] however, as we will show, Plato, in this dialogue, has already shown that the logic Anytus deploys to distinguish the sophist from the Athenian gentleman was inherently sophistic.[9] Plato's conception of sophistry, both as demagoguery and as teaching for pay, and this is our working definition, can be reduced to this: sophistry (re)produces the 'false conceit of wisdom'.[10] Education, Plato insists, consists in clearing the soul of this conceit (Sph. 231b). In the *Apology*, Socrates' three accusers are described as being representative of all facets of the Athenian state: Socrates notes that 'Meletus is aggrieved on behalf of the poets; Anytus the professional men and politicians; Lycon the orators' (Ap. 23e). As we will see, the conception Plato has of sophistry extends way beyond the simplistic, decidedly liberal notion that they were 'freelance, mostly non-Athenian independent teachers who travelled throughout Ancient Greece from city to city making their living out of the new demand for education'.[11]

Regardless of the chronology of the dialogues it would not be incorrect to say that the entire effort of the Platonic corpus consists of Plato drawing a diagonal line so to speak, just like the one Socrates draws for the slave boy in the *Meno*, from the foundational dialogue the *Apology* to the ideal city of the *Republic*. This diagonal line is that traced by Socratic enquiry and it can be seen to run both ways at once.[12] For now, it suffices to note that the diagonal is at once *irrational* in mathematical and political senses, as it connects points that should have no direct communication in the geometry of the state and, in doing so, is literally *unpresentable* according to every established form of computation. Yet its existence and power cannot simply be denied or explained away. Our contention in this chapter is that for Plato, and precisely because of that which is 'explained away', the state of the Athenian situation is sophistic.[13]

Situation and state

Badiou argues, and we will explain these terms below, that in the context of 'historical situations' what constitutes their *state* is the knowledge which determines the order, rule and distribution of the elements or inhabitants that are present in this situation – whatever it might be. It so happens that for us this determined situation is Athens, or more specifically the 'Athens of the dialogues'. Presciently, Badiou refers to this knowledge as the encyclopaedia (BE, 327/361). As our introductory remarks suggest, for Plato, the state that put Socrates to trial and convicted him of being as nothing to education is a state ruled and ordered, not by a discourse of truth, but at best by its imitation.[14] In the Platonic dialogues which present to us the situation of Athens, sophistry is what provides the rule by which what is known can be known, and what is not known cannot be known. These 'sophists', as Socrates has told us, do not tell the truth and as Callicles, 'a man', Socrates says, 'of sound education', shows in the *Gorgias* they actively seek to refrain from its pursuit the better to pursue the interests of the state (Grg. 487d). Obviously, and Callicles mentions this explicitly, it is of this rule that Plato's Socrates falls foul and as such it is this rule Plato seeks to undermine by a deliberate and sustained analysis centred upon the 'failure' of the Socratic figure to be 'sophistic'. Plato, on the basis of the Socratic encounter with the sophistic state, reveals the 'Athenian state' to be constituted by a 'lack of truth'. We can put this into a formula which has the virtue of being both descriptive and prescriptive at once: what Socrates does not know is what sophistry knows as knowledge. It is within this 'sophistic', encyclopaedic state that the greater part of our thesis will unfold. Therefore, in order to establish something about Plato's take on sophistry, we must set its parameters.[15]

For Badiou, a situation is a structured presentation. What it presents are multiples of some sort. These in turn present other multiples. In its being, a situation is infinite – there can be no set of all sets, no greatest ordinal, no greatest cardinal. Infinity, for Badiou, is a 'banal reality'. 'Situation' names an immanently 'structured' collection of this infinite multiplicity. A situation presents a multiple of multiplicity as a structured consistency relative to that for which it is a situation. Each element is counted as a one-multiple (a structured infinity) and the collection of these one-multiples is equivalent to the situation which presents them as such. The relation that structures the multiple in this way, that organises their singular collective appearance, is called *belonging*. It denotes the original *form* of multiple collection. This form neither denotes nor distinguishes a difference between the multiples themselves. Belonging denotes the indifference of the collective as such. The 'counted' multiples *belong* to the situation which counts them for no other reason than that the one that they are is presented as such. In-difference, *equality* at the level of presentation, is the rule of belonging. This is not to say that these elements are not different. What a situation presents is any number of elements distinct from each other. The critical factor is that their difference in no way determines the form of the presentation. At the level of presentation or structure it is their consistency relative to the situation that matters. The structure of a situation is simply that which makes the situation *this* one rather than that – a school and not a factory, a factory and not family, and so on. The reciprocity between the structure and the elements it presents establishes a certain univocity. What structure attests to is that the elements it presents are presented elements of that situation and no other. Whatever is counted to exist in this situation does so as subject to the form of its existence and at the same time the form of existence denotes that what exists (there) does so by virtue of its form. A consequence of this is that *to be presented* denotes also the existence of *what is not* presented. A situation as a form of structure, an articulation of consistency, a count as one, is understood therefore as an operation (cf. MP, 22). It is an operation upon that which is-not-one. Any 'one' in this schema has become so. It is the result of the operation of structure or the count. For Badiou, following what he argues set-theory discerns, 'the one is not' (BE, 23/31). If it *is* not then 'nothing' or that which is not one *is*. Being for Badiou, that-which-is-not-one is infinite multiplicity or pure inconsistency. That the one-is-not must be understood as being relevant to every situation.

For our reading of the Platonic corpus 'Athens' is the name for the situation which presents the elements of the dialogues. We will call this alternately the Athens of the dialogues or Plato's Athens. If Athens is a situation then it is simply: 'the multiple made up of circumstances, language, and objects wherein some truth can be said to operate' (TW, 121). To pre-empt somewhat, this undifferentiated collection of multiples structured purely in terms of their belonging, and thus equally present, equally there *as* the situation, can be understood as the model form for the counter-state that Plato attempts to think 'constitutionally', under the name *Republic*. In a certain sense the onto-logic of the situation prescribes the proper form for the relations that will structure this ideal city. Plato is explicit in saying that the ideal city will model itself on justice. This can only mean the egalitarian distribution of place undifferentiated in the first instance by any other consideration. In the penultimate chapter of *Being and Event* Badiou will note that the ability to force an equality, establish the veracity of a new subset of an existing situation, depends entirely on the arrangement of a prior belonging (BE, 414/453). This is to say, then, that Athens will remain the crucial focus for Plato of everything that takes place in the dialogues. We could say that the sophistic state, working upon the same multiple elements, organises itself around a certain 'misrecognition' of this situation. Indeed, its very representational form implies this. Plato's goal on the contrary is to establish a city consistent with its very constitution.

In this sense we can say that belonging is the generic *form*. It names the fundamental reciprocity between element and structure. All elements counted to exist in the Athens of the dialogues exist equally, simply because at the level of structure nothing is known of them other than that presented as such, they belong. In Badiou's terms, 'the *identity* of multiples is founded on the *indifference* of belonging' (BE, 61/74). At the level of presentation therefore, the basic structure of situations, an ideal form of equality presents itself. We have, in a sense, a pure collection cut from what is otherwise uncollected. The latter, as we noted, points to the infinite multiplicity, the *being* qua being of every presented situation. Speaking retroactively, and ideally, and again pre-emptively in regard to our thesis, we can say that the being of the 'truth' of any situation is the equivalence between elements at the level of their presentation which the operation of belonging ensures. The real problem, as Badiou asserts, is 'to make such truths manifest', for at the level of presentation this (form of) 'truth' remains *indiscernible*. What the corpus shows is that 'there is no truth apart from the generic [indiscernible], because only a faithful generic procedure aims at the one of situational being' (BE, 339/374). That is to say, the subjective educational trajectory Plato's Socrates enacts within this situation keeps its eye on this *form*. As Plato notes in the *Cratylus*, 'I think we have to turn back frequently to what we've already said, in order to test it by looking at it backwards and forwards simultaneously' (Crat. 428d): thus *back* to the relation of belonging – or situational being – and forward to that truth which manifests itself in accord with its situation. For now we will simply assert that the Athens that Plato's corpus presents to us can be understood as a situation. Athens is simply a term of structure. The more important task for us is to establish the state form of Athens.

Two procedures

Our claim is that the state form of Athens is sophistry. As we said, sophistry organises itself as a set of attitudes, practices and determinations. In this sense it can be understood as a particular operation within and upon the Athenian situation. This collection of practices and attitudes has a unifying logic, a *knowledge* manifest in its operation and distinct from what Badiou (and Plato) regard as truth. In Badiou's words, 'everything is at stake in the thought of the truth/knowledge couple' (BE, 361/327).

As 'state knowledge' sophistry brings together two procedures: as 'representation' it marks the redistribution of the elements originally presented into a collection of parts, which is to say it counts this original count and determines its known order. However, as we will see, it remains fundamentally vulnerable to presentation. The state depends entirely on that which is presented but this relation or this form of the relation is not reciprocal.[16] Simultaneously, and in order to secure against what presentation fails to count – *presentation* itself – it organises these parts in regard to a rule (BE, 287/318). A simple ontological rule prescribes that there is an excess of parts over elements – one element can be counted as a part of many parts. Within our non-ontological situation this excess plays a crucial role for both the state and for the possibility of its interruption. In order to 'in-determine its indeterminacy', the state forecloses its interruptive possibilities by submitting this excess to a rule. It is not contradictory to say that the rule brought to bear by sophistry is that which effectively generates the *character* of this excess. We need to show that this rule of excess, the unifying logic or 'knowledge' which sophistry brings to bear as the state of the Athenian situation, which is to say as the educator to all Athens, is 'interest'. Indeed, sophistic knowledge, subject to interest, has a real quantitative aspect to it. Plato, hardly ever fails to mention how much money the sophists earn and how quantitatively pernicious are their offspring. To use Marx's terms, money seems to occupy the place of a 'general equivalent' within sophistic education. As we said, it is by this rule of interest that the sophistic excess or conceit is shaped.

This rule can be comprehended as uniting three aspects:

1. *End.* A sophistic education provides the youth with the necessary knowledge for making one's way in the state. It has a repetitious function and a reproductive intent.
2. *Practice.* The sophist teaches for money and thus transmission is reduced to the exchange of goods. The a priori assumption is of a subject already properly constituted (citizen) and thus capable of discerning what is true or not true concerning knowledge.
3. *Theory.* Discursively, the 'keynote' of a sophistic education is sounded by Protagoras:[17] 'Of all things the measure is Man, of the things that are, that they are and of the things that are not, that they are not'.[18] Although scholarly debate does not agree on the meaning of this maxim, for Plato, it was quite clear: predicated on an un-thought conceit – that it knows what is and what is not – it authorised the free reign of interest at the expense of truth.

Category of the state

Our first task is to illustrate the *fact* of this excess – what Plato refers to as a 'conceit'. The elaboration of the rule that supports it is a more complex task. Although the conflation of ontological and philosophical discourse is fraught, when determining the concept of excess it will help to make use of the basic set-theoretical articulation between set and power set.[19] It is akin, perhaps, to Socrates drawing squares in the sand in order to demonstrate to Meno that he does not teach. All we want to do is illustrate that the excess of parts is a simple rule of representation. The conceptualisation of this rule as it operates in a specific situation, Athens, will come next.

Excess

Take a simple set (a, b, c). In non-ontological terminology this is a situation. We can see that each element is presented as one element of the set which presents them as one. All that can be 'known' of these elements is that they are presented by the set. This is to say that what it is that 'makes up these elements' is not presented by this situation. Now, if there is a situation or set (a, b, c), there is also this set's subsets and, more critically, the set of its subsets or 'power set'.

Simply, it is possible to configure the original set into several subsets or parts, all of which can be collected up into one set. Thus we have the power set (or state) of (a, b, c,) = ((a), (b), (c), (a, b), (b, c), (a, c) (a, b, c)Ø). In non-ontological terms the power set, the set of all the subsets, is the 'state of the situation'. There are three things to note. First, it organises all the elements of the original set into the possible order of their appearing, accounting for any and all manifestations – (a, b), (a), (a, c), etc. Secondly, it counts the original set as a subset itself ((a, b, c)) thus securing (and obscuring) the original one-effect provided by the original operation of structure. (To re-emphasise: structure is not itself structured (structure cannot *present* itself) and so what is secured against is the possible 'return of the void' or the inconsistency that consistency (presented element) 'is'. We will return to this (BE, 280/309).) Thirdly, it counts this collection as *one* set, i.e. its state. Combined, what happens is that what was counted to exist as such and thus as *belonging* is now secured in its existence in regard to how it is situated in relation to other subsets under a rule particular to the kind of situation it is (i.e. school, family, nation, cinema, etc.). In the original form of the situation the element was *articulated with structure alone*; now the state mediates this articulation and organises it in *relation to a rule* concerning its parts. This new relation is *inclusion.*

What is immediately observable is that the power set ((a), (b), (c), (a, b), (b, c), (a, c) (a, b, c)Ø) is distinctly larger than the original set. In our finite set the excess of the power set over the original set is immediately countable. But when the set is infinite as any open or 'historical' situation is, the gap between the original set and the set of its subsets or between the situation and its state is literally immeasurable. To put it enigmatically, due to the excess of parts the 'void', which is included in every set and thus, constituting as it does the original insistence of inconsistent multiplicity, has more places to hide. If there is an excess between that which is presented and the proper order of its representation, and excess by definition escapes measure, then inconsistency, that which is uncounted, remains a threat. The *rule* of the state, if I can put it that way, is to make sure that this excess is delimited in such a way that the threat of the void remains dormant (BE, 109/126). We will return to this.

Strictly speaking there are no new elements in the power set, only specific iterations of the first three a, b, c (and the void – which these elements present and is as such 'included in every set').[20] What this means, as has been inferred, is that the original form of presentation is not negated so much as occluded in favour of the representative form. The original multiples do not cease to exist (and neither does their un-known 'quality' the void) but under the 'encyclopaedic' determinations of the state, the rule by which it operates, they are known only in terms of their 'singletons', i.e. *a* becomes or 'is known as' (a); or in a classroom situation *students* are included as 'meritorious' or 'poor scholars' – an A student or an F student (the latter subject to all the force the norm of the institutional situation can muster). However, there is a further question concerning the regulation of this excess. As we said, in infinite situations, this excess (between a set and its power set) is unmeasurable. The ruled control of this errancy is precisely, the province of the state. Given that the existence of excess is not in question what becomes pertinent is the means of its control. What we want to remark on here is that in a particular type of situation the possibility of its measure exists. This is to say, that in such a situation the chance of subverting the rule that governs this excess will also exist.

'Historical' situation

Badiou argues that it is possible to identify three types of situations: natural, neutral and historical. On the one hand, the distinction is straightforward: neither natural nor neutral situations present singular multiples, that is multiples which are not represented. Accordingly, in a natural situation all the elements will be both presented and represented. Of neutral situations Badiou remains rather enigmatic. He says of them only that they *distribute* a mix of 'singular, normal and excrescent terms' but they '[bear] neither a natural multiple nor an evental site (a presented yet unrepresented element specific to historical situations).[21] In effect, a neutral situation is something like a situation in general – one that, as he says, is neither natural nor historical, but denotes the 'gigantic reservoir from which our existence is woven' (BE, 177/197).

A historical situation is distinguished simply by its determinate lack of normalcy – being neither natural (normal) nor neutral. The distinction turns on it presenting at least one singular, abnormal or 'strange' multiple, a multiple presented by the situation but whose parts the state cannot count. In other words, the proper order or place of these parts is not known to the state. Such a multiple is termed a 'site'. We will see the importance of this 'site' in Chapter 2.

For now, we can posit three things:

1. In historical situations the excessive rule of representation is founded on a limit. There exists (although indiscernibly) a multiple which cannot be represented. Only its abnormality can be marked.
2. Plato's Athens is such a situation simply because Plato has already firmly established in the *Apology* that within his Athens there is something unknown and non-sophistic at work. The state has noted this immanent anomaly and determined that the nothing that it is must not be.
3. Because the rule of representation cannot properly account for this singularity – even as it tries to – its excessive nature becomes apparent (i.e. the conviction of Socrates) and the possibility of measuring its excess is opened up.

The particular features of this movement, which are specific to historical situations, are examined in the coming chapters. Let us note that an obvious instance of this type of distinction between the Athenian situation and the sophistic state of this situation is discernible in the *Crito*. In this dialogue – famous for confounding scholars due to Socrates' praise of the Athens that condemns him – the Socratic figure avoids the sophistic state and addresses his enquiry directly at the situation itself. The Laws, with whom he speaks, simply denote the generic or constitutional principles, indiscernible names and conditions that *belong* to the Athenian situation. Socrates bypasses the demagogic rule and sophistic representation of this constitution in order to speak both to what Athens *is* 'beneath sophistry' as it were and, as he does in the 'next dialogue', the *Phaedo*, to orient his friends toward the city that Athens 'will have been' without sophistry. Socrates, recall, never speaks to the polis per se; he reminds us constantly that 'in such a city' he is incapable of politics and in the *Apology* he notes that at seventy, this will be the first time he speaks in the law courts. He maintains that he is a *stranger* to the discourse common to such a place (Ap. 17d). In the *Crito* therefore he speaks past this 'polis' to what in the *Phaedo* he terms 'the world to come' – which, in Lacanian terms is 'that which is in Athens more than it knows'.[22] In the final chapter we will elaborate on this 'new place' wherein what is true of the Athenian situation is made manifest.

In sum, this distinction between presentation and representation, belonging and inclusion, situation and state, pertains to all situations (BE, 103/119). At its most benign the state is merely the operation that secures the situation by putting into circulation a knowledge of the organisation of its parts. The parts, as we saw, are always in excess over their elements or terms. The state is simply that which counts these parts as one, providing a structural integrity to what is effectively an errancy not counted in the original structure – which counts only terms. The re-presentation of the terms into a single set of parts is necessary 'because their excess over the terms, escaping the initial count, designates a potential place for the fixation of the void (BE, 109/123). A historical situation is always one in which a 'new' measure of this excess might be taken – a place wherein the 'wandering' void may be fixed by an event and indexed to a point within the situation. It is in this context that Socrates' 'historical' remark in the *Phaedrus* might be taken as a threat. In reply to Phaedrus' prophetic observation that here, outside the walls of Athens, Socrates appears to be a stranger, the latter replies, 'forgive me, my friend. I am devoted to learning; landscapes and trees have nothing to teach me – only the people in the city can do that' (Phdr. 230d). Socrates prefers to perpetrate his strangeness within the city constituting therein a threat to sophistry as the mark of its conceit.

Rule of excess

What we need to do now is establish the rule that characterises sophistic excess and binds Plato's Athens into the state that it is. What this entails is an articulation of this rule and showing that this rule constitutes its educational (sophistical) apparatus. Badiou contends that what he calls the 'orientation of constructivist thought' is that which 'prevails in established situations' (BE, 328/362). What we want to do is give a summary account such that we can recognise in this orientation the rudiments of sophistic practice, theory and ends. The essential features of this orientation are three for Badiou: language, discernment and classification. The function of language is to indicate that this or that element of the situation contains a certain property. Immediately, we can see that language somehow intercedes between presented elements and their representation. It expresses the criterion of the former's inclusion by the latter. Badiou calls the *capacity* language has for marking out these properties 'knowledge'. 'In the last analysis, the constitutive operations of every domain of knowledge are *discernment* (such a presented or thinkable multiple possesses such and such a property) and *classification* (I can group together, and designate by their common property, those multiples that I discern as having a nameable characteristic in common)' (BE, 328/362). In the case of discernment the situation itself is supposed such that its elements present properties specific to it. If an element can be *discerned* as such it is on the basis of this element belonging to the situation – it is presented as such. Thus language, so the constructivist position assumes, nominates only based on what exists. The assumption is that nothing external to the situation is imposed in and through such discernment. This would, after all, suggest the *existence* (and therefore the being) of that which cannot be named. If such a property is discerned within the multiple the latter is immediately classifiable in the sense that via its 'common' name it can be included with others similarly discerned. Badiou notes that the capacity of language to achieve this commensurability between an existent or belonging multiple and an included rule of its 'inclusion' is the means by which language is able to police the excess inherent to the representative relation. 'It is this bond, this *proximity* that language builds between presentation and representation, which grounds the conviction that the state does not exceed the situation by *too much* . . .' (BE, 288/319). To control errancy – the possible site of the void – by means of binding belonging to inclusion, elements and parts as tightly as possible through the specification of nomination is the goal of the 'constructivist' orientation Badiou argues. 'Knowledge' names the coordinated movement of these three functions. The functions of discernment and classification are further grounded in capacities supposed inherent in the constructivist subject: discernment is grounded in the capacity to judge, classification in the capacity to link such judgments.

To judge is not to decide but to speak *correctly* or to make sense insofar as what is picked out conforms to and confirms the situational order, which is to say the power of language in this case, the point being that for the constructivist vis-à-vis the situation nothing else is sayable.[23] 'Knowledge' does not speak of what is not presented precisely because it is impossible to ascribe to 'nothing' an existent property of the situation and to count it as such. 'If all difference is attributed on the basis of language and not on the basis of being, *presented* in-difference is impossible' (BE, 319/353). Plato has Protagoras put the same thing like this: 'It is impossible to judge what is not, or to judge anything other than what one is experiencing, and what one is immediately experiencing is always true' (Tht. 167ab). The 'difference' between Leibniz, Badiou's arch-constructivist, and Protagoras is essentially that for the former God is the universal measure while for Protagoras the individual qua state provides the rule. The link between the constitution of the individual and his state is paradigmatic for Plato. To de-sophisticate this link, thus acknowledging its motive force, is Plato's task.

Badiou goes on to say that 'knowledge is realised as encyclo*paedia*' (BE, 328/362: emphasis added), that is to say the 'summation of judgments' made concerning what exists for the situation such that they are all counted, or grouped by a 'common determinant'. This 'encyclopaedic' determinant organises the judged elements into parts based solely on the ascribed property. In turn, then, 'one can designate each of these parts by the property in question and thereby determine it within the language' (BE, 329/363). In sum, knowledge solely determines existence in the form of its nomination. A consistency is supposed at work; or rather a law already orders the thinking of the situation such that certain (non-)attributes can have no possible means of appearing. In his critique of Leibniz Badiou points out that what this orientation excludes as impossible to the formulas of a well-made language, a language in which what exists conforms to the reason of its existence, is the 'indiscernible' (BE, 320/354). The indiscernible is such that no reason for the existence of what it divides can be given and thus 'language' as nomination through rule is contradicted. As Badiou notes, Leibniz himself says, '*if the void exists, language is incomplete*, for a difference is missing from it inasmuch as it allows some indifference to be' (BE, 321/355). Constructivist thought is founded on the impossibility of the existence of the void qua situation, which is to say the indiscernible and that which presents it. As this suggests, to not know the void is not a matter of knowledge but of constitution (BE, 294/325).[24]

Interest and conceit

Our claim is that 'interest' is the organising term of sophistic Athens. It is its 'educational ethic' and, like any constructivist universe, it has the virtue of securing its elements to the state, affording them a protection against the *thought of* errancy (the being of excess) and the actuality of disorder, *and* ensuring the concord of interest between the state and the elements of its situation. In Badiou's words this 'programmatic vision occupies the necessary role, in the field of politics, of reformatory moderation. It is a mediation of the State, in that it attempts to formulate, in an accepted language, what the State is capable of' (BE, 293/324). Against and through this repetition and its reproducing effects, effects which *seem like* 'transformation', the typical task of Socratic enquiry is to show that the sophist fails to know precisely what it is they profess to know. Moreover, as the *Sophist* proves – precisely by way of the 'long detour' it takes in refuting Parmenides' claims regarding the being of that which is not[25] – to not know or to be in error is the very essence of sophistic subjectivity. To be *a* sophist is *to be* in error. However, for Plato, error like truth is not a matter of being per se but a matter of one's orientation concerning the latter. In short, if truth and error both have being and being is not becoming then truth and error (which is not knowledge) exist and can be distinguished not at the level of linguistic judgment but in terms of their form.[26]

In the sophistic conception of things, as Protagoras signals, there is only opinion – judgment conceived in perception. Repeatedly, Plato contends that the poets – Homer, Hesiod, Simonides et al. – the 'pre-Socratics' – Heraclitus, Empedocles, etc. – and the contemporary Protagoreans are aligned as 'patrons of the flux' (Tht. 160d–e and Crt. 402bcd). For them, to claim the truth of a distinction was an error against the right of perception (Tht. 152e). The two categories of knowledge for Protagoras are ultimately 'better' and 'worse'. When Socrates asks Protagoras what the youth Hippocrates will receive from the master in exchange for his money the master answers 'young man, if you come to me, your gain will be this: the very day you join me, you will go home a better man and the same the next day. Each day you will make progress towards a better state' (Prt. 318a).[27] A Protagorean education is in strict accord with its philo-sophistic position, a position which pointedly refuses to account for the being of things on the premise that such things, that they are, cannot be known and if they cannot be known then they are not. Protagoras' assertion concerning the gods is exemplary: 'I am unable to know whether they exist or do not exist or what they are like in form; for there are many hindrances to knowledge, the *obscurity* of the subject and the brevity of human life' (Diog. Lae. 9.41, emphasis added).

The consistency between the thought and the practice, or rather, as Plato points out, between practice and language, is important because Plato's criticism of sophistry turns on two related things; ignorance and conceit. What the sophist is ignorant of is that his belief or opinion (they are the same thing) is not knowledge. In this sense the sophist imitates in ignorance of the fact that he imitates (Sph. 267d). The sophist is not a figure who knows but fails to correctly transmit his knowledge. In terms of affect, he is far from being a poor *teacher*. Rather, as an imitator, he fails to know. The real conceit of sophistic knowledge then is its ignorance of its own lack. For the sophistic position error, simply, cannot exist. One is simply a better or worse judge. The wisest will be the one whose judgment results in the proper classification of the objects present to him. Thus the sophist might be the best teacher of the lack of truth (something contemporary debates on education fail to take into account). As we will discuss more fully later, Meno (the well known *mercenary* from Xenophon's *Anabasis* here, as Plato notes, fighting for Gorgias and not the Persian King)[28] famously put this 'ignorance' in terms of a question: 'How can I know what I do not know when I do not know what it is' (Men. 80d)?

This ignorance, as Plato deems it, is both compounded and retroactively confirmed as a conceit by the sophist's willingness to sell, transmit and thus reproduce this ignorance. What the sophist considers his true wisdom, that one cannot know what one cannot perceive and name, is for Plato the mark of *his* ignorance. Note the sophist is not without knowledge in a general or ordinary sense (one thinks of the polymath Hippias as an extreme example, or Prodicus, 'godlike in his universal knowledge') (Prt. 316a). He does possess a *technē*, or as Plato notes sarcastically a 'knack'. This is what allows Plato to hint at a certain level of cynicism in the sophistic position. He is not an innocent and so 'sincere imitator' but is one who, conditioned by his practice of speeches and dispute, worries that he may not in fact know what he professes too (Sph. 268a). On first pass, this looks like a contradiction. Plato establishes that the sophist does not know but believes he does and then he supposes that the sophist is knowledgeable enough to know that he might not know. In fact this too is imitation. If the sophist is ultimately the imitator of the wise man, as his name suggests, then he also imitates the practice of the wise man who is always concerned to know what he does not. Thus the practice of imitating the wise man 'discursively' (demagogue) or engaging in 'refutation' (sophist) conditions him to imitate concern over the state of his knowledge. Again, this is not a knowing imitation but an ignorant one.

Imitation

Given this context of imitation it is worth noting the extent of the imitative tradition in which Plato's Socrates is intervening. In the dialogues, as we have argued, Plato presents the sophist as the paradigm figure of the knowledge of Athens. The sophist by his own admission has inherited this position from the poet (Prt. 316c–317c). As Havelock says, 'The function of the poet was primarily to repeat and in part to enlarge the tradition', the latter pertaining to what Havelock calls 'the Greek ethos' – ostensibly the set of public and private laws, techniques, history and so on, linguistically identified and stated, and transmissible as such.[29] In *Handbook of Inaesthetics*, Badiou refers to the 'alliance' between Simonides the poet – the first poet to be paid for his verse – and Protagoras, in terms of the latter's designation 'of an artistic [poetical] apprenticeship as the key to education' (HB, 1). The latter, in Badiou's view, Socrates tries to thwart (cf. Prt. 339+) and Plato considers a subterfuge, precisely because Plato, he says, designates art to be the 'charm of a semblance of truth' (HB, 1–2). In Havelock's analysis, the poet's educational effect is verified in the form of a 'psychological identification'. The youth is the nodal point of the coming together of the poetry – the form of transmission – and the ethos which provides its content. Havelock says two crucial things here: 'The content of the poetic statement had to be formed in such a way as to allow this identification. This means it could deal with action and event only involving persons.'[30] The Greek ethos, which is already a representational set of occurrences and interpretation of occurrences, is set to a form of transmission whose effect is measured by its ability to 'charm' the youth to an identification with the original representation. This form of transmission in the Homeric works and in the work of the tragedians turns around the moral character of representational figures, individuals whose reactions to events form the core of a universal moral education. We see in these works the concentration of moral principle and lack of the same in individuals, gods, and men and women alike. It is thus, through *the interest* these figures are displayed as having in the events that surround them that we know of these events at all. The poet captures in verse, in rhyme, rhythm and meter this interest on two levels: the verse of the poet creates a narrative of events and they represent (what should be and thus what is to be) the emotive, psychological investment of these figures in these events and in reaction to them. The poet gives an immediate character, a presence if you will, to the events he narrates. They are memorisable, so become memorable, and so retain an immediacy whose effect is to provoke the youth to identify with the interest of these figures (cf. SP, 44). Through this 'memorable' identification the youth is to be brought to 'right action' or 'right feeling' which these figures have been represented as displaying. In short, the poet/sophist has the task of charming the youth. So charmed, the youth will publicly exhibit as affect the reproduction of the Greek ethos. A certain continuity, recognised through effect, itself the guarantee that a certain reproduction is in place, has seemed to take place, is assured and verified.

For Plato, this psychological identification measured by its registered effects in respect to the continuity of a tradition was not the same thing as an *education*. For Plato, immediate identifications are the point at which one begins enquiry. They are not, as we will see, confirmations of subjectivity by any means. To decide for and to participate in such an enquiry necessarily disjoins one from identification with the rule of the state. This disjunction is constituted in a single point and is, as such, a *real* point for what will be an infinite series of division. This division is manifest as both the procedures undertaken as enquiry and in terms of the orientation of the thought of that enquiry. The question of Plato's Socrates to any profession of knowledge put into practice as 'education' is 'is it by truths or by interest?' This is the impasse of non-sophistry and its double, the Republic and Athens.

The sophist is the heir and ally to this tradition and as such takes on the role of transmitting the 'knowledge of the state', but his mode of operation is no longer poetical per se. The sophist 'sublates' art – the 'charm of a semblance of truth' – to his teaching. In the teaching of rhetoric and oratory and so on, the sophist serves the state in the form of its repetition. The particularity of this repetition and its veracity lies in the fact that it has a quantifiable result. In effect, it serves to multiply the number of identifications which can be made between the state and the youth. At the same time as these identifications are multiplied they remain nevertheless under the shadow of the overarching concept of the state. Why is it that the sophist, this 'money-making' and 'many-sided animal' producing multiple forms of identification between the youth and the state, can get away with making the claims it does in regard to teaching the youth all he needs to know in order to make his way in the state (Sph. 226a)? After all, this claim would seem to have to take into account all the contingencies of life in the polis: from trade, commerce, politics, war, law and beyond.[31]

The claim of the sophist here registers its real effect precisely at the level of affect. This is to say that sophistic teaching, at the level of practical effects, at the level of the reproduction of the interests of the state, has at the same time an effect of foreclosure. This effect of foreclosure mimics or rather is the reverse of the Platonic displacement of sophistry. The sophistic foreclosure amounts to the refusal to admit that non-sophistry even exists whereas the Platonic displacement assigns sophistry *to* its 'proper place' (thus where Socrates is neurotic, sophistry, 'repressed', is psychotic).[32] These two forms of displacement come together at the site of education. In other words, Socrates and sophistry come together over the youth of Athens. We return to this in Chapter 3.

Lack of not knowing

The claim of the sophist to equip the youth with all they need to make their way in the state is simply the claim to teach state-knowledge. Certainly, the sophist calls this virtue, wherein the man best fitted to the state will result in the best state for such a man. The reciprocity here is derived from the very constructivist form of the sophistic teaching. The predicate which allows the equation of youth and state, as we repeatedly see, is interest. We said that for Plato sophistry turns on ignorance and conceit. It is ignorant not of what it knows nor really of what it doesn't know but rather of the fact that it doesn't know. That is to say, for the sophist there is only what it knows and this includes what it doesn't know which it registers as what cannot (must not) be knowledge. The sophistic type of knowledge incorporates the anxiety of maintaining itself in such a position – as master of what is known and of what is knowable. With imitating the wise comes the burden of sustaining the imitation. The sophist must continually acquire new 'knowledge', in this sophistic sense, thus maintaining the 'apparatus of discernment' (BE, 292/324). The sophist as imitator has to deal with a certain form of excess. In his re-presentation of wisdom he cannot help but include the very thing he cannot know – that truth or wisdom, if you like, exists as something other than sophistic representation. This is the constant anxiety that haunts the sophist, that what he professes to know will be found out to be *nothing* at all, the nothing perhaps that Socrates *knows* to exist. So, figuratively speaking, what constitutes excess for the sophistic state of the situation is the sophist's *lack of not knowing*.

We have established an image of our state of the situation. The question is: how does 'sophistics' (demagogue and sophist) ward off this anxiety or 'peril' of the void? Mind, this anxiety, the threat of the void, of non-knowledge, 'wanders about' the state, gadfly like, and could be exposed at any point, through any encounter. As such, the sophistic premise forestalling this void must be one that is able to both collect up all possible appearances and do so in a way that does not ruin the consistency of presentation. The sophist must establish the rule by which all that belongs to Athens can also be shown as included. To put this less abstractly, the sophist must educate the youth in the maintenance of the state. Doing so forecloses the indiscernible nothing of the Socratic position – that which (for the sophistic state) is not education – and augments sophistry's own rule.

Essentially the sophist (as the state) cannot admit the existence of what it does not know, and by implication *that* it does not know. For the state, there is an a priori limit to enquiry. The demagogic and sophist teachers agree on this. Whereas the latter figures such as Gorgias, Protagoras and Prodicus all seek to match the language of perception to the form of existence, the former, figures such as Thrasymachus, Callicles and Anytus, all affirm that what comes to be counted as just within the state is what is of interest to the stronger. The stronger the 'perception' (and strength is a matter both of force and numbers), the more exacting, far reaching and secure the existence. Every state, the demagogues note, has *its own perceptions* (R. 339). This is the sophistic equivalent of virtue: 'And since the state is the master of language, one must recognise that for the constructivist [sophist] change and diversity do not depend upon presentational primordiality, but upon representative functions. The key to mutations and differences resides in the State' (BE, 291/322). Difference, devoid of all content, is paradigmatic for the sophist and thus for sophistry any notion of the same occurs as an imposition and must accord with interest.

To a degree, this accounts for the popularity of the sophists among certain sections of the democracy insofar as they could provide for the undermining of traditions. At the same time it accounts for their unpopularity with certain sections of the oligarchy. However, as we will see, all are caught within the logic of sophistry for Plato. Against sophistry and its internal divisions Plato declares that it is the same and not difference, the interests of all and not of each, that is foundational. That is to say, that as difference is ubiquitous – and Plato accepts the sophist's assertions in this regard – it is only upon what *is* the same that a new constitution may be thought.

Sophistic logic

The strange logic that sees oligarchic figures oppose the sophists and yet be themselves sophistic is worth following. What we see is that the demagogue and the sophist concur on the knowledge of knowledge, if not the method of its insistence. Thus, when Anytus rails against the sophist in the *Meno*, Plato makes it very clear that method and not logic is at issue (Men. 91c). What we see is a specific example of how judgment works. Near the end of this dialogue Meno and Socrates run into Anytus. Anytus is one of the accusers of Socrates in the trial (he is 'aggrieved on behalf of the professional men' (Ap. 24a)) and as usual Plato does not fail to make allusion (for the second time in this dialogue) to Socrates' fragile existence in the state (Men. 80b, 94e). The conversation continues to consider whether virtue can be taught. Anytus is sure it can, and, as in the *Apology*, he considers that any good Athenian will make a youth 'a *better* man than the sophist would' (Men. 92e, emphasis added). Meno will later suggest that common opinion is vague on the value of the sophist as teacher. In a comment which conforms to the Protagorean ethic he says 'that sometimes they are considered teachers, sometimes they are not' (Men. 95c). Anytus, on the other hand, is adamant: 'They are the manifest ruin and corruption of anyone who comes into contact with them' (Men. 91c).[33] Socrates appears shocked at this outburst and asks whether he has been wronged by one. Anytus answers, 'Heavens, no! I've never in my life had anything to do with a single one of them.' To which Socrates replies: 'How can you know what is good or bad in something when you have no experience of it?' Anytus retorts that 'he knows their *kind*'. Socrates suggests Anytus has a 'second sight'[34] for 'how else you know about them, judging from what you tell me yourself, I can't imagine' (Men. 92bd). The key to Anytus' claim is that what he does know is the correct property that one must possess in order to be, in this case, counted as a teacher of virtue. His lack of experience of the sophist is the very basis of his knowledge precisely because there is no other knowledge to be had of this figure than that which is the consequence of judgment and discernment in regard to a well established norm. The norm of the Athenian polis, for Anytus here, is the citizen. Anytus claims that any city that 'allows them [sophists] to come in' is mad. This is not a racist slur but a political claim. Foreigners, like women and slaves, were not citizens; they were not 'Athenians of the polis' so to speak. For Anytus, the whole question of virtue and the good is inextricably linked to one's place in the polity – democratic or not.[35] In a similar vein Socrates has occasion to chide Phaedrus: 'You seem to consider not whether a thing is or is not true, but who the speaker is and from what country the tale comes' (Phdr. 276c and Phd. 91bc). In the *Meno* Anytus is emphasising that one's place in the polis, who one is (as he says), the place of enunciation in other words, rather than what one is (an unanswerable question) is what matters in regard to what one can know and can teach. In effect, Anytus is claiming to know everything at once – without enquiry – and this is legitimated by the fact that, as Socrates makes a point of mentioning, he has been elected by the majority to the highest office (Men. 90ab). For Anytus, there is no need to enquire into the claims of the sophist precisely because he already knows what a good man is and that is a citizen of the polis. Or, conversely, the logic here is, one cannot enquire into what one's knowledge does not recognise to exist. With regard to virtue, the sophist, for Anytus, can be nothing. Socrates, the man who will not take part in his city's politics, ultimately inhabits this same position for Anytus. He is the absolute foreigner, more dangerous than any other because he *belongs* to the city.

The sophist is simply a foreign type, a stranger; such is why Socrates defends him against Anytus. Thus the figures not of the polity are essentially figures of the margin that appear only in terms of their use or their lack of use. The constant link Plato makes between the wealth accrued from slavery, the character of the city that is sustained by it, and the money spent on sophists is worth recalling here (as is Socrates' own *impious* discussion – on what is not known – with the slave in the very same dialogue).[36] For Anytus, the power to determine or to name an existence is given by one's position as citizen, which *by definition* is the place of (unconsidered) virtue. That Anytus includes Socrates with the sophists is not to say that Anytus recognises Socrates as a practitioner of sophistry per se but that he is situated within Anytus' statist conception to be equally placed, which is to say of the same part as the sophist.[37] They are of the same *kind* in the sense that they both are judged by Anytus to be incapable of virtue and classified therefore to have the 'part of no part' in virtue.

We can see that what Plato insists on is that what unifies the sophistic position, whether it be demagogue or professional teacher or the public itself, despite the diversity of opinion on show, is a commitment in some way to the Protagorean ethic in which a norm is posited such that whatever is perceived to contain a property conforming to that norm can thereby be named as such to belong as a part to the situation at hand. Whatever cannot be named cannot exist other than as, in Leibnizean terms, that which is a striving to exist for that situation – thus as potential part. Obviously, Socrates does not conform to either conception. Rather, as mentioned, Socrates' separation from the state is constituted by an entirely different make-up and Anytus is not the philosopher enough to see that the sameness he supposes is only re-presentable and that the real difference between sophist and non-sophist (the logic here is classical: recall, Socrates is the only non-sophist) is at the level of Form.[38] That is to say, it is not a matter of knowledge but of *constitution*.

What the above analysis helps to confirm is that, as Plato conceives it, the norm of the sophistic state is interest. This term is appropriate to both the demagogue *and* sophist and so covers both figures that appear throughout the dialogues as the proponents of a 'generalised sophistry'. In every dialogue Socrates interrogates these figures either directly or in the form of a surrogate, and we should recall too that these figures cover all types of states: the timocratic, the oligarchic, the despotic and the democratic.[39]

Exchange as interest in interest

One of the consistent definitions ascribed to the sophist is that of a teacher for money. Their wealth is constantly noted, the scale of their fees, who pays the most and, as we mentioned, where the money comes from. The demagogue, similarly, Plato claims, seeks office for personal gain. Both argue that their gain will benefit everyone – thus what is in their interests is in the interests of all. It is what politicians today designate by the phrase 'national interest'. Thus we have something like ideology. The constant reminder of the proximity the sophist has to money is not just done to distinguish the Socratic from the sophistic positions. It is an effect in itself. Plato seems to want to emphasise that the relation of exchange is predicated on the assumption of distinct gain – that interest can force the bond between the two. The general dialectic is that one's knowledge will translate into better wealth and one's wealth into better knowledge. Education is seen as the proper pursuit of the individual subject's interest in accord with the rule of the state. For the latter, interest is the object of reflection proper to any 'educated' subject. To know, in short, is to be properly instructed in an interest in interest. In other words, the sophistic teacher is one who represents the interests of the state to the youth as 'in their interest'. In light of this we can twist the Protagorean maxim into the educational ethic of sophistry. It states: 'The limits of my knowledge are the limits of my interest.'[40] The expectation is that this interest in interest will lead to an increase in value for both. Moreover, as the logic of Thrasymachus tells us, to be interested in interest is a property common to every state and what constitutes education in the sophistic state is simply the individual realisation of one's own interest according to this general rule.[41]

The negative proof that interest is the term that names education for the sophistic state is given, as usual, when considering the single, proscribed, non-sophist educator. Obviously, this figure marks a sort of limit point to the excessive power of the sophistic state. We can surmise that the sophistic rule must cease to function at this point. So the question can be posed as: 'What is it Socrates lacks in regard to the state?' That is to say, why does the state fail to recognise this figure except as an exception whose existence cannot be tolerated? What does Socrates fail to do in regard to the youth? What rule does he fail to satisfy? We know already that he fails to educate but what is the reason why? The simple answer is of course that Socrates has no interest in this state of things, no interest in this form of knowledge insofar as it is the *state* of the Athenian situation. For this singular figure, what is in the interest of all is the very basis of all thought and discourse and not the contingent fabrication of a particular knowledge founded on excessive conceit and an ignorant rule.

We will leave off pursuing Socrates as this development is the object of the remaining chapters. Instead, we should note that an interest in interest is a generative or re-productive notion. F. M. Cornford notes that the word *tokos* has two related meanings in Greek. It means offspring and interest on a loan.[42] In the *Republic* Plato uses it to make a pun which revolves around Socrates bringing these terms together and cautioning Glaucon to beware he doesn't inadvertently cheat him with false coin. Cornford's gloss on this combination in translation is 'a breed from barren metal' (R. 506). Consistent to the entire thematic of the Socratic procedure the *Republic* proposes the possibility of 'testing the metal' of those who would belong to the ideal state and those also who belong to other types of state. It is akin with Socrates' midwifery wherein the souls of those who come to him are tested to see whether they are pregnant with truths or with 'wind-eggs'. Thus the pun here alludes to both this testing for true offspring (the sun as the offspring of the good in the intelligible world (R. 508c)) and to the sophistic practice of monetary exchange.[43] Moreover, this division extends into the analysis of existing constitutions. For Plato, 'constitution' refers to both man and state (and this shouldn't be overlooked in thinking about the non-sophist), and what is at issue in the four states where reason is submitted to the rule of interest – to ambition and position in the timocracy, to money in the oligarchy, to the free reign of the appetites in the democracy, and to the free use of power in the despotic – is the progressive failure of an education by truths.[44] In fact what we have is the hereditary progress of the simulacrum of this education. Through each state of the decline the subject's interest in interest grows. This is of course the mirror image of the self-conception of the Athenian state where the reproduction entailed by an interest in interest is the very mark of virtue and thus of a good education.

Derrida's chimera

For the sake of comparison and in the spirit of engaging with and working through sophistry we turn now to Derrida's reading of this notion of offspring. It is not one that agrees with ours. Indeed, Derrida finds that this term serves the perpetuation of a type of sovereignty that *un-reasonably* denotes all orders of value. Derrida purports to discover a 'law of the father' in Plato, one which is intriguing, perhaps shocking, not because it is unique but precisely because by ascribing logos to the paternal position Plato has consecrated his foundational philosophy to a 'structural constraint' which precedes it.[45] The breadth and subtleties of the argument cannot be covered here. We will pick it up in the middle and drop it well before the end just as Derrida does with the speech of the king from the *Phaedrus*. We will give an exposition of this position and weave in a response attentive to our conception of the 'sophistic' state.

The setting for this section of Derrida's essay is the question of the value of writing. The central text Derrida reads is the relevant sections of the *Phaedrus*. Derrida picks up on the concord we have mentioned between interest and offspring part way into section two. Briefly, Derrida sets his analysis in the context of a 'father *logos*' wherein the familiarity of the former is given to us by relation to the latter: 'Logos represents what is indebted to: the father who is also the chief, capital, and goods. Or rather the chief, the capital, the goods' (Dis. 82).[46] The Good as it is proposed in the *Republic* is this figure of the *patēr*-father, *patēr* in Greek being synonymous with all the above (Dis. 86). In a real sense, the logos is the presentation of itself to the father who will authorise it and assign to it the value of what it is.

Derrida says Plato introduces this reproductive connection in his critique of writing. For Derrida, it is not tied to the demand inherent in sophistic exchange as it is for us, but to the Good. The good, the father, capital, is the source of all value and thus sophistic exchange, in Platonic terms, would be a mere semblance of that which is generated under a 'logos indebted to the father'. *Tokos* in Derrida's translation and definition refers strictly to the domain of reproduction or procreation. The term, in this fashion, covers 'agriculture, kinship relations and fiduciary operations' (Dis. 87). The offspring is the 'child' of any such relations: it is the 'return or revenue' Derrida says. However, we should note that what returns as interest is not a generic production per se but is truly a reproduction in the sense that it is the return of a difference under the conditions of the same. If we think capital, for example, what returns with interest is capital as profit, capital and capital itself as the offspring of the relation capital has with its conditions. Derrida remarks on the passage from the *Republic* where Plato, noting the role of 'capital' in his picture of the democratic state, says: 'Meanwhile the usurers, intent upon their own business, seem unaware of their [the poor "who long for revolution"][47] existence; they are too busy planting their stings into any fresh victim who offers an opening to inject the poison of their money; and while they multiply their capital by usury they are also multiplying the drones and the paupers' (R. 555e).

For Derrida, this passage shows the meaning of *patēr* 'inflected in the exclusive sense of financial capital'. As we see, Capital, in the place of the King, is set as the value by which the poor exist on the one hand (as without capital, yet eager to associate with it) and the usurer who is marked by Capital as the representative figure of the latter's existence. Derrida suggests that the good, the father and thus Capital is analogical to the sun in the Cave metaphor (Plato directly states the latter); one cannot look directly into its face, thus a clear sight of it is refused (Dis. 87). It is this notion that knowledge is withheld (in plain sight as it were) and that the father is the metaphor (or metonym, maybe) of this withholding in the sovereignty of logos that Derrida seeks to address. The good, sun, father is the source of offspring, of logos and the attendant *logoi*. Derrida argues that because the good or capital cannot be confronted face to face then what authorises one to speak as such cannot be spoken of – and thus all that can be addressed of the Good is its Idea, which Derrida is equating with the son of the father or logos (Dis. 88–9). The Idea for Derrida remains resolutely metaphysical.

Derrida's reading here, concerned as it is with subverting what he takes for the paradigmatic form of the Platonic logos, has the virtue of returning us to the constitutive split between the philosopher, who for Plato, works by truths, and the sophist, our subjective figure of interest.[48] Derrida's position on this is extremely interesting because he identifies the split between sophist and philosopher in a constitutive sense not unlike our own. He too takes his cue from the search for the sophist imitator which inadvertently reveals the philosopher model. However, for us, this split is not one of sovereignty but of procedure; moreover, the idea which Derrida conceives in terms of the son of an unspeakable father is not in thrall to the father, but the sole form of manifestation of that which is not present, but which is not at all a presence – present or not. If we accept this notion of the father-logos as a working metaphor, which is merely another way of speaking about the Truth – which in our Badiouean terms is an 'entirely empty category' (C, 66) and is as such commensurate with the lack of truth of the Platonic state – then there are two orientations, both of which produce 'offspring'.

There is the Socratic procedure, which, as we have seen, is fundamentally a-structured by the sophistic procedure which, in the *Phaedrus*, is the procedure of those who write and then leave their offspring undefended. The offspring of this generic or Socratic procedure, working as such from 'nothing', is not individuals making their way into the light per se but a new constitution of what it means to live outside the shadow of the state, or, analogously, to live in the half-light of the idea.

In this sense, the Good is a demand that issues in logos: but it is nothing except that which is realised through the 'Socratic procedure', which, as Derrida says, is that of knowing oneself, by oneself (Dis. 80). What Derrida does, through the logic of exchange, semantically at least, by insisting on the predication of logos (the presence of its place) is equate the predicative interest of the market, 'the service of goods', with the *void* truth of the Platonic procedure. This he does perhaps despite himself, for he does not concern himself with the concept of exchange per se. However, to speak of interest, of offspring as we mentioned, is to presuppose the relation that must support the procreation of this interest (recall that Socrates, paradoxically, defends the sophist as one who enters into exchange with the youth *by* taking money). The latter is simply the return of one thing (money) as another (knowledge qua capital): as that *which it is* under the guise of that *which it is not*. As we have argued, based on Plato's own showing, exchange is the relation the teacher-sophist establishes with the pupil-consumer in support of the production of an 'interest in interest'. It is a condition, in other words, of knowing to knowledge which institutes the certainty of its return whereas Socrates' relation to logos and to his associates is mediated through non-knowledge under the condition of love – which in Lacan's terms, whose general purport Plato shares, 'is giving what you do not have to someone who does not want it', in other words of giving the lack of knowledge (thus the very basis of all knowledge) to those who do not want it.[49]

Under the Platonic condition for truth, which is here love *of* wisdom (Plato carefully separates the lover from the object in the *Phaedrus*), one desires what one does not have, whereas exchange already presupposes the possession of goods, on the one hand, and on the other, a knowledge of the good of these goods, a knowledge of these goods and their 'proven effect' – which one equates with a capital sum. In Lacan's terms the sophist and his 'offspring' are well ensconced in *le service des biens*.[50] Unsurprisingly, Plato does not fail to mention this love of goods, which is antithetical to the love of the Good, in his discussion of the democratic man and in his discussion of the quality of the teachings the merchant sophist sells in the early stages of the *Protagoras* (Prt. 313c–314c). To put it in contemporary terms 'selling is what selling sells'.[51]

What organises the normal conditions for transmission or exchange under a regime of generalised sophistry is interest. Using Derrida's reading, exchange, when considered as the *sophistic* programme, would form an equivalence between the disparate forms of sophistic teaching and Socratic enquiry. Exchange, then, appears as the underside of Derrida's desire to subvert the Platonic logos, reducing the latter's interruptive force – occasioned by the lack of presence rather than the presence of lack as Derrida has it – to a mere reoccurrence of the sophistic form: an imitative discourse in its own right and a form of exchange. By equating the Platonic form with the sophistic in this way, Derrida has done the work of the state in ensuring that the incoherence that inheres between the interventional logic of the Platonic discourse and the mediatory logic of sophistics can be thought safely under a single nomination: exchange considered as the medium of the rule of interest.

We would suggest that Derrida's reading, as strong and as

inventive as it may be, is only possible if one reads the Platonic corpus as situated in the place of the sovereign. But given the real place of non-sophistry within the sovereign state of Athens, the time after all of the genesis of the corpus, we insist that the corpus must be read anew as that which subtracts itself from all sovereignty – and in particular, given that this is what conditions the corpus, sovereignty constituted by a generalised sophistry. Thus, as we will see, Plato's assertion of *logos* is the result of a drawing under and away from; it cannot be construed as something like a transcendental imposition. The Platonic corpus does not come in over the top but arrives from within. It seems to us unjust to read Plato in terms of result alone – or as if the *Republic* were a sovereign state announcing a sovereign reign rather than the result that it is of an eventally founded, generic re-collection of the terms which Athens presents. One must read the corpus in terms of its constitution.[52]

The sophistic equation

Despite all we have said, we need to make a clarification in regard to what it is Plato objects to in the current state. This is because his objection is not of a type recognised by the current state for what it is. Plato's objection to sophistic practice is not therefore that the sophists are in service to the state or that they take money for this service. Nor was Plato objecting to the sophist selling the knowledge of what it was the state required, nor to his purporting to teach *that* particular knowledge. In constructivist terms it is hardly objectionable to train or school a subject in the art of making its way in the world as it is. Nor was the Platonic objection aimed at the obvious fact that this training was only available to those who could afford it, thereby continuing the access of the privileged to the access to privileges.

The greater objection to the sophist that Plato held was not that they sold their wares, but that they entangled this selling with wisdom. That is, it was not just that they claimed to be selling wisdom, that they subjected even this to the demands of 'callous cash payment', but more than this, that they, by their very practice, established these two in relation. It is this latter aspect that draws Plato's continued fire and this because exchange demands equivalence as its conceptual foundation. Equivalence would mark that, under the rule of interest, reciprocity is founded between wisdom and money. Socrates makes this plain when he tells Hippocrates: 'If you pay [the sophist] sufficient to persuade him, he will make you wise too' (Prt. 310d). We should not overlook the term persuasion here, for it is money which persuades the sophist to teach the youth the art of persuasion, the extent of the latter being the mark of wisdom for the 'imitative' class. However, what founds this foundation is not intrinsic to the couple 'wisdom and money' but is extrinsic. What makes wisdom, the sophistic commodity, and money reciprocal is the form of the state itself, which is to say the set of relations that organise the world for which the sophist is educator and for which sophistry is education.

For Plato, there is no possible calculation, no measure, which could engender equivalence between truth and interest as it is manifest in the form of exchange existing within the sophistic state. While the state manages a situation in which such exchange is everyday carried out subject to the laws of tradition and the market, truth has no immediate relation to this state of affairs. Exchange, determined as the modality of equivalence and administered by the state, is the name for and the mechanism of foreclosure. That is to say, what must be is that Socrates, a figure who bluntly refuses this logic of exchange, whose disinterest in interest is well remarked and emphasised as the negative constitution of virtue, *must not be*. As such, truth is decidedly not that which can be put into circulation by the market (Socrates circulates within the market*place*, but not within the market itself) nor does truth support this circulation.[53]

What the above reflects is the structural form of state knowledge as Plato conceives it. If there is nothing but the state, then interest is both the category of existence and at the same time the object of knowledge. The sophistic procedure, as the *Sophist* shows, is a self-reflexive, self-perpetuating procedure of production whose fatal flaw is the excessive conceit it has in its ability to know. When Protagoras tells Hippocrates 'after each day with him he will go home a better man, more ably adapted to the city, than the day before and so on ever after' (Prt. 318a) this is merely indicative.

The thing itself

To finish it is worthwhile proposing a summary of this sophistic position. It is gleaned from reading the *Euthydemus* but encompasses the essence of the seven-line division we see in both the *Sophist* and *Statesman*: divisions which analyse the specific detail, predicates and practices of the sophist and demagogue alike. The series of these divisions each includes an immanently separated instance which is simply the Socratic position.

In the *Euthydemus* two brothers stage a show of eristic 'philosophy'. They profess themselves capable of refuting anyone on any topic. They have no concern for truth, only victory. However, while satirising these two and this show as a type of philosophy, Plato aims his most severe criticism not at the brothers but at a 'man of the law courts'. This man, a writer of fine speeches for others, has just come away from 'watching' this performance where Crito's 'friend', Socrates, has 'put himself in the hands of men who just grapple with every phrase and don't care what they say'. In reply to Crito's retort that 'surely philosophy is a fine thing', he says, 'it is of no value whatever', and yet, he says, alluding to the 'sophistic' interlocutors, these are 'some of the most powerful men of the day' (Euthd. 305a).

Using Prodicus' terms Socrates counters that these men (of the law courts) are the 'frontiersmen between philosophy and politics'; as such, they know just enough about either to be 'moderately well up' on both. This knowledge enables them to 'keep clear of both danger and conflict' while enjoying 'the fruits of wisdom'. In reply to Crito's suggestion that the accounts such men give of philosophy seem plausible (this in relation to the performance just witnessed), Socrates says, recalling the similar comment from the *Phaedo*, 'plausibility [or seeming] is just what it does have, Crito, rather than truth' (Euthd. 305c–e). Socrates proceeds to dissect the 'man of the law courts' in these terms. He is just enough divided from either philosophy or politics to be less than either. Alluding to his claims that philosophy is nothing and the system that allows it to take place is similarly worthless, Socrates says, 'it is only if such a figure is between two evils that he seems better than both'. What occurs here is a classic Platonic division: the man of the law courts is reduced to being less than the two goods, philosophy and politics, by virtue of his refusal to truly, which is to say subjectively, partake of either. What he does is *approach* both, but for Plato, this approach, characterised in terms of verisimilitude, remains a semblance of real engagement as it lacks all courage, a necessary virtue. This writer of fine speeches seeks the gain associated with being 'like' either but in the face of the dangerous consequences fidelity exposes one to he retreats. As neither, he is other to both. The dialogue ends with Crito expressing his confusion and asking Socrates how he should educate his sons.[54] Socrates replies 'pay no attention to the practitioners of philosophy, whether good or bad. Rather give serious consideration to the thing itself' (Euthd. 307bc).

Finally, we are in a position to establish the essential features of the sophistic state. The rest of our enquiry will be devoted to tracing Plato's Socrates in his efforts to separate out from this state a thinking of non-sophistry whose present indiscernibility is the very constitution of a new form of the state. These essential features are: (a) the sophist is concerned with the art of dialectic only insofar as it promises gain. This is dialectic, but in its eristic sense only, with concern being for the victory refutation brings; (b) the sophist is an intrinsic and extensive figure of the state, foreclosing the demands of truth for the logic of interests; (c) from this position they act as the conduit by which the right measure of the latter can result in the gain of the former, and as such, they can profess to teach 'what is required' for a young man to make his way in the state; (d) in ethical terms this 'immoderation' in regard to their professions of knowledge amounts to a lack of courage. The sophist, concerning the truth, must be a man of perspective rather than conviction, of judgment rather than thought, of interest and not principle. The truth as a mark of rigorous division, rather than sophistic dissemination, by which opinions 'true' or 'false' lose their utility and their veracity, is anathema to the sophist for it puts at risk his stake in interest; (e) thus, avoidance of this risk (of the true) is the necessary condition for enjoying the 'fruits of [this] wisdom' (obviously Socrates 'shows' the result of the 'risk': no money, no property, etc.) or in other words the profit of this interest, and it is this which gives the sophist their modal power in the state; (f) finally, that the sophist is a figure of semblances, of opinion and never of that which is 'by truths'.

This summary leaves us with the complete picture of the sophistic state. Its knowledge, rule, and practice will form the backdrop of the Socratic procedure we will follow across the coming chapters. Our goal here was to read the character of this state in and through what Plato shows it to be. We have not sought to interpret the dialogues so much as demonstrate that under the condition of Badiou's distinction between the situation and its state the possible place for the arrival of something other than the rule of interest and the conceit of knowledge might be found. In the next chapter we will establish the existence of such a place and establish that it is the foundation for all the encounters of the dialogues and the enquiries pursued thereby.

Notes

1. Jacques Lacan, 'Kant with Sade', *Ecrits*, pp. 660/782.
2. John Sellars, '"The problem of Socrates", Review of Sarah Kofman, *Socrates: Fictions of* a *Philosopher*', pp. 267–75.
3. Alexander Nehamas points out that both Isocrates (in his *Helen*) and Aeschines include Socrates under the term 'sophist'. The former, Nehamas says, writing fifty years after Socrates' death felt no need to justify this categorisation. The inference is that it was well accepted. See 'Plato on philosophy and sophistry', *The Virtues of Authenticity*, p. 108.
4. Badiou develops this logic in reference to Saint Paul. However, it is clear to see that this opening gambit of the *Apology* is central to Plato's situating of Socrates. For Plato, it is Socrates who is the true citizen.
5. Diogenes Laertius relates a story of Justus of Tiberius from his 'Garland' that Plato ascended the tribune and said 'I men of Athens, being the youngest of all those who have mounted the tribune . . .' Plato was then shouted down by the judges who cried 'κατάβα, κατάβα', that is to say 'Come down' (in John Ferguson, *Socrates: A Source Book*, p. 27; hereafter all references to Diogenes Laertius will be to this source and appear in the text, taking the form Diog. Lae. followed by verse number and page number).
6. With this conviction and execution the Athenian jury literally turns the strange figure of Socrates – strange because he signifies that which is not (*known* as) 'Athenian' – into the Athenian stranger: the figure who returns again and again in an effort to turn the city toward the pursuit of truth. This return is always a return to education and to the city wherein such a possibility exists (Phdr. 230d).
7. Cf. Gramsci: '. . . The entire function of the state has been transformed: the state has become an "educator" . . .' Antonio Gramsci, *Selections from the Prison Notebooks*, p. 260.
8. In the *Statesman* the Visitor says: 'We must remove those who participate in all these constitutions, except for the one based on knowledge, as being, not statesmen but experts in faction; we may say that, as presiding over insubstantial images, on the largest scale, they are themselves of the same sort, and that as the greatest imitators and magicians they turn out to be the greatest sophists among the sophists' (Stm. 303c; cf. Euthd. 305c+). This is an interesting turn of phrase for it suggests that the individual sophist is between the experts of the faction, the man of the polis and the youth. The relation between Callicles, Gorgias and Polus in the *Gorgias* appears to be the salutary example. For how close to the state many sophists were – writing constitutions, serving as ambassadors, etc. – see G. B. Kerferd, *The Sophistic Movement* and Mario Untersteiner, *The Sophists*. Badiou's reading of Saint-John Perse

in *The Century* comes to mind here: 'I write stanzas on exile and the impermanence of human things, but I allow no one to ignore that I am under-secretary to the Emperor' (TC, 84).

9. Kerferd claims that public attacks on the sophists – and there were more sophists of course than appear in Plato –were political attacks on Pericles himself who, Kerferd argues, was in fact the 'patron of the sophists' (Kerferd, *The Sophistic Movement*, p. 22).
10. This phrase has many variations throughout the dialogues. This particular confection is from Cornford's gloss on the role of the 'noble sophist' as given in the seven-line division of the dialogue the *Sophist* (Plato, *Plato's Theory of Knowledge: The Theaetetus and the Sophist*, p. 170; see Sph. 231b).
11. Patricia O'Grady, 'What is a sophist?', in *The Sophists: An Introduction*, p. 12. O'Grady, tellingly –'democratically' – gives this definition as one 'free of Plato's dogmatism and malevolence'.
12. The 'diagonal' is important in Cantor's proof that the cardinality of real numbers exceeds that of the cardinality of the natural numbers. It is by tracing a diagonal across the graph of correspondence that new numbers are formed that escaped the one-to-one correspondence that the graph posits. This proof has its implication in set theory in terms of sets, subsets and the set of all subsets, the upshot being there can be no set of all sets, no 'highest aleph'. *There is* incommensurability and it may be traced. See Mary Tiles, *The Philosophy of Set Theory: An Introduction to Cantor's Paradise*, p. 64, p. 110. See also Meditation 26 of *Being and Event*.
13. See Barbara Cassin, 'From organism to picnic, which consensus for which city?', pp. 21–38. Cassin argues for the bond of consensus as fundamental to the constitution of the city. The best efforts of the sophists sought this. For Badiou, the philosopher is suspicious of consensus and the constitution of any consensus is what the philosopher must investigate. '*Since Plato*, philosophy has meant a rupture with opinion, and is meant to examine everything which is spontaneously considered as *normal*. Everything consensual is suspicious as far as the philosopher is concerned' (M, 78).
14. Socrates was convicted by a majority. The concept of 'majority' will return periodically in the dialogues. It is always in terms that pose the singularity of truth against the opinions of the majority. The 'paradox' is that a truth is always already *for all* in a way that majority opinion, obviously, cannot be.
15. '. . . to think the new in a situation we also have to think the situation, and thus we have to think what is repetition, what is the old, what is not new, and after that we have to think the new again' (Badiou and Bosteels, CCT, 253).
16. Jacob Klein presents exactly this form of non-reciprocity in discussing

Plato's distinction between sensible and insensible numbers of things. '[W]hatever furnishes the *foundation* for something else (in our case for the ordinary numbers), whatever makes the being of another possible, is also more meaningful, more powerful in its being, than this other. The being of that which is the foundation takes precedence over that which is so founded, i.e., it is prior, because the second cannot be without the first, but the first can be without the second.' Further, he says that Aristotle refers to Plato's use of this distinction in such a way as to signify that it was characteristic of Plato (Jacob Klein, *Greek Mathematical Thought and the Origin of Algebra*, p. 71).

17. Protagoras is critical to the sophistic tradition in four ways: (a) he was a good friend of Pericles and wrote constitutions for him; (b) he claimed that he belonged to the great sophistic tradition which included the poets Homer, Hesiod and so on who, for him, were sophists even though they hid their true profession under other names (thus the problem of speaking in one's own name is paramount in sophistry); (c) Plato devotes at least three dialogues to the 'problem of Protagoras'; (d) the great scene in the dialogue which bears his name sees all the prominent sophists of the day, a collection of demagogues, hangers-on and others, attend a gathering at Callias' house in his honour. Indeed, his very name suggests these connections: 'First man of the city', basically.
18. De Romilly, *The Great Sophists of Periclean Athens*, p. 98. Plato counters this with explicit comments at R. 604b, L. 716c and Tht. 161c.
19. The full exposition of the distinction Badiou makes between the ontological and the metaontological realms of discourse is beyond the scope of this work. There are pertinent critiques of Badiou's distinction (and 'conflation') especially insofar as for Badiou, an ontological situation deals with elements and sets and as such with signs and abstractions while all other situations deal with 'things'. See Ray Brassier, 'Presentation as anti-phenomenon in Alain Badiou's *Being and Event*', pp. 59–77; Justin Clemens, 'Doubles of nothing: the problem of binding truth to being in the work of Alain Badiou', pp. 21–35; Zachary Luke Fraser's excellent study of Sartre and Badiou, *This Infinite, Unanimous Dissonance: A Study in Mathematical Existentialism, Through the Work of Jean-Paul Sartre and Alain Badiou*, esp. pp. 73–8.
20. The void is the proper name of being (BE, 52).
21. See the introduction to *Infinite Thought* where Feltham and Clemens deftly avoid having to describe what Badiou means by 'neutral situation' (IT, 25).
22. Jacques Lacan, *The Four Fundamental Concepts of Psychoanalysis, Seminar XI*, p. 263.
23. Badiou makes the point that the constructivist vision is compelling and on its own terms irrefutable (BE, 289/320). Certainly, the dialogues

illustrate this 'capacity'. The sophist is an ever retreating figure, turning counter examples into his own proofs; making a virtue from suspending conversation and refusing to go on; passing the baton of conversation to others to preserve one's own position, among many other displays.

24. Cf. B. Madison-Mount, 'The Cantorian revolution', pp. 41–91.
25. Cf. D, 26–9, and Gilles Deleuze, 'The simulacrum and ancient philosophy, appendices to *The Logic of Sense*', esp. p. 262; hereafter LoS.
26. As Heidegger points out, Plato is confronted with two possibilities with regard to the sophist: either assent to the dogma of the Parmenidean tradition that says that 'non-beings are not' or in 'ruthless opposition to all pre-established theory' accept the fact of the sophist's existence, and this includes the facts of 'deception', 'distortion' and 'misrepresentation' (Heidegger's terms). The sophist is a copy, an imitation of the wise, but against Parmenidean tradition Plato takes up the task of making μή ὀν of the ψεὖδος intelligible. For Heidegger, as for Badiou, the sophist has the positive effect of 'making visible the phenomena which further investigation can latch onto'. These alternatives, Heidegger continues, between the submission to the tradition and ruthlessness toward it (further investigation) recurs in every philosophical investigation conscious of itself. He concludes by saying that such 'ruthlessness' is 'reverence toward the past' (Martin Heidegger, *Plato's Sophist*, pp. 285–6).
27. In his semi-mock recapitulation of Protagoras' ideas in *Theaetetus*, Socrates has Protagoras state that 'In education what we have to do is to change a worse state into a better one . . . the professional teacher does it by use of words' (Tht. 167a). He goes on to say that if the teacher can achieve this he is worthy of his large fees (Tht. 167d). Cf. Ap. 20bc. Citing Apelt citing the *Dialexis* (an anonymous summary of arguments believed to be based on the lectures of fifth-century sophists) Cornford notes they really did believe that mastery of eristic discourse gave them the means to pronounce upon any matter from medicine to law to the running of the city and the ordering of men (Plato, *Plato's Theory of Knowledge: The Theaetetus and the Sophist*, p. 191, fn 3).
28. Socrates says that 'According to Meno the hereditary guest friend of the Great King virtue is the *acquisition* of gold and silver' (Meno. 78d) – 'justly' of course he is invited to add! As we will see, from the sophist one must learn precisely this: the just acquisition of goods.
29. Eric Havelock, *Preface to Plato*, p. 234.
30. Havelock, *Preface to Plato*, p. 234.
31. Cf. Isocrates: 'But these professors have gone so far in their lack of scruple that they attempt to persuade our young men that if they will only study under them they will know what to do in life and through this knowledge will become happy and prosperous. More than that, although they set themselves up as masters and dispensers of goods

so precious, they are not ashamed of asking for them a price of three or four minae! Why, if they were to sell any other commodity for so trifling a fraction of its worth they would not deny their folly; nevertheless, although they set so insignificant a price on the whole stock of virtue and happiness, they pretend to wisdom and assume the right to instruct the rest of the world. Furthermore, although they say that they do not want money and speak contemptuously of wealth as filthy lucre," they hold their hands out for a trifling gain and promise to make their disciples all but immortal!' (Isocrates, 'Against the Sophists', in *Isocrates: On the Peace*, p. 72). In Untersteiner's inexact terms 'the sophists must be given the credit of having conceded to man the right to a human life, human speech, and human thought' (Mario Untersteiner, *The Sophists*, p. xvi).

32. To be exact, what Badiou says is that that philosophy must not give in to anti-sophistic extremism: 'Non, le sophiste doit être seulement assigné *à sa place*' (C, 73). It is critical to note the sophist must only be assigned to *his* (or *her*) place (*à sa place*) and not to a place in general. The *place* of the sophist is an effect of sophistry being, in this case, displaced by that which is 'to come', by the generic procedure or the education by truths. No *one* in particular assigns the sophist his/her place. The sophist's place is itself a retroactive fiction. For a different view see Cassin, 'Who's afraid of the Sophists? Against ethical correctness', p. 105.
33. It is worth comparing the cases of Callicles in the *Gorgias*, Thrasymachus in the *Republic* and the 'man of the law courts' in *Euthydemus*. Against all three Socrates defends the practising sophist. What unifies these instances is that he does so by demonstrating the sophistry of each.
34. Grube uses 'wizard': *Plato: Complete Works*, p. 891; also *Plato: The Collected Dialogues*, p. 376. The above translation is Guthrie's *Protagoras and Meno*.
35. The histories tell us of Anytus and Meletus' sycophantic and murderous behaviour under the tyranny. This notion that what it meant to be Greek was to be a 'man of the polis' is repeated ad nauseam in texts from across the spectrum of disciplines that deal with (and fetishise) ancient Greece. Cf. 'Yes that is how a democracy comes to be established, whether by force of arms or because the other party is terrorised into giving way' (R. 557a). One never learns *that* in school.
36. It is repeated several times in various dialogues that Callias is the Athenian who has spent more on sophists than anyone else. The glorious gathering of sophists depicted in the *Protagoras* takes place at his house. Anyway, it should be noted that Callias' money comes from his father Hipponicus (his mother was an ex-wife of Pericles). Hipponicus' father was Callias II who made his money in the silver

mines of Larium. He was the biggest slave owner. Of added interest is that Hipponicus' other son Hermogenes (different mother) is the interlocutor in the *Cratylus* and his name means son of Hermes, the god of wealth (elsewhere Pluto gets this crown). Hermogenes is not so well favoured though and he is one of the few who we could reasonably say was 'corrupted' by Socrates (positively connected to an enquiry) (Cr. 407d–408a; see Chapter 3). By inference, he is no son of Hipponicus' *type* – unlike Callias. The latter, rich off the back of slavery, is in slavish thrall to sophistry whose wisdom is slavish in its rigor and which prospers from the receipts of slavery.

37. Socrates says the same thing: in reverse! 'I believe that I am one of the few Athenians – so as not to say I'm the only one, but the only one among our contemporaries – to take up the true political craft and practise true politics.' His reason is that he does not make speeches that flatter but aim at the truth (cf. Ap. 17a and Grg. 521c–522a).
38. This is in line with the conclusion reached between the Stranger and Theaetetus in the *Sophist*, that 'when not or non are added to the names of things they indicate not a contrary but that the thing is other than the things to which the names following the negation are applied' (Sph. 257c).
39. As examples: in the *Meno*, Meno speaks from a Gorgianic position; in *Theatetus*, after Theodorus gives up Socrates himself speaks as Protagoras; and in the *Republic* Thrasymachus even speaks in the language of the 'actual' Athenian Ambassadors to Melos as related by Thucydides (R. 339).
40. This certainly recalls Wittgenstein's proposition 5:6 from the *Tractatus* that 'the limits of my language mean the limits of my world.' For Badiou, Wittgenstein is 'our Gorgias' (C, 7).
41. H. D. Rankin in *Sophists, Socratics and Cynics*, p. 14, notes that one effect of the sophists was to 'free' the youth from a traditional morality enabling them to pursue 'success without remorse of conscience'. But of course the new economic and social position of Athens demanded just that. The sophists were not opposed to the state in any way but played their part in the re-form of the state. We are not the first to point out that the sophists share certain critical features with postmodernism. What links them is the conflation of truth with authority or tradition and thus they fall to privileging a cultural laissez-faire over justice.
42. *The Republic of Plato*, fn 2, p. 217.
43. Plato notes that, 'the mercenary skirmishers of debate' are the direct 'offspring' of the Protagorean ethic of measure (Tht. 165de).
44. In Badiou's ethics, evil is the failure of the good. As the sophist is the ignorant imitator of the wise, so evil is a simulacrum of truth for Badiou. This distinction precipitates Badiou's extension of subjectivity in *Logiques des Mondes*.

45. Jacques Derrida, *Dissemination*, pp. 80–2; hereafter in text as Dis.
46. Derrida comments that neither translators nor commentators have accounted for the play of these schemas. This may be true in French translation and commentary but Cornford picks this up in his translation and commentary of the *Republic*.
47. I. Bernard Cohen notes that the Greeks did not have a single word for revolution and used many approximations depending on context. He argues that they were certainly well aware of the act itself. He notes that Aristotle in the *Politics* uses the confection *metabole*, which he translates as 'change with uprising'. *Revolutions in Science*, p. 54.
48. In terms taken from Badiou's *Logiques des Mondes*, the sophist, as the philosopher's perverse twin, would be situated within the 'subjective space' opened by an evental occurrence, as a 'reactive subject'. 'The reactive subject works on the basis of a denial (*déni*) of the novelty inherent to a generic process and in favour of statist categorisations. The reactive subject works on the faithful to settle for 'what is' (the lack of a present Badiou calls it) and the 'ways of doing' that produce this 'what is' (repetition and reproduction) (LM, 82, my translation).
49. Derrida is of course very concerned with the status of writing. In the *Phaedrus*, ostensibly a dialogue on love, Plato distinguishes between that which is 'written (or *inscribed*) in the soul' and as such is the discourse of all such souls, and the writings that affect only to persuade one way or another. The first belong not to the wise, he says, but to the lovers of wisdom. Thus Plato is not here talking of a father logos but of a procedure which loves, a procedure which by that love makes reason manifest in the world. The philosopher induces the offspring of reason; he produces nothing. The famous statement of Lacan that 'love comes to supplement the lack of sexual rapport' is entirely appropriate here. It is probable that he was influenced in this conception by the *Symposium*. See Lorenzo Chiesa, 'Le resort de l'amour: Lacan's theory of love in his reading of Plato's Symposium', pp. 61–80. In *Théorie du sujet* Badiou appropriates this saying and reformulates it as a motif of courage as the condition for justice: 'Amiez ce que jamais vous ne croirez deux fois' ('Love what you will never believe twice') (TS, 339–46).
50. Jacques Lacan, *Seminar VII, The Ethics of Psychoanalysis, 1959–60*, p. 303.
51. The Clash, 'Car Jam', *Combat Rock*, CBS, 1982.
52. At the risk of being gratuitous, we note the following from Friedrich Kittler: 'Nonetheless . . . when it came to discussing ancient Greek history, Derrida had no idea at all about the actual historical or philosophical contexts he considered in his writings. It is for this reason that I have reservations about Derrida's historical interpretations of philosophers such as Plato' (John Armitage, 'From discourse networks to cultural mathematics: an interview with Friedrich A. Kittler', p. 7).

53. Cf. Badiou: 'There is no commercial philosophy' (BE, 340–1/375–6). This is reflected in the *Republic* where philosopher kings are forbidden to own property or engage in business. Their only intercourse is with the Good. The Good is not a relative term.
54. Crito's concern, matched by other 'fathers' in other dialogues, and of course generalised in the corpus itself, seems to signify that this form of the Sophist predominated and was considered to be the obvious figure in the education of the youth.

CHAPTER 2

Site

> 'Now, in every matter it is of great moment to start at the right point in accordance with the subject.' (T. 29b)

> 'Le commencement sont mesurés par ce qu'ils autorisent de re-commencements.' (LM, 396)

Given that the dialogues present a clear disjunction between the figure of Socrates and that of sophistry, the *question* of this disjunction emerges. That is to say, if Socrates is not 'of education' insofar as education is 'by the state', then what is it in the 'Athens of the dialogues' that this figure names? What we have seen so far is that with regard to education he is not a part of the sophistic state and yet he is convicted as a singular threat to the very constitution of this state due to the very paradoxical (non-)relation he maintains with the youth and with others – 'anyone at all' as he contends. So what does 'Socrates' name in the Athens of the dialogues? More specifically, what is presented there (but lacking in the re-presentation that would see it included) as an essential part of the sophistic regime? The facts are that this knowledge of what 'Socrates' names will *come to be* known, but as yet we are constrained to conceive of this unpresented 'part' without full knowledge of what it *will have been*. What we do have is the certainty that what he does name is what the state is not: he names what to the state is nothing. It is too early to say that Socrates 'knows nothing' but what we can see is that this nothing can be conceived precisely because there is nothing else, with regard to education, that Socrates can be seen to name. Thus, if nothing else, his is the name in the state for what is not a sophistic 'education'. Education therefore is the very thing that founds the disjunction between the Socratic figure and his sophistic double and as we will see, education, ultimately, can only be non-sophistic.

A point of passage

If one casts an eye over Badiou's work of the past forty years one can identify three instances of the site. It appears in an early though unformulated way in the 1982 work *Théorie du sujet*; it forms the core of the articulation of being *and* event in 1988's *L'être et l'événement*; and in 2007's *Logiques des mondes* the site is the reflexive space through which the new passes in appearance. Within each work this 'element' plays a fundamental role in organising Badiou's philosophical conception of how the new appears in situations and coincidently how *being* is situated therein. As we argued in the introduction we are not convinced that the 'categories *Being and Event* deploys' have indeed been 'practiced across the entirety of the contemporary system of reference' (BE, 4/10) nor have the consequences been drawn regarding the 'history of the metaphysical text' wherein these categories, 'though at work there', go 'unnamed' (BE, 435/475). To this end we will concentrate on the conception of the site as it appears in this work.

As Badiou readily admits, 'the theory of the site is fairly complex' (CCT, 254). Symptomatic of this complexity is Badiou's own reorganisation of the concept as alluded to above. This is further marked throughout Badiou's post-*Being and Event* oeuvre and into the secondary commentary by its appearing, usually without comment, as either event-site or void-site. Conceptually, the cause of this complexity is that the site marks a transition point, a point of passage, which bridges the being of a situation (its 'void') to the establishment of its truth (post-event). The site is at once the last measure of presented consistency and yet at the same time precisely because of the type of element *that it is*, will have constituted the material basis for any event – that which ruptures with all situational consistency. The question the site poses is of an element that is consistent with its situational structure and at the same time is that which exposes its situation to the perils of inconsistency.

Schema of the site

As important as this concept is to Badiou's oeuvre, our goal is simply to provide a working explanation of how the site functions within Badiou's conception of a truth procedure sufficient to applying it to the Platonic corpus. This does require some original work on the function and 'make-up' of the site but it is by no means complete.

In order to reign in some of the complexity we will take the measure of the site through the following series of quotes.

1. I will term *evental site* an entirely abnormal multiple, that is a multiple such that none of its elements are presented in the situation (BE, 175/195).
2. [S]uch a multiple . . . is *on the edge of the void*. [It] is therefore the *minimal* effect of structure which can be conceived (BE, 175/195).
3. [The site] is the totally unforeseeable beginning of a rupture (LS, 142).
4. [A site is] a disassembled gathering . . . the provisional territory of some protocols of thought (P, 195).

From this we can form a description. The site is: abnormal, disassembled, unforeseeable, minimal and provisional.

If we schematise this description we can then draw out a few fundamental points which will serve both our exposition and the analysis of the dialogues.

- Like any multiple the site exists insofar as it is presented as such by a situation. That it is characterised as 'abnormal' or 'unnatural' simply denotes there is something particular about this multiple in relation to the others that the situation presents.
- Disassembly denotes that elements which make up the site, though 'real', are not presentable as such by the situation which presents the site. The forms of structure particular to the situation have no means for assembling these abnormal elements into a consistent form. The site is the presented term of their disassembly.
- Given their relative inconsistency the situation has no means for recognising them as anything other than nothing. Although *this* site-multiple is not 'empty' as is its ontological counterpart, the elements the site presents are void *for the situation*.
- In such a situation, the site will be the minimally structured element. It will be counted once, not twice. This is to say, the elements of the site are not effects of structure. It is possible to say these void elements found the situation.
- As beneath this situational order the elements which a site presents remain latent, not in terms of their intrinsic potential as individual elements but in relation to the fact that they lack the form of their gathering. From an analytic perspective, a perspective outside the situation itself, we can know that these formless elements are the provisional material of the event. In combination with the latter,

which is to say retroactively, they establish disassembly as a capacity.

Ontological provenance

Before we move on to develop this schema, it is important to note the ontological provenance of this term 'site'. By denoting that which 'presents what is unpresented' or, indeed, that which is nothing to the situation, the term 'site' is the literal transcription into the philosophical (metaontological) lexicon of the ontological name of the 'void'. In passing let's note that the relation is not one of mere analogy. If ontology thinks, for Badiou, then philosophy thinks it as thought. The latter is constrained to do so in its own language and through the invention of concepts appropriate to its discourse and history. For Badiou at least, these inventions are thoroughly conditioned by the rigorous and systematic thinking of pure multiplicity established in ZFC set theory. The singular outcome of ZFC, adopted by Badiou, is to show that the *one* of every appearance is intrinsically *multiple*. The fundamental thought Badiou draws from the latter, as we mentioned, is that the 'one is not' and, as such, *the nothing is* (BE, 35/45). 'Nothing' (Badiou's term) is the general regime of non-presentation.

We have seen already that what appears of being does so as a situation, as a structured multiple. Through the operation of the latter a consistency is established. In set theory, these operations are functions of the axiom system which prescribes the variety and context by which what is nothing comes to *be* thought. However, the great universe that set theory establishes relies on an assertion of existence which is itself axiomatic. If the nothing is – 'a multiple without one' – then set theory, being a situation in its own right and thus having its own law of structure, must mark this inexistence. The result is that that which is nothing is named void. Given that it cannot be one, nothing can only *appear* as the one of the multiplicity that it is: 'It is thus ruled out that the nothing – which here names the pure will-have-been-counted as distinguishable from the effect of the count, and thus distinguishable from presentation – be taken as a term. There is not a-nothing, there is "nothing", phantom of inconsistency' (BE, 54–5/68–9). Set theory assigns inconsistency or pure multiplicity or nothing, a mark of itself. The mark localises, for a situation, the general regime of that which is un-presented or nothing. The void, simply, is the 'proper name of Being' (BE, 59/72). This name or mark Ø refers uniquely to 'nothing', making 'being' thinkable in situations.

Accordingly, set theory draws its entire form from this presentation of the multiple. It determines a thinking of being which has in no way to know, identify or qualitatively differentiate its terms in order to think and thus to multiply them. It is a rule of this thought that multiples be treated on the basis of their belonging to a situation and not as the reflection of some transcendental mark or imposed nomination. The situation, whose ontological basis is always the same, simply cannot recognise such impositions. Knowledge, of any sort, is not presupposed; the existence of the void set is a decision on the unpresentable.

The importance of the void-site for thinking *historical situations* is established when we consider two fundamental aspects. As a term, which is not represented, it marks a point of escape from statist rule. Secondly, if it escapes this rule then its existence as such must be predicated in terms of belonging alone. We can say, then, that the one of presentation continues to insist in the situation through the singularity of the site. The latter guards the lack of the rule of the state. This 'lack' is a capacity common to all situated elements (inhabitants). This common capacity is something we shall return too. Suffice to say for now that it concerns the central problem of the universal, recognisable in our terms as education for all. It is fundamental that it be understood that an education by truths can only be one that addresses this lack. The very essence of the sophistic position is that such a capacity is dependent upon or secondary to its mode of determination. As we saw, the Protagorean ethic is that which holds good for every city. However, this is not to say the Protagorean ethic is the good of every city. For sophistry, any education first passes through the determinations of the state yet, as we see, the site guarantees the place of its lack. In other words, that a non-state education not appear for the state is what the site guarantees.

Singularity, eventality, gathering

From our five-part schema above it is possible to derive three central features of the site: singularity, eventality and gathering. The analysis of each will help to show how the site serves to help facilitate the invention of a new form or, in other words, how that which is *nothing* to the situation becomes *everything*.

- *Singularity* can be understood as the pre-evental form of the site within a given situation (BE, 522/556). This is not to suggest we can identify the site per se, as this or that feature of a situation, only its 'multiple form'. The abnormality of this multiple is its singularity. Nothing of what makes it up appears as one in the situation. The latter, as Badiou says, is 'an essential attribute of the site'.

- The site is *evental* precisely because this multiple which presents nothing marks the only possible site for an event. Eventality thus names the latent void power of this most minimally structured multiple.
- We adopt the term *gathering* because what the site qua singularity presents are what *will be* the elements of the event, which is to say that the nothing which properly 'belongs' to the site is the very material of the event. Even more importantly, these un-(re-)presented elements that the site presents are precisely elements of *this* site. Badiou says: 'The site designates the local type of the multiplicity "concerned" by an event. It is not because the site exists in the situation that there is an event. But *for* there to be an event, there must be the local determination of a site; that is, a situation in which at least one multiple on the edge of the void is presented' (BE, 179/200).

The 'type of multiplicity concerned' is not just any 'nothing at all' but is the inconsistency that *will have been* consistent with the site that presents these elements as consequences, retroactively speaking, of an event. These elements are typical of the multiplicity concerned. Thus, while the *form* or the assembly of these elements is unpresentable in *this* situation as it is (without evental 'supplement'), that which these elements *will present as*, though void, is absolutely a *part* of that situation. In this context the site can be understood as the gathering point of all the non-presented elements of this situation. This gathering is ideal in the sense that the collection of these elements is a formal supposition. What is supposed is that, as with any other form multiple that which is unpresented, the universal nothing of the situation, will, if it were presented, be presented as one. Literally, then, these elements are unknown parts of the situation whose inexistence is marked by the site. An event will determine that 'they have been gathered'. In the consequent work of the subject these elements will become known as those which were of this site, those which were critical, in our terms, to the procedure of a non-sophistic education.

We need first to distinguish singularity from eventality. This is because even though a site is a singular multiple, a singular multiple is not a site strictly speaking. Rather, a site is the in-situational guarantee of its appearance. To clarify this distinction will help clarify in turn a common misconception of Badiou's work that links the existence of the site to the necessity of the event. Moreover, it might be suggestive in thinking the strangeness of the decision to execute Socrates at seventy after a lifetime's work. We might say that it is when what is singular illuminates *its* site that the failure of the state to name this multiple becomes a question for that state.

Singular

We said that the singular multiple is the in-situational guarantee of the site's appearing. What does this mean? As noted, the singular multiple can be realised to exist solely on the basis of a rigorously defined typology of situations. The existence of the singular multiple founds the historicity of a situation, Badiou notes, and as such only a historical or non-natural situation admits a singular multiple (BE, 174/194). It is the very instability of singularity which gives a situation its historical definition, for the singular multiple is such only because in this situation it is not also represented. The same multiple presented in other situations might indeed be 'normal'. Again, what this highlights is the very specificity of the term situation. It is always *a* situation specifying types of multiples particular to it.

Evental

On the other hand, 'a site' Badiou says 'is only "evental" insofar as it is retroactively qualified as such by the occurrence of an event' (BE, 179/200). Thus analytically speaking the site and its singularity are split, as it were, by the occurrence of the event itself. The event convokes the eventality of the site on the basis that such a retroactive designation is materially guaranteed by the existence of a particular form of multiple appearing – which is of course singularity. We could say that 'eventality' names the latency of the singular multiple – to be a site for an event – a multiple whose historical existence is in turn the sole guarantee of the possibility of an event. Given that the event realises the site, we could say that the latter is something like the first consequence of the singular multiple's 'illegality' vis-à-vis the state. We have seen that in the statist vision what is not represented, what is not determined by a term of the encyclopaedia, cannot have the status of existing for that situation. To be singular is not only unnatural but illegitimate. It subverts the rule which establishes the currency and expression of 'sophistic' knowledge. The singular multiple will be exposed to the state as the lack of its name.

Gathering

What is latent or evental about the singular multiple is the *presentation* of the void elements that make it up. The singular multiple is the *actual in situ* 'gathering' point of these 'void' or 'disassembled' multiples. The term 'site' names this point once an event, having occurred, is *decided* to have occurred. The temporal logic which rules all multiple appearing is evident here. Singularity anticipates the real gathering together of elements hitherto unpresented by this situation, while the site will be seen, retroactively, to have 'gathered' that unknown 'disassembled' gathering. The event, in effect, supplements this disassembly, it authorises, for a subject, that this disassembly is counted as one, and gives positive content to what up until then can only be thought as that which is not of the situation. In terms that will be explained later, in 'mobilising' this disassembled gathering and making the form of their multiplicity possible, the event *subtracts* them from the order of the state. In a 'positive' sense, the event negates this order. That is to say, it is not a negation of the state which is at stake – the event does not take its rule from the state – rather, subtraction is the affirmation of an existence and the possibility of its form. Again, when we turn to the dialogues we will see how this works – how, for example, Socratic corruption is entirely affirmative. Because the site is ultimately a positive term of the *eventally* conditioned situation and not a term of the state, it comes late to the situation. What we can say is that the site will have named the combination of the singular multiples' lack of situational presentation and the latency of that which it presents. Because the site names this point only post-eventally, the site and the singular while materially indistinct are syntactically divisible.[1]

Sum and rule

There are several points to be gleaned from this exposition. A single multiple constitutes the limit of the state of the situation. The state of the situation can in no way support the positive existence of these elements. The site is an immanent and an exceptional multiple. We could even say that although it belongs there, it is uniquely strange nevertheless. Its very lack of representation (the disassembly that is its gathering) suggests that in a non or pre-consequential sense, it is already a break with situational order. To sum up: (a) structurally, singularity signifies the point of immanent impasse for the rule of the state; (b) eventally, the site gathers the materiality of this impasse as the latent capacity of an event; (c) as the limit of the situation the site is also the possible space for the foundation of the new.

We have four general rules:

1. Only a historical situation admits an event.
2. *If* an event happens it will do so at a site.
3. This site is materially situated within the historical situation, and as the mark of unpresentation, it touches every element.
4. The disassembled, elemental matter constitutive of the singular multiple, which situates the site *for the situation*, will be the material presented or gathered by the event.

Nothing in common

We want to turn back now to our claim that the site designates a capacity common to all. We know that the site is the term marking the general distribution of what that situation regards as nothing. What is unique about the void is that it belongs to no situation. Thus while our 'site' qua element does, what it presents – nothing – does not. However, its very 'attribute' of not belonging to any situation is the reason for its universal inclusion. Having no elements that can distinguish it from any other set/situation the void cannot not be a part of every set. As the void has no belonging in terms of the situation it in essence wanders about the situation as a part of every elemental appearance. While these theses are essentially mathematical or ontological ones, their 'transitivity' matters here.

As noted, the site is the ideal localisation of this wandering spectre of the void. But its real (re)collection per se is only post-evental. The crux of the matter is that what is unpresented of a situation is a part of every element of the situation. It is in this sense that we identify this as a latent and universal capacity. To describe the void-site this way is not to step outside the ontological prescription that authorises this thought. The void set, once asserted, falls under the determinations of the axiom schema like any other multiple. It accords with Aristotle's maxim that 'it is of the essence of being to appear'. Badiou says in turn 'the essence of the multiple is to multiply itself in an immanent manner, and such is the mode of the coming-forth of being for whoever thinks *closely* (εγγυθεν) on the basis of the non-being of the one' (BE, 33/43). What is latent (in our sense), is this 'generative force' whose character Badiou names the indiscernible. We remarked in the last chapter that what we called the 'Socratic position' is that which is both properly immanent to, and indiscernible for, the sophistic state.

To call it a capacity is in truth a retroactive designation. It is a determination from the perspective of knowledge, and in terms of the void as such there is no knowledge. The most we can really say is that the void is universally included. And it is this universal condition that matters, for what we need to establish in terms of the sophistic situation is precisely that that which is not sophistic knowledge is that which is for all. This is no simple inversion. Although Callicles is right to assert that if Socrates had his way the world would be turned upside down this does not simply happen (Grg. 481c). If that which is not known to the sophistic state (that it doesn't know what it professes to know) is nevertheless included in every part it counts as one then what we have is the disassembled or un-gathered capacity for something non-sophistic, or for the realisation in thought and discourse of something that is the established result of its withdrawal from sophistry in all its forms.

In our conceptual situation the site is that which designates the *place* of thought. It is, as Badiou notes, 'the unforseeable beginning of a rupture', the first mark of the thinking of that which is not and yet, being for all, is already 'universal'. Analogous to the conceptualisation of the site on the basis of the void, we can posit that Badiou's 'event' performs the axiomatic role in the historical situation. Like the axiom, it breaks or ruptures with what has been in its assertion of what is.[2] This event designates what is specific to the site insofar as it is the site for a particular situation. Thus given that the site designates the inherent but void capacity of all for what it is that this all can do –'what they, the people, are capable of . . ., and with respect to the surplus-capacity of the State' (BE, 293/324) – then it has to be the case that what is shared among the parts is something particular to that situation. It is some-thing of that situation even as it is of that situation's unpresentation (cf. TS, 25). That is to say, if the situation were a school which presented a site then what was void to the situation would be that which could be found to be what was essential to it being a school. What is essential is that which makes it a school for all and thus a school at all. If this is lacking, if the school favours some over others in accord with some determination which is extrinsic or tangential to what it is 'to educate', then the situation presents an injustice in the sense that it is unfaithful to the 'thought of its being'. In other words, what the state forecloses is not the presented existence of elements – these alone are its basis – but rather the *model* form of presentation itself. This foreclosure entails an excess – the conceit that knows this form as nothing – which in fact registers as a lack. In statist representation, therefore, there is the lack of a non-sophistic education.

In this context the site simply designates that which is foreclosed from situational representation – which is its presented form. The real importance here is that what is foreclosed *has to be worked out*. As this form is not known, which is to say it does not fall under any statist or encyclopaedic determination, but whose concept form *can be thought*, it can only be subject to a procedure or enquiry which will or will not determine the shape and extent of its existence.

Such an enquiry proceeds precisely on the basis that 'of this', they 'know nothing'. If these enquiries avoid the encyclopaedia – by, in Platonic terms, 'keeping their eye on the real' and not the semblent – what they retroactively determine is that a situation is itself that which 'makes space' for a new (generic) determination of what it presents. The split or gap between the situation (model) and its state (simulacrum) is retroactively confirmed as this procedure institutes itself between the two, so to speak. Figuratively speaking, we often see in the dialogues that Plato situates the Socratic figure between the youth (or some other interlocutor) and the state.[3] We should stress that this is in no way a proposal for some return to origin or an exemplary state of nature. Belonging, the originary form of appearing, is precisely that, a Form. Any post-evental subjective procedure or act of generic construction manifests itself on the basis of this Form and not on the presence of any particular element.

Badiou notes that what is common to the 'human animal' is the capacity for this type of thought, more extensively, that given the occurrence of an event the human is such that it has the capacity to enter into the thoughtful construction of the truth of this situation (IT, 71).[4] To do so is to become 'subject', a designation not limited to human beings in Badiou's philosophical apparatus but to anything which supports the truth procedure. In this context the site can be deemed the thought-full, though unknowing, anticipation of the event and the truth procedure is something like this event being thought through. Badiou says that a thought is 'nothing other than the desire to finish with the exorbitant excess of the state' (BE, 282/312) and thus we can extrapolate that the site is the situational mark of such a desire. In the context noted above and in obvious conformity to the procedure of the discussants in the *Republic* what must be thought is the justice of the situation, that which is for all – and appropriately, as with Plato's cave-subject, this thought must concern itself with its situation.

The name of the site is 'education'

It is time to put this in our 'Platonic' terms. In the Platonic situation the name of the site is 'education'. This term is recognised by the situation and is used by the state to describe its own practices. As a term-part of the situation it can, Badiou notes, enter into 'consistent combinations with other presented multiples' but what it presents cannot (BE, 175/195). All the sophists profess to educate and to enter into the recognised field of practice designated by this term. However, education is under the injunction of truth. This is our orienting maxim but it is already prescribed in the dialogues that the only education is an education by truths. Recall that as 'late' as the *Laws* Plato repeats this injunction (L. 644a–b). It is the insistent problem and, as he says, he is not 'quibbling over a name'. Each dialogue addresses this *real* lack of a non-sophistic education. As the name of the site education marks the void link between the sophistic practice and its Socratic rival. In this context education should be understood as the foundational term for the undoing of the sophistic state. Indeed, Plato's expulsion of the poet/sophist from the ideal city is predicated on the fact that in terms of education these figures simply reproduce its lack. The 'Homeric mind' is, by both how and what it teaches, insufficient to bequeath its followers a 'way of life' (R. 600b). Plato juxtaposes this lack to that of the Pythagoreans who he says established just that.[5] This is no subtle hint that his corpus has taken up this task.

The public dialogue and the dialogue the *Republic*

In the examples that follow, we seek to emphasise the singular position of education. We want this illustration to attest to the fact that for the Athenian state that which constitutes a non-state education cannot be presented in the state. It is presented there as a term but what makes it up is void. The existence of the void-site is indicated to us by the Socratic figure, but as a figure of corruption what he signifies to the state is only what cannot be. It is true to say that Socrates is a singular figure of the Athenian scene, but as we have seen singularity is an effect of structure and not of nature. So although the signifier Socrates is on trial and the life of the mortal body attached to it at stake, the real target of the trial is the need to protect the state from the exposure to its void. Badiou notes that '*the State is not founded upon the social bond, which it would express, but rather upon un-binding, which it prohibits*' (BE, 109/125). In short the Socratic position, that of education as *only* by truths, must not be exposed as being a part of the state, for it threatens this prohibition. In terms of *our* exposition, what this means is that the name 'Socrates' must be understood as distinct from that which the trial seeks to have done with. On the other hand, it is an integral part of the sophistic position that it cannot distinguish the enunciation from that which is enunciated – we have noted this above – and such is why it ultimately seeks to silence that which speaks in the vain hope of silencing what is spoken. In the coming chapters we will further separate the Socratic body from its name and from what it names. Here, any reference to Socrates is a reference to what is not a sophistic education.

We will confine our reading to the *Apology* and to the *Republic.* In the first, it is the sophistic state which ultimately determines the insistence of the lack of a non-sophistic education. For the state what presents *as education* is what *there is* of education. The state recognises nothing non-sophistic and yet, in Socrates, whom the state does recognise, it discerns the threat of this lack. In the *Republic* Plato confirms the singularity of education. Whereas the sophistic state approaches this site from the perspective of knowing 'what must not be' in regard to what it presents, Plato's approach is to begin at just this point. He insists, if you like, that this lack insists and that education is the site for the realisation of that which is for all. The two trajectories, sophistic and Platonic, diverge at the site.

The *Apology*[6] begins with Socrates addressing the jury. He has never done this before. At the age of seventy, an Athenian citizen, war veteran and educated man, he finds himself 'a complete stranger to the language of this place' (Ap. 17e). To have taken no part in the legitimate form of Athenian politics is strange enough; to profess not to speak its language is to mark himself a foreigner (Ap. 18a and cf. R. 496a–e). The manner in which he does so is critical. Although he intends to reply to the accusation he notes that his incapacity as a speaker means he will not do so in the same 'flowery' or 'embroidered' language of his accusers. The imputation that he is a fine speaker like them is a lie, he says, which will be refuted by the manner of his speech. He claims that from him they will hear only the truth: if this makes him an orator then so be it; but he is one '*not after their pattern*' (Ap. 17a–c, emphasis added). The language Socrates speaks is not that of the typical orator. Thus the very term orator is subtracted from its sophistic meaning by Socrates and given a generic form. It means now simply 'to speak' and 'what is' spoken, rather than how or by whom, becomes what is important. As he points out (and *this* is irony), his manner of speaking will be irrelevant. He will say whatever occurs to him in the first words that come to mind. He can do this precisely because 'his cause is just' (Ap. 17c). Socrates is noting that to speak from justice is not specific to him but is already the capacity of all (Ap. 23b) As he will go on to say, it just so happens that as yet he is the only one who has tried to realise this in an extensive way – 'in the *open* spaces of the city' (Ap. 17cd, emphasis added).

The central accusers of Socrates, or at least those in whose name the accusation stands, are Meletus, Anytus and Lycon. They are, as we noted, 'aggrieved' on behalf of the poets, politicians and professional men, and orators respectively (the appearance on the list of these latter two, Anytus and Lycon, appears to have been crucial in getting the numbers for conviction) (Ap. 36b).[7] However, Socrates notes very early in his defence that he is more afraid of the cumulative effect of the accusations consistently made against him over the years. These, he says, insinuating themselves at an impressionable age, have more likely infected the minds of the jury than those of the three accusers – 'formidable as they are' (Ap. 18e). Socrates sums up the accusation of this unnamed multitude, whose 'untruths' have been repeated down the years, as an accusation of impiety. He says they have whispered it about that there is a 'clever man' who has 'theories about the heavens' and knows of things 'below the earth' and 'who can make the weaker argument defeat the stronger' (Ap. 18bc).[8]

Socrates points out that he has been at odds with the state of the situation for his whole life. As such, his 'impiety' consists in two things: what his enquiries concern and the 'divine' ability to turn the weak into the strong. He rejects these charges. However, there is a real truth in them (which is why Plato brings them up). As Socrates points out, he is not Anaxagoras who did enquire into the 'natural' world and the heavens and who was indicted for impiety for claiming the sun was a red-hot piece of metal (cf. Diog. Lae. II, 12–14). If it is true Socrates was Anaxagoras' student we might then say that Socrates has 'internalised' Anaxagoras' cosmology, albeit through Archelaus' theory of 'mutuality' (Diog. Lae. II 17–19). He maintains theories of the soul and of its relations to the body and these relations can be analogously applied to the form of the state best suited for such a creature. Nevertheless, as he says, no one has heard me speak of *these* things in which I have no interest (Ap. 19d). What he 'makes strong', as he has already said in the opening remarks, is the true argument whose position is always the weakest.[9] Set against the sophistic backdrop of the presence of knowledge, what is true therefore is always that which must come to be so as that which *is* for all. The truth is the least apparent of all arguments. For Socrates, in terms of what is real as opposed to what seems to be, truth is the *strongest* of all possible arguments and so the accusation is false. However, the world must be turned upside down before this realisation is truly possible. In a world where appearance is true, truth can only appear as weak, singular and 'against the numbers'.

The trick of the Platonic vision is always that we are reading two sides at once. We must read Socrates from the perspective of what Badiou calls the 'generic extension', which is to say from the side of the 'world to come', where appearance is *not* the rule. Conversely, we must read the Athenian state as the place where appearance is true and any challenge to this truth is impious as a thought and corrupt as a practice. This is the situation Socrates invokes when he says – ironically – that in giving his defence he hopes the result will be that he has rid their minds of 'a false impression which is the work of many years' (Ap. 19a and 31b). This false impression extends to the slander against his method. He makes it plain that he has never professed to educate or take a fee and declares it the 'finest of things' if one is qualified at such an art. He names Prodicus, Hippias, Gorgias and Evenus as those inhuman 'geniuses', capable of encouraging the youth to be educated by them and to pay for the privilege – thus leaving behind their 'fellow citizens' many of whom can be associated with for no charge (Ap. 20ab). Socrates notes that he feels that Evenus, who according to Callias charges 500 drachmae for the privilege, really should be congratulated as a master of that art.[10] But as for Socrates, he says he does not understand *that* art. Using the rhetorical form, Socrates asks why, if he is not such a figure, this misrepresentation has occurred. If his behaviour had not been abnormal, he would surely not be in this position (Ap. 20c).

What constitutes this abnormality is that such wisdom as he has is nothing at all like that of these geniuses. He says pointedly, he has 'no knowledge of such wisdom' (Ap. 20e). To accuse him of this is to commit lying and slander. This is of course the result of his enquiries pursuant to the Delphic 'axiom' that no one was wiser than he. In essence, Socrates set out from this axiom to check its veracity against the wisdom both apparent and verified by the rule of the city. This is to say, the wise were obviously those who held key positions by the strength of the numbers, votes and drachmae alike, and so it was to those he went to test the principle. As we know, what Socrates presented to them was not amenable to their knowledge.

What makes no sense to the 'wise' is the Socratic proclamation of the knowledge of ignorance. This made no sense to the poets and craftsmen each of whom, possessed as they were of specific technical knowledge, assumed that this ensured that they knew about everything else as well. Similarly, it made no sense to the sophists and politicians who presumed already to know what it was to know something, and this included what was not to be known (Ap. 21b–22e). As we see in this, Socrates clearly notes the excessive rule of the sophistic position whose error in presumption 'clearly outweighs their positive wisdom' (Ap. 22d). Against all of these positions, which constitute the entirety of the city – apart from slaves and women – Socrates sets himself as the 'spokesman for the oracle' 'being neither wise with their wisdom or stupid with their stupidity' (Ap. 22de). Moreover, he carries out his enquiries without regard to the authority of the polis, the assembly or the law courts: he induces hearers without the sanction, in a formal sense, of the state; and he speaks to any and all comers for free and 'without qualification' (cf. BE, 408/447). As a 'citizen' he refuses to attend the polis either in the democracy or the tyranny; and, as in this trial, the two other times he is summoned before the state he is each time singled out: under the tyranny he refused orders to arrest Leon of Salamis, but instead, taking the advice recommended in the *Republic* to good men, he went home (R. 496d), and after the disaster at Syracuse he refused to support the illegal group trial of the fleet admirals.[11]

For the third time Socrates repeats the charges against him. These are specific to the philosopher he says, and are made by those who are loathe to admit the truth of their ignorance for fear of reputation. Such types are 'energetic'[12] and numerically strong, and have a well-worked case against him (Ap. 23d and cf. R.327c+). Socrates now addresses the specific charges of Meletus et al. These are essentially the same, of course, but he specifies them now in order to interrogate Meletus. As always, he wants his interlocutor to speak 'in their own name' and with their own words. In this way, the truth of what is said is put to enquiry. Having addressed the general accusations, he now subjects the specific claims to his 'method'. The corruption of the youth comes first: Socrates starts by saying that as Meletus has discovered what it is that is pernicious concerning the education of the youth he must then know what is good.[13]

This brings us to the central and profound cut made at the trial. Continuing the above line of questioning Socrates finally asks Meletus the following: 'Then it would seem that the whole population of Athens has a refining effect upon the young, except myself; I alone demoralise them. Is that your meaning?' Meletus answers, 'Most emphatically yes!' (Ap. 25a).

This is the fundamental point for us. Certainly, Socrates goes on to offer a refutation of Meletus' position – one that does not spare the blushes of the accusers or the jurors (Ap. 34d), the sophistic nature of which soon becomes known. Along the way the Socratic method offers itself as reproof to the sophistic process when, for example, Socrates says that if he has committed this wrong out of ignorance (which is the only way anyway) there is no need for the law courts, just some enlightenment.[14] However, this is all grist to the sophistic mill. It is as if Meletus is 'right' and that all Athens *is* non-Socratic. This, of course, is what Plato is showing us. This is not to make a hero out of Socrates but precisely to show that what is not a sophistic education, like all truth, unfolds as it were from a single point in a situation. Socrates' comment that what he needs is enlightenment points to the significance of education as the site for this truth procedure. Indeed, it points directly to the metaphor of the Cave wherein a fundamental evental turn occurring at the 'cave-site' is a requirement of moving step by step toward the sun. Education is the site for the turn, which for Plato is the turn to that which is of the situation despite its state. Only this 'Socratic' (or perhaps *Platocratic*) procedure can make manifest (assemble, gather and deploy) those elements which properly belong to the education site. It is clear, as Socrates 'discovers' at the trial, that nowhere is this education manifest in an Athens that concerns itself above all else with 'acquiring as much money,' 'reputation and honour' as is possible (Ap. 29e). The Socratic corruption, as he says, consists finally in this: in encouraging whomever he meets to put aside the concern for their bodies and attend to the welfare of their souls (Ap. 30a). To attend to the latter is to bring 'wealth' to the former – interest is thereby put under the rule of reason, the capacity of all – but for Plato this is not a reciprocal relation, what Socrates means by wealth is not 'making money'. What we do know is that there is no 'logic of exchange' underpinning this.

It is well known how the public dialogue plays out from here. We should just note that Socrates continues to differentiate himself or, rather, *what he names*. Explicitly, he continues to relate all that renders him suspect to the city, all that renders him 'different from the normal run of humankind'. What differentiates him ultimately is his decisive subjection to the prescription of the oracle, for to 'know thyself' is precisely to subtract oneself, enquiry by enquiry, courageously (Ap. 28e), from the knowledge of the state. Implicitly, he persists in maintaining fidelity to that which is non-sophistic both before conviction and after, and again before and after the decision on the death penalty. Indeed, his stance seems to become even more provocative in light of the circumstances. Socrates notes this, and claims it is not a matter of *his* stance but of the appearance by which it is conditioned. *He* is simply being consistent – speaking the truth despite the circumstances. What makes this truth seem more provocative is simply a sophistically grounded assumption that to die is a bad thing. He asserts that he is ignorant of what constitutes death and therefore to cry about it or fear it is to act as if one knows what one does not – to be, in short, sophistic. He accuses them explicitly of condemning him for not speaking to them in their own language, in terms that would have given them most pleasure (Ap. 38e). Truth itself, he says, will convict his accusers (Ap. 39D).[15] This again invokes what will become the theme of the *Phaedo*: that truth insists *despite* the existence of any man.

We will look only briefly at the *Republic* and at one section. Our only intention is to confirm that what Plato insists on is that education can only be non-sophistic and that as such, given the sophistic state of the situation, it must inexist for this state. In the *Apology* we saw Socrates differentiate his thought and his practice from all Athens and all Athens from him. He proclaimed his subjection to the Delphic axiom and his inner conviction to be both his alone and the basis of elaborating that which is for all. The Athenian state proclaimed exactly the same thing, but from the 'other side'. For them, it was 'all Athens', representative Athens, who educated and the Socratic position, being the mark of what was *singular*, sowed only corruption in the polis. The general context of our passage from the *Republic* is a discussion dealing with the possible corruption of the 'philosophical nature'. The larger context is of course the quest to found a city built on the doctrine of fair shares, a doctrine only a non-sophistic education can support (Grg. 508a). The assumption here is that such a thing as the 'philosophical' nature exists but the conditions of its realisation are lacking. Such a nature, given the lack of its proper conditions, will in fact be brought down by the very qualities which pertain to it. Its temperance, courage, love of truth will be diverted by the rewards and temptations of the goods of the city.[16] Plato says that unless some 'miraculous interposition' takes place, such will be the fate of the philosophical nature (R. 492e). This section of the text begins with Adeimantus proposing to Socrates that those who practise philosophy – which we can say is the *form* an education by truths takes (in the dialogues at least) – seem to become useless to society.[17] Socrates says he agrees with this. Then why, Adeimantus asks, can you be proposing a city run by philosophers (R. 487de)? Plato here invokes his second favourite motif of the ship of state.[18] The master of this ship is the 'worthy' demos. It is however, short sighted, a little deaf and deficient in seamanship. The crew are politicians and demagogues all equally lacking in the knowledge of navigation and helmsmanship and, worse, declaim that it cannot be taught in any case. The latter seduce the master by opiates and flattery into letting them steer. This 'steering class' compete with each other, killing or throwing overboard those who take their chance at the helm. Such a voyage amounts to a 'drunken carousal' but the sum of all these activities is the norm and skill in making one's way in such a 'state' and one is rewarded and praised accordingly. 'Every other kind of man they regard as useless', Socrates says (R. 487e–488e). To this crew Socrates juxtaposes the 'useless visionary' (R. 489c): the one who has spent time studying the 'science of navigation', learning the seasons, the stars, the winds and so on, and who has by instruction or practice learned to control the helm and steer a course. The useless visionary is of course the philosopher (a distinction acquired, we must note, by those who have spent the necessary thirty-five years studying 'navigation'). The essential trait which distinguishes him from the crew, the *individuals* of the demos and from those who *profess* to follow a philosophic way of life is his disposition toward truth, 'which he must always and everywhere follow or else be an impostor with no part in true philosophy'. Such a figure is 'born to strive toward reality, [and] cannot linger among the multiplicity of things which men believe to be real, but holds on his way with a passion that won't faint or fail . . .' (R. 490a).

There are now two types who fasten onto philosophy: the type who pursue truth faithfully and those who profess too. It is the latter, Socrates suggests, who give philosophy its *bad name*. Now, what happens here is that the latter become those who set the conditions whereby the rarer figure of the philosopher might 'run aground'. Once again, we have the force of numbers and their determinative ability set against what is singular – the many-headed hydra of appearance against the universal singularity of the true is the analogy or perhaps the metaphor insisted on. Again, we need to note that the philosopher in this instance is only so as he who is subject to the decision that, given an event, there are truths. It is the actual singularity of the pursuit of such indiscernible truths that constitutes the rarity (and uselessness) of the philosopher. Plato's philosopher is simply a participant in this procedure, this way of life. For Plato, education consists in this pursuit, while for the state, such a pursuit, being foreign and useless to what it demands of its crew, cannot be educational at all. Plato makes it clear that what passes for education in such a state is that 'life*style*' which such a state demands. The 'education' pursued by the non-sophist-philosopher, being a '*way* of life', cannot be presented there – the conditions of its existence are foreclosed by the encyclopaedic ship of state. In addition, this is ultimately the 'fault' Socrates claims, of those who profess to know.

The crux of the matter is again as we showed in Chapter 1. It is not the individual sophist per se who is at fault: Plato chides Adeimantus; you don't hold the popular belief that certain young men are demoralised by the private instructions of some individual sophist (R. 492a)?[19] Clearly, he refers to his own position as much as that of the sophists. Recall that on philosophical grounds he has defended the genus *philo-sopher* against the type *soph-ist* in *Meno* and *Euthydemus* and separated them as such in the *Sophist*. The problem highlighted again here is very much the state of the situation itself. Does the influence of the individual sophist amount to much?' he asks rhetorically. 'Is not the public itself the greatest of all sophists, training up young and old, men and women alike, into the most accomplished specimens of the character it desires to produce' (R. 492ab)? This training up, he says, happens wherever the public gathers, in the assembly, the law courts, the theatre or the camp (today the school). The populace crowds together, 'clamouring its approval or disapproval, both alike *excessive*, of whatever is said and done' (R. 492b, emphasis added). To hold out against such teaching is near to impossible and no individual instruction will be enough to counter 'the force of such a torrent'. The young man will come to be just as they are. In other words, the state reproduces itself in and through the manner of its education. It is worth noting that in a proto-Althusserian fashion Plato claims that if anyone doesn't succumb to the 'present state of society' by means of this educational process then there are fines, punishments and even death for those who fail to achieve the correct *qualifications*[20] – qualifications, we should note, that the subject (in Badiou's sense) disqualifies in relation to the situation to come (BE, 408–9/447).

At this point Plato reinstitutes his critical and consistent division between the sophistic educational practice and that which is not-sophistry. If the individual sophist cannot counter the clamorous teaching of the public, it is because the former serves the latter. The sophists teach nothing other than the *opinions* current in the state (R. 493a). The sophist has the knack only of assuaging and cajoling the humours of the 'great beast', the public. This knack acquired by 'long familiarity' he calls 'wisdom' which he 'reduce[s] to a system' in order to set up a school (R. 493bc and cf. Grg. 489d). Recalling again the Protagorean ethic of relative measure, Socrates insists that what is taught in this way conforms to desires already manifest. That is to say, what is clamoured for is the pleasure received in having one's already existing knowledge confirmed. The *love* of wisdom alone does not conform to this measure. In the *Symposium* Socrates admits to knowing something. He knows about love. We know that what Socrates knows is not what the state knows and so we know that the state is incapable of love. Moreover, this is the case because love, as we noted, is always for that which you do not possess (or know – they are in this sense the same thing). On the contrary, the sophistic art is conditioned not by love but by exchange, and amounts to turning flattery into pedagogy in return for money, prophecy into profit we might say; the latter merely legitimates the process. The dialectic of sophistry can be summed up by saying 'no one buys an unknown product'. Plato concludes the substance of his argument by saying the sophist, blinded by this frenzied activity of the world of goods, cannot tell 'how great the real difference is between what must be [conforming to the demands of the state][21] and what ought to be [the demands of truth]'. Such a person, *constitutionally* unable to decide for truth, 'would offer only a queer sort of education' (R. 493c, emphasis added).[22]

THE TRUE COUPLE

Although these passages reveal a good many things about the Dialogues, not least their constant self-referentiality, and thus, perhaps, something of their systematic nature, our concern is whether they illustrate that education can be conceived as a site. There are two things that matter here:

1. We have shown that education is presented in the dialogues but, under the purely imitative effects of sophistry, nothing that makes it up is similarly presented.
2. The sophistic state, by trying and convicting Socrates, has, paradoxically, drawn notice to this site. Simply, 'Socrates' in naming nothing for the state which is known to the state must therefore name that which the state cannot know. The state cannot know the elements of the site. These elements are what will have been a 'Socratic education', which will have been the only education worthy of the name.

What this amounts to is that we have done enough to show that education is the site for an event. We cannot prove the latter from the perspective of the situation. A site is always retroactively qualified as such *by an event*. What we have shown is that Plato splits the dialogues in two at the point at which sophistry fails to know what it professes to know. Sophistry, and what is not sophistry, is bound by nothing. The former knows nothing of its ignorance and the latter knows only the ignorance of the former. Education is the void term for this point of immanent and minimal difference. In the *Apology*, Plato carefully evokes the foundational importance of this difference and sets out the schema for tracing its consequences across the corpus. The *Apology* and the excerpt from the *Republic* – the true *couple* of the entire Corpus – both confirm that the sophistic state takes up the educational theme. In the *Apology* Socrates gives the history to his efforts to enlighten and educate the citizenry of Athens. At every turn, he sees his practice denied and disavowed. The elements that would make up this 'Socratic' education are not a part of the sophistic state. It is not that they are refused as such, but that they cannot be recognised as educational because they do not lead to, and thus presume, the polis, the market, the school or the stage. The *only* education is, for the state, no education at all. The emphatic coalition between the individual sophists and the society they serve constitutes a torrent of positivism connecting their practice with a place already well marked in the city. Such a connection is affirmed in the *Republic*. For Socrates, the exiled citizen of the latter within the Athenian state, the place of the non-sophist is first to hide from the torrent, to recognise the necessity of division and to invent from out of nowhere a new constitution of its place (cf. Grg. 486a–d). In the next chapter, we start to elaborate this new constitution.

Notes

1. For a discussion of Badiou's use of the distinction between semantics and syntax, particularly in his early work *The Concept of Model*, see Ray Brassier, 'Badiou's materialist epistemology of mathematics', pp. 135–50. In a not unrelated way Deleuze, in the *Logic of Sense*, talks about the child in relation to language and how on its leaving the 'depressive position' (which elsewhere in this text *is* Platonism), it does so by the Voice of the mother tongue; not its semantics but its phonemics allows this for Deleuze. 'In the continuous flow of the voice which comes from above the child cuts out elements . . .', it individuates, its evental singularity is cut out from the voice and a freedom of a sort ensues (LoS, 230). We can see here a mix of Nietzschean and Heideggerian attitudes to Plato: the genealogical desire to seek out the point of decline, to seek the phoneme prior to its semantic reformulation, and the designation of a turning point at which the veil comes down and truth goes unconcealed in the idea.
2. Aristotle's definition of the axiom is appropriate: 'that which is necessary in order to learn something else' (*Nicomachean Ethics*, Book VI, p. 114). In *Metaphysics* Aristotle says, 'The axioms are most universal and are principles of all things. And if it is not the business of the philosopher, to whom else will it belong to inquire what is true and what is untrue about them?' (*Metaphysics*, Book 3, 997a 10, in *The Complete Works of Aristotle*, p. 1557). It is worth comparing what Heidegger says about 'the good' here. In terms very similar to Aristotle above, he notes that 'in Greek thought τὸ ἀγαθόν means that which is capable of something and enables another to be capable of something.' Every ἰδέα, the visible form of something, provides a look at what a being is in each case. 'The ideas', he continues, 'enable something to appear' and 'the ideas are what is in everything that is' (Heidegger, 'Plato's doctrine of truth', in Pathmarks, pp. 174–5).
3. This is illustrated in a most literal way in *Lysis* wherein Socrates meets several boys on the way to the *palaestra* where their sophist Miccus – 'no ordinary man' – awaits them. He engages them in conversation, preventing them from reaching their Sophist (Lys. 204a). The inverse of this initial act of separation is shown in the *Symposium*

when Alcibiades, adopted son of Pericles, himself torn between his love for the Socratic agalma and his desire for the 'pleasures of the flesh', and in fact mistaking one for the other, enters the gathering, takes his seat on the couch and in so doing divides Socrates from Agathon (the Good). Moreover, is not the figure of Socrates here treated as precisely nothing? Alcibiades, his eyes covered by garlands, does not notice Socrates until, and this is critical, he has put the – good, promising, as yet unconnected – youth at a distance from the philosopher – the *lover* of wisdom.

4. It is in this text that Badiou quotes from point 4 of the Cultural Revolution's sixteen-point decision calling it 'Mao's thesis on the immanent self-education of the revolutionary masses' (IT, 72). 'Let the masses educate themselves in this great revolutionary movement, let them determine themselves the distinction between what is just and what is not' (IT, 71). See for the full text Mao Tse-Tung, 'The sixteen point decision', Point 4 (Appendix to Jean Daubier, *History of the Chinese Cultural Revolution*, p. 300).
5. In his notes to the *Parmenides* Cornford remarks that this passage from the *Republic* refers directly to the *Timaeus* (90b) where, he says, the Pythagorean 'converse' is reproduced by Plato. It is also obvious that this passage, concerned as it is with once again dividing interest from truth, refers to Socrates' own claim in regard to his *daemon* – the immortal in us (see also Tht. 151e and L. 713e) (*Plato and Parmenides: Parmenides' Way of Truth and Plato's Parmenides*, p. 27). As we will see Badiou's conception of the subject has recourse to a similar 'obedience' (see E, 47, 67 and 71).
6. In this section all translations from the *Apology* are taken from *The Last Days of Socrates*.
7. Lycon is not heard from and Anytus is spoken of by Socrates as 'hedging'. He says Anytus has said, either Socrates should not be on trial at all but, given that he is, he must be put to death. According to Plutarch, Anytus was in love with Alcibiades. The latter treated him 'cavalierly' and 'with great insolence'. Perhaps this 'fact' adds to the intrigue. (Plutarch, *The Rise and Fall of Athens: Nine Greek Lives*, pp. 248–9.)
8. He refers to a certain poet, which is likely to be Aristophanes whose *satire* claimed he made the worse appear stronger. The question of Aristophanes' depiction of Socrates in *The Clouds* is interesting, for he contends that as the arch-sophist Socrates teaches the 'art of winning law-suits'. Even though Socrates had not been brought to trial when the play was composed the notion is patently absurd. Thus the depiction is perhaps more ironic, more a commentary on sophistic Athens than on the philosopher? Aristophanes' appearance in the *Symposium* certainly suggests that the two were not enemies.

9. Apropos of Lacan's remarks concerning the impossibility of saying the 'all of truth' and, as such, aligning it with castration and an inherent incapacity or weakness, Badiou says that 'truth is bearable for thought . . . philosophically loveable, only in so far as one attempts to grasp it in what drives its subtractive dimension, as opposed to seeking its plenitude or complete saying' (TW, 120).
10. Five hundred drachmae are equivalent roughly to a year and half's wages for a day labourer (Vincent J. Rosivach, 'Some Athenian presuppositions about the poor', *Greece and Rome*, pp. 189–98). One should recall Socrates' own sarcasm and backhanded 'compliments' to the jury in his trial. Indeed, in arguing that he is not a teacher (all other Athenians are), that he could not therefore corrupt (notice the real irony here), he offers, in a very un-Athenian way, evidence for his truth in the form of his 'poverty' (Ap. 31c). See also the analysis of the *Cratylus* below.
11. See Alcibiades story from the *Symposium* recounting how Socrates' bravery goes unrewarded and indeed how Alcibiades, the paradigmatic man-of-the-city, is rewarded in his stead. Socrates' 'inexistence' is consistently recounted by Plato. Our greater point here, one Plato makes obvious by showing precisely Socrates' 'over-conformity', is that Socrates is not opposed to Athens. What Plato shows is that the Athens of the dialogues *is* qua state implacably and irreversibly opposed to that which Socrates names. Cf. Debra Nails, *The People of Plato: A Prosopography of Plato and other Socratics*, p. 199.
12. Grube has 'ambitious' (*Plato: The Complete Works*).
13. Cf. Badiou's *Ethics*.
14. His refutation of the accusation of impiety similarly follows the 'Socratic method' (Ap. 25d–27a).
15. Not long after Socrates' death a public mourning was awarded him and Anytus and Meletus were harshly dealt with, though not necessarily – indeed, probably not – for their accusations against Socrates. What the former shows is not the polis coming to its senses but is further evidence of the indiscipline and mutability of sophistic thinking.
16. In his 'La (Re)tour de la philosophie elle-même' (C, 64–70) Badiou accuses Plato of 'going bad' in just this way. We disagree with Badiou's premise. See our Conclusion.
17. We use the term philosopher only when speaking of the *Republic*. Otherwise, we stick with non-sophist or non-sophistry. This is because the *Republic* is the 'world turned upside down' (Grg. 481bc).
18. Medical analogies appear to be Plato's favourite generally (i.e. R. 403–412). This suggests an analogy between education and political health (an analogy with a long and corrupt history in front of it!). Plato seems well aware of this 'history', for he warned against submitting to 'doctors' in the same way he warned against submitting to sophists.

19. Cf. Althusser's discussion of education as the dominant, contemporary Ideological State Apparatus (ISA), where he makes a point of exempting certain teachers (Louis Althusser, 'Ideology and the state', p. 106).
20. For Althusser, the ISA relies ultimately on the Repressive State Apparatus (RSA) for its extensive effects – the military, the courts, the cops, etc. ('Ideology and the state', pp. 98–9). In the USA today this interrelation is being felt in yet another variation. Many ex-military personnel, certainly without the rigorous training of Plato's Guardians, are being hired as principals and administrators of state and privately-run schools in order to bring capitalist (the logic of interest) order and 'family values' to the 'unconvinced'. See the collection of essays in Saltman and Gabbard's *Education as Enforcement: The Militarization and Corporatization of Schools*. A recent Australian education policy document noted that those who 'fail' to be so educated constitute a threat to themselves and to the economic future of the state (see Queensland Department of Education and Training, 'New Basics Project', http://education.qld.gov.au/corproate/newbasics, accessed 17 January 2011).
21. In relation to the sophist Plato calls this 'necessity'. Grube/Reeve, more contextually minded, translate it as 'compulsion'(*Plato: Complete Works*). There is no doubt that Plato is playing on the non-philosophical character of the sophist here. This figure even mistakes the nature of necessity. Recall that at the end of the *Republic* Plato relates the Myth of Er in which is featured the Spindle of Necessity where souls are displayed as what they were, what they are and what they will be. The dead must *choose* (R. 617d–e).
22. The Grube /Reeve translation (*Plato: Complete Works*) has 'strange sort of educator'. This is an appropriate inversion. In the subsequent passage Plato extends this act of submitting oneself to the state to poets, painters and politicians, thus equating them as all imitators and flatterers going out of their way to seek approval and thus avoiding the question of what is or is not just.

CHAPTER 3

Event/Intervention

> 'Truth is no road to fortune, and the people dispenses no ambassadorships, nor professorships, nor pensions.'[1]

We have seen that the state of the sophistic situation constitutes the normality of Plato's Athens. Sophistry is the sole and ubiquitous figure of education. We have also established that this name 'education' – despite it belonging to the sophists' discourse – marks a permanent and disavowed ambiguity there. The trial of Socrates shows both that education must not take any other form than that of sophistry but also that this very act signifies a certain anxiety the state has in regard to its own knowledge. On the basis of this we established that education in the Athens of the dialogues could be understood as a site. Conceived in this way, education is what is void to the sophistic state, even as this state deploys the term, institutes a set of practices in its name and seeks to monopolise all knowledge pertaining to it. What sophistry thereby produces is the lack of a non-sophistic education.

In this context the Socratic figure is seen to mark a real point of distinction between the sophistic educational apparatus and the disavowed 'Socratic' form. The insistence of such a point, one that recurs in each dialogue, calls for enquiry. To enquire, for Badiou as for Plato, supposes an event: something 'unknown' but encountered provokes the thought of something being amiss. Where there was a path, there is now an impasse. The state, constituted as it is by the rule of excess, encounters no such impasse but it does encounter its effects. That is to say, the state cannot concede that it does not know: it must continue to know for this is what it means to be the 'state', that any existence or belonging submit inexorably to the order of parts, to its representative form and thus to its language. However, as we will see, that an encounter *takes place* necessarily catches the attention of the state. As we have said, this knowledge, the normal reign of the encyclopaedia, extends to the point of knowing what must not be known. In order to break with the impasse that the site represents between 'state knowledge' and 'situational presentation', Plato's 'miraculous interposition' is required (R. 492e). We will see that the event is in fact not a miracle – its basis is entirely situational – but it is something precarious, fraught and indecisive. In order for a non-sophistic education to have any purchase in the situation – an education, we have shown, that is properly 'for all' – something must happen which establishes the trial of its impossibility.

Two categorical concerns

We have two categorical concerns in this chapter: event and intervention. In the simplest terms, the event is what happens without determination, a chance occurrence, an unexpected encounter. The intervention is the initial act in the procedure that decides or recognises that what happened by chance *belongs* to the situation. It declares the event as something other than nothing and registers this with a name. Analytically speaking, what complexity there is between something happening and deciding that it happened is reducible to two points:

1. An event is an abnormal occurrence *for* a situation. Its abnormality consists in two things: if it happens, it happens at a site and thus it draws it resources from the void. This is why, for the situation, it appears by 'chance'. The situation cannot know the void nor, by inference, account for the event. Secondly, and entirely due to this, the event belongs to itself. The event consists both of the void elements it mobilises *and* of its disappeared self.
2. The intervention must declare that what happened was not what normally happens, that it was in fact 'new', and yet that it happened. This means there is something at stake for the situation in which the event/intervention happens. The pure abnormality of the event, precisely its newness, means that the intervention is enacted as a *decision*. No criteria exist by which to discern its place within the structure or to calculate the range or detail of its effects; ergo, a decision must be made. To mark the insistence of this exceptionality, its 'trace', and to provide a point of orientation, the intervention produces a name. Given that the situation has rejected the event's novelty, this name must also be 'new'. To put it a little enigmatically, the newness that the event signifies

will register through the name. In this context, the name, while being a matter of language, will be 'unheard of.'

The event as 'what happens'

Badiou schematises the event in the following matheme: $e_x = \{x \in X, e_x\}$. This reads 'the event (e_x) is a one-multiple ($\{x \in X, e_x\}$) made up of, on the one hand, all the multiples (x) which belong to its site (X), and on the other hand, the event (e_x) itself' (BE, 179/200). Again, we should read this like the squares traced in the sand in the *Meno* – at once illustrative and yet fundamental. There are two critical parts to this one-multiple: its attachment to its site and its supernumerary or 'belonging to itself' status. Badiou is keen also to establish the actuality or advent of the event which the matheme inscribes. That is to say 'it does happen' or 'will have happened' (as we will see). Despite what follows from the event, whether the consequences are taken up, whether it is disavowed as an anomaly or assimilated to the normality of the situation, it is never possible to say that 'nothing happened'. However, what happens is not necessarily, or rather is very rarely, an event. The *eventality* of the event, just like the eventality of the site (the latter becoming true on the basis of its event) is subject to the incessant logic of the future anterior. Badiou evokes this logic at the beginning of his meditation on the event saying, in terms of its conceptual construction, that 'it can only be *thought* by anticipating its abstract form, and it can only be *revealed* in the retroaction of an interventional practice which is itself entirely thought through' (BE, 178/199). The not particularly clarifying matheme is an example of its abstract form, yet Badiou does show in the subsequent meditation on the intervention that this matheme is derivable from the circumstances peculiar to the occurrence of the event and is not, in his terms, a luxury (BE, 179/200). Before we move on we will try to flesh out the event on its own terms, most particularly its relation to the site whose elements it mobilises. It is true to say, however, that these articulations only really become evident retroactively.

The event and itself

What is peculiar to the event is that its very essence is to disappear. Its real situational importance is its impact at its site and in looking forward to 'the subject'. We know that the elements of the site are (or *will have provided*) the material basis for the event's appearing while the site itself as the sole presented element which presents these elements gives the event its situational currency (BE, 179/200). These elements have no stake in the situation in terms of presentation or representation, but, as we saw, as nothing they are nevertheless constitutive of an unknown, indiscernible part (BE, 174/194 and TW, 99). In its advent the 'event' 'supplements' the unpresented or disassembled elements of its site. The event opens the closed world of the situation's presentative regime long enough to expose what was nothing to the chance at being the something *which it is* for the situation (TW, 101).

This is all it is in this pre-interventional stage – a contingent encounter: a meeting on the docks, a late arrival at a dinner, a knock at the door. Its eventality, that it is *an event*, is entirely aleatory in regard to the effects of the sophistic rule. It provides, in the situation at its site, an instance of chance by drawing on, through the site, the very being of the situation. In this way, the event can be said to present the elements of its site as Other than the nothing that they are for the situation (TW, 101). By cutting through the normalcy of the situation the event/encounter supplements what is otherwise lacking in presentation with a minimum of existence. As what happens it provides the elements of the site with an immediate (and universal) form for the consistency it lacks (TW, 147). Otherwise, as we have seen, these elements are simply unapparent, disassembled, of no calculable interest. The site, however, is not the all of the event. The event is also made up of itself.

This simply means that an event presents itself in its occurring. Nothing of the situation can do this. If 'what happens' can be presented or represented as a multiple by the situation or its state then really nothing unnatural has happened. If the event becomes an event, or becomes *evental*, the situation is itself broken with and the logic which provides its coherence loses all currency. The consequences of an event are not internal reform but conceptual invention and (meta) structural change. We should note here that it is these consequences of the event that will have transformed the state of the situation and not the event per se. This is not a miracle but a subtractive, affirmative praxis. The event, as aleatory, contingent, illogical, unknown to the state, punches, we might say, only an initial hole. What is at stake is summed up in our maxim: an education is that which 'establishes the effect of an encounter as a transformation'.

The event escapes the return to normalcy by the two features that make up its singularity: its attachment to the site and by presenting its own presentation. To illustrate this duality, Badiou provides an image of the French Revolution. We will give another image below, but what is derived from these is an intuitive understanding. For Badiou, the term 'French Revolution' names whatever one can think that pertains to its historic construction: peasants, the guillotine, Robespierre, the Jacobin clubs, reactionaries and so on. However, if the multiplication of such a historical inventory was all there was to it, then its status, as an event, as the foundation point for a new orientation to the world, is consumed under a larger logic of history or politics, for example. This, Badiou notes, may 'well lead to the one of the event being undone to the point of being no more than the forever infinite numbering of the gestures, things and words that co-existed with it' (BE, 180/201). Such logics admit no break into their historicising retrojections, none that cannot be recuperated as confirmation of that same logic at least. Badiou argues that what halts this dissemination of pure facts is '*the mode in which the Revolution is a central term of the Revolution itself* [emphasis in original]; that is, the manner in which the conscience of the times – and the retroactive intervention of our own – *filters the entire site through the one of its evental qualification* [emphasis added]' (BE, 180/20). The term 'Revolution' is a term of the revolution itself and not of the situation or of the encyclopaedia in general. This is to say, the name as figure of presentation presents precisely that which it is. 'Of the French Revolution as event it must be said that it both presents the infinite multiple of the sequence of facts situated between 1789 and 1794, and, *moreover*, that it presents itself as an immanent résumé and one-mark of its own multiple' (BE, 180/201).

To illustrate this latter aspect in another image we must think of the event firstly and simply as 'what happens'. Yet when what happens *happens*, there is no longer only what happens, there is also 'that it happened'. 'That it happened' is the signifier for 'what happens'. The former, 'that it happened', presents 'what happens'. The signifier has no prior existence. It is the presentation of 'what happened' and at the same time it is not 'what happened'. Moreover, 'what happened' is known to have happened due only to the immediacy of its signifier. Here is an approximate image and one should ignore the subjective aspect: I click my fingers. The clicking of the fingers is 'what happens' at its site. 'That it happened' is the sign of its appearing there. 'That it happened' is the signifier of the clicked fingers – which, empirically speaking, is no more. So, 'that it happened' is a matter of *its* happening and as such the former can only belong to the latter. That is, the signifier 'event' can only be a presentation of the event itself – made up of the clicking of the fingers. In this sense, the event presents itself to itself or it belongs to itself. By presenting *itself* in this fashion and coupled to the fact that in occurring it presents what is nothing to the situation, the event precludes the state from nullifying its self-presentation. As we will see, the state effectively knows nothing of the event (though it can register its 'strangeness') and cannot intervene in its self-presentation one way or another – although it can block its extension. 'The event is thus clearly the multiple which both presents its entire site, and, by means of the pure signifier of itself immanent to its own multiple, manages to present the presentation itself, that is, the one of the infinite multiple that it is' (BE, 180/201).

The question of the *eventality* of the event, that is the question of its effect, is ultimately a matter for the intervention. The latter decides that as a 'presented multiple' it belongs to the situation of its site while at the same time its self belonging distinguishes it from its site. Badiou argues that if the event does belong to its situation then there are conclusions to be made concerning its relation to its site. We noted above that internal to the event are two relations. On the one hand the event as occurrence presents the void elements of the site. On the other it is presented by its own signifier. This dual relation allows Badiou to denote the event as 'supernumerary' or 'ultra-one' (we will return to this).

What this means in regard to the relation the event has to the site is that the event puts itself at the smallest distance from its site. The site is a presented multiple of the situation. The event escapes presentation by the situation by happening at the site beneath situational presentation. That is to say, by having non-presented elements as its elements the event cannot be counted as a part of the situation. However, precisely by presenting itself it becomes a presented multiple. Badiou says, 'the event blocks its *total* singularisation by the belonging of its signifier to the multiple that it is. In other words, an event is not (does not coincide with) an evental-site. It 'mobilises' the elements of its site, but it adds its own presentation to the mix (BE, 182/ 203). It is in presenting the elements of the site that the event also presents itself. In doing so it puts itself at a distance from the site, or from the 'edge-of-the-void'. The distinction that must be made here is almost indistinct and this is so because we are effectively talking about a *point*. That the event presents itself frees it in a certain sense from the situational constraint and thus its relation to the multiples of the site is distinct from the relation the site has to these same elements. Whereas the site stabilises the disassembly of these multiples the event disassembles this stability. If the event is decided by the intervention to belong to the situation then it is on the basis of its division from the site by itself. It is properly understood then to be the 'advent of a situated multiple' which 'wrests a site from its founded inclusion' (TW, 101). In other words, it mobilises the elements of the site (by *force* as we will see) in avoidance of the statist determination – a determination which includes the determination of the site as a presented multiple – whose entire excessive function is that of accounting for whatever strangeness occurs.

What we have so far is an evanescent appearance whose status in terms of the situation is unfounded. The state of the situation has no basis for including such a multiple and the abnormality of the multiple itself therefore precludes its situational presentation. The full significance of the event therefore, which by no means has to be something spectacular or obvious, concerns the event belonging to the situation to which its site belongs. Although we have described the form of its occurrence and provided its basic articulation in relation to its site and itself, in terms of such an occurrence being *evental* – in the sense that the consequences it initiates are extensive enough to retroactively confer event status upon it, thus at the same time confirming that it was an event *for* that situation – we have some work still to do. Before this it is worth sketching out a typology of this event encounter as it appears in the dialogues. Without wanting to complicate things we can identify three event appearances or, rather, one Idea and three instances of its appearing in the Athens of the dialogues.

Plato's typology of the encounter

It is our assertion that the entirety of the dialogues is structured by this event/encounter between Socrates, nominally speaking, and the sophistic state. As we argued, both the state (of the Athenian situation) and Plato consider Socrates to be a figure separated from the procedures of teaching and learning that take place within this Athens. The state negates Socrates in this context, removing him from the polis as an abnormality without representation, while Plato affirms this separation, nominally as the stranger, the exile and, consequentially as we will see, the model figure of his counter-state the Republic. We divide the encounter into both Idea and instance because each dialogue stages its own specific encounter, each of which partakes of the Ideal encounter which forms the structural basis of the corpus. This encounter between the invariant Socratic figure and the variety of figures of sophistry has a foundational status for the corpus. The *Apology* shows this and the *Republic* both confirms this and draws its consequences. We cannot address each dialogue in turn but it is clear that each plays out the same rivalry, from the point of the encounter particular to it. Whether it is a dialogue on love, politics, etymology, virtue, speechmaking or justice, the same structural positions ensue: Socrates, the exemplary figure of thought, versus the sophists, the exemplary figures of interest. The Idea therefore denotes this foundational encounter which underpins each distinct dialogic manifestation. We are certainly not saying that Plato had a *theory* of the event, but we are saying that in Plato there is an event – Socrates' encounter with the sophists and therefore the state.

Not every dialogue stages an *explicit* staging of an encounter. As such, we can identify three general types:

- Where the encounter is implied.
- Where a 'minor' encounter involving characters who may or may not reappear precedes the encounter itself and, as such, signifies what is implied.
- Where Socrates encounters someone in the street, be it his central interlocutor or someone else. This type can itself be divided into implied and minor.

The dialogues wherein the Idea of the encounter is *implied* rather than *explicit* include *Apology*, *Crito*, *Philebus*, *Laches*, *Euthydemus*, *Meno* and *Laws*. For example, in the *Philebus* we enter into the middle of a conversation at the point where Philebus (pleasure seeker) is leaving and Protarchus (son of Callias) is to take over. In the *Apology* we enter the dialogues as Socrates is beginning his reply to his accusers. The encounter has *taken* place. Its *taking* place is, as we enter, being established precisely on the basis of what has implicitly taken place. In the *Meno*, Meno without preliminary launches straight into a question on the teaching of virtue: a question Socrates recognises later as premised on 'a debater's paradox' (Men. 80e). As a student of Gorgias, a guest of Anytus and a figure whose unscrupulous military career would have been known to the Athenian readers of the dialogue,[2] the structural disjunction between the two positions is already clearly implied in the opening question. In these dialogues the stakes of encounter are quickly made clear. The general subject matter, the interlocutors and the latter's subjective positions soon become apparent. The only difference in these dialogues is that Plato doesn't stage an encounter but presupposes it to us.

The minor type are those in which Plato stages a sort of pre-encounter. Certain characters chance upon each other. They then proceed to discuss the circumstances surrounding '*the* encounter'. Plato, with great metaphorical economy, actually enumerates the parameters and form of the conversation to come in these preliminary discussions. That is, these minor pre-encounters contain the generic marks of their fuller elaboration, the real substance of the dialogue, such that if one re-reads these minor conversations again, after the philosophical elaboration which they prefigure, the affinities become apparent and are profound in themselves. We can also see that this staging of a pre-encounter signifies in itself the significance of the event/encounter to the unfolding of the dialogue. That is to say, it is that these stagings cannot be considered purely in terms of theatrics but must be understood as a matter of formalisation. They establish and prefigure the form of the break to be pursued across the dialogue as it is across the corpus. Examples include *Phaedo*, *Theatetus*, *Sophist*, *Statesmen* (these last two 'carry on' from the *Theatetus* and as such the encounter is renewed), *Parmenides* and *Symposium*.[3]

The third type are those where it is Socrates himself who encounters someone by chance. These are *Cratylus*, *Phaedrus*, *Lysis*, *Gorgias*, *Greater Hippias*, *Ion*, *Menexenus*, *Timaeus*, *Charmides*,[4] *Protagoras*[5] and the *Republic*. It is worth sketching the shape of the encounter from this last dialogue.

The torch relay

The opening encounter of the *Republic* has two identifiable stages. In the first, Socrates and Glaucon are returning from the harbour where they have just witnessed the procession of the Thracian goddess Bendis. They are accosted by Polemarchus' slave and asked to wait. Polemarchus and his friends catch up and the latter tells Socrates that as they are so many, Socrates is no match for them and must stay. To this show of strength by number Socrates asks if there is an alternative: if he may convince them to let him go. The band replies that he cannot convince them if they refuse to listen. To this Socrates replies that he refuses to stay. Adeimantus interposes: '"Don't you even know that in the evening there is going to be a torch race on horseback in honour of the goddess?" "On horseback!" [Socrates] exclaimed; "that is something new. How will they do it? Are the riders going to race with torches and hand them on to one another?" "Just so," said Polemarchus' (R. 328ab).[6]

Straightaway some of the main themes of the dialogue are displayed and so too of the position of Socrates in the polis. Let's go through it. He is accosted. It is requested he stop moving. This motif is common in the dialogues. His gadfly-like quality is described in the *Apology*. He claims 'he never ceases to settle' chasing down the truth of what is professed by the figures of the polis. Later, in the *Republic*, he will chide his friends for 'holding him up', telling them that by doing so a swarm of questions has been stirred up (R.450a). Similarly, Socrates is often accused of shifting registers or changing the topic like the statues of Daedalus from whose line he is descended.[7] Thrasymachus will accuse him of his 'usual' dissembling early in their encounter. Socrates will argue that conversation moves of its own accord, and it is he who seeks to 'tie it down'. In this exchange he will accuse Thrasymachus of setting the limits to his responses and he gives a mathematical example. He says that Thrasymachus would ask him for the factors of twelve and yet forbid him to answer 'it is twice six, or three times four, or six times two and so on'. Very tellingly Thrasymachus claims this is an 'unfair analogy' – a general refrain of sophistry vis-à-vis mathematics. Socrates' point is that it is not he who dissembles by giving true answers even if the answer is 'I do not know', but the sophist who rejects these and demands untrue answers in their place (R. 337a–c). The threat of numbers is again a central motif. It is by numbers he is convicted and by numbers that he is singular. Numbers and strength are used as sophistic arguments to ground justice in the *Republic*. By working through various scenarios Socrates will attempt to convince his auditors that neither is suitable. The implication here is that no one will listen. This is, was and had been true throughout the Athens of the dialogues where demagogue and poet speak together on this (cf. Grg. 471e–472c). Socrates, as at his trial, nevertheless refuses to give way on such grounds and challenges the group to do something about this situation.

At this point in our minor Socratic encounter, the reference to the 'new idea' which will come on horseback and by night occurs. Set against what has just been implied, that the use of numbers, force and persuasion have all failed, what Plato intimates is that the 'laws' of the day, those of the current state, have failed to render an understanding of justice, either in terms of a definition or in its practice. The introduction of this new idea – from the harbour where the new idea appears *to* the city where it will be manifest – has several features. The notion of horseback, while being of interest to Adeimantus because of his profession, is also to signal the wildness of the new idea on the one hand and that it is tameable on the other (cf. *Phaedrus*' opposite horses – 'this means chariot-driving is inevitably a painfully difficult business' (Phdr. 246b)). It is tameable, precisely by hand-to-hand or face-to-face engagement: *polemos*. What is lazily taken today as cliché – the light of the idea – is a central motif of the *Republic* which needs to be returned to over and again rather than be summarily dismissed as quaint.[8]

In the second stage, the conversation shifts to the house of Polemarchus. The 'torch-relay' will take place among those gathered in the house. We have seen some preliminary topical set up, now we will see addressed the question of (sophistic) genealogy. The three speakers who lead us through these introductory conversations represent three positions relative to the idea of justice: Cephalus speaks of the aristocratic tradition of the polis where to act rightly according to circumstance prevails; Polemarchus, the son and heir, gives this its more contemporary poetic cum Protagorean twist only to discover that, depending on the 'interpretation' one puts on this notion, one may or may not be just – it offers no guide as to how we should live; Thrasymachus represents the logic of the demagogue and of empire which, as noted, Thucydides exemplifies in the mouths of the Athenian ambassadors to Melos.

We have three figures: the traditionalist, the poet and the demagogue. All hold positions which cannot be justified in their own terms. That none is amenable to a real definition of justice means, of course, they will not be accommodated in the just city as they are. It is important to note, though, that these positions are not abandoned, but *worked through*. Indeed, these positions equate to the stages of degeneration *away from* the ideal state – the timorous-cum-oligarchic form, the democratic and the tyrannical. The central motifs discernible in the introductory conversation, to 'tell the truth', to 'pay what one owes', to 'give what is due' and to 'serve one's interest' will all return and be extensively elaborated in the dialogue. Each will help form the new idea of justice and, 'turned upside down' so to speak, will reappear estranged from the Protagorean ethic of which they are a part. In short they will take a new form, recognised only by those who care to see. What Plato's Socrates does, here, as throughout the dialogues, as subject to this encounter, is subtract these motifs from their particularity and instead consider them as local sites of universal import.

A model encounter

There are two things to extract from this typology: one, as we said, is simply to note that the staging of an encounter between the Socratic and sophistic positions is a fundamental aspect of the Platonic dialogues. The significant encounter of the *Apology*, an encounter that affected Plato so profoundly, recurs as the model for each dialogue. Plato makes a point of showing us that what takes place in each dialogue is subject to this very encounter. Not only are the dialogues the set of *consequences* of this initial encounter but the encounter itself is repeated and affirmed as essential. The break with the sophistic state is localised by Plato for each and every dialogue at the same specific point: the site. This is to say, every encounter opens the dialogue to the 'corruptive' force of what is void to it – a 'Socratic education' – one whose elements remain otherwise foreclosed. The event introduces the possible pass of these elements as the encounter itself halts the steady progress of the sophist, often literally, in teaching the youth to make their way in the state. The attempt to draw the consequences of the encounter between the sophist and non-sophist over education then forms the underlying struggle of each dialogue. Plato makes sure that the variety of sophistic and demagogic opinions are brought to bear to forestall, discredit and reject both the centrality of the encounter and its possible extension. Often, Socrates is arranged against several sophistic positions simultaneously. In *Gorgias* in similar fashion to the *Republic* he confronts master (Gorgias), student (Polus) and patron/demagogue (Callicles) in turn; in *Euthydemus* he spars with the eristic players, Euthydemus and Dionysodorus, and then confronts the 'man of the law courts' (cf. Tht. 175c). Moreover, as we will argue below, as a consequence of the same encounter, the corpus can be seen in its entirety to establish the very model of 'the lack of a non-sophistic education', which is to say, in a world other than that of sophistry, an education by truths.

The second thing to note is how the pre-encounters establish the model for the proper enquiry that the dialogue unfolds. Again, this seems to be a re-affirmation by Plato of the centrality of the original encounter. The example above from the *Republic* is telling insofar as that dialogue is the most complete attempt to withdraw from the determinations of the Athenian state and to indeed construct what is not a sophistic state faithful entirely to the idea that in Athens a non-sophistic education is lacking 'for all'. So when Plato stages the pre-encounter he not only institutes a cut into normal proceedings, opening a new trajectory and exposing the situation to its Socratic, or more accurately non-sophistic, elements, he also prefigures the essential form and content of the coming enquiry which serves to reaffirm the overall structure of the corpus, that it is subject to the event of the encounter between the sophistic state and the singular non-sophist, displayed most spectacularly and decisively at the trial. All the iterations of the founding event, the structuring event, which occur in the specific dialogues work to both orient the singular enquiry specific to that dialogue and also affirm the Idea of the event – that in some unfounded manner the state be broken with at the specific point of education. As Plato's entire trajectory shows, from the *Republic* founded on the withdrawal *through* sophistry to the Academy and even by the dialogue form itself, it is from this localised point of the encounter that the subjective procedure will extend itself. The state is not done away with at once but by *enquiry*. Such an enquiry is always a *process*. As subject to the event, the enquiry now has the space and the material with which to work a trajectory through the sophistic state, a trajectory guided by the 'void' of this state which denotes the shared lack of a non-sophistic education. Plato's commitment to the series of points noted in this trajectory should be understood as a mark of his fidelity not to the individual Socrates but to the procedure of enquiry established in his name that proceeds step by step and is oriented through an encounter at a single point.

The context of intervention

In order to establish the event in the foundational sense that we have alluded to above, there needs to be an intervention. In a real sense it is the first stage of enquiry and as such belongs to what we call the 'complex of the subject'. The intervention will establish two things with regard to the event: first that it is indeed an evental multiple, which means, as we have seen, that it forms a one from the elements of the site and from its presentation of itself; secondly, that it belongs to the situation of its site. The necessity of this attests to the inherent undecidability of the event. It is undecidable in the sense of its happening – is it an *event* or not? This is never 'solvable' one way or another. It is subject to verification at best. The event harbours no miraculous powers. It is also undecidable in terms of its situation. Does it, or does it not, *belong* to the situation of its site? Given what we know of the event from our reading of its abstract form we know that nothing of the situation or of its state can provide the event with such recognition. Thus no inhabitant of the situation can apply a calculation to this strange occurrence in such a way that its significance be known. What is needed here is a decision on its undecidability. One should note that such a decision does not retroactively change the status of the event as undecidable; it simply decides that what happened, happened and thus belongs to the situation. In Badiou's terms the work of the intervention consists in recognising a multiple *as* an event (BE, 202/224). The series of enquiries carried out by those 'faithful' to the decision will proceed on this basis alone.

As the first stage in the complex of the subject the intervention marks the arrival of Badiou's 'subject'. In Chapters 4 and 5 we deal more fully with the complex of the subject. As we will see the subject need not be human, in the sense that what it is that supports the praxis of investigation into the post-evental situation is not constrained to be mortal, even though it provides the investigation with a finite form for its expression. Curiously, the case of the subject and its name here mirrors somewhat the case of the event and its name. Whereas 'Socrates' names the encounter between sophistry and non-sophistry, Plato, retroactively, adds his own name to the subject of this encounter. The latter is known universally as the 'Platonic corpus', or as we will say the 'subject body' of the Socratic event. In this corpus Plato essentially re-collects the various instances of the Socratic encounter with sophistry and formalises this recollection as an education by truths. However, we do not want to get ahead of ourselves.

'Who' intervenes?

At this point, confronted by the exposition of the intervention, we need to mention what or who it is that intervenes. Given that the essence of intervention is to decide, what is at stake here is not, initially anyway, knowledge. In absolutely Socratic fashion, it is a decision for that which one doesn't know. To come to know what we do not know is the simple ethic which underpins the subject, yet, as we have seen, to admit the existence of what is not known is a fraught exercise for any figure of the state, any figure that is whose subjective presence is staked in the consistency of the state. In retrospect we can see that Plato is the figure who faithfully grasps the educational profundity of this Socratic point. The corpus is not only the expression of such fidelity but its faithful extension also. We posit then that Plato is the figure who intervenes to decide on the belonging of the *Ideal* event. If we exclude the epistles, Plato appears himself twice only in the corpus. As mentioned above, he is named in the *Phaedo* as being ill on the day of Socrates' execution and is therefore unable to attend the final conversation in the prison. Why does Plato note that he is absent at the death? We discuss the *Phaedo* in Chapter 5 but what we will say is that, as with the *Phaedo* itself, what is of concern to Plato is the life of philosophy. By marking his absence Plato suggests to us that he is concerned singularly with the future of this 'way of life' – just as Socrates is looking forward to a philosophical future without the constraints of his current 'bodily' state. To put it in Badiou's words, 'no death is an event' (IT, 128).

In the *Apology* Plato twice announces his own presence at the trial. In the first instance Socrates is summing up his defence. In doing so he cites several figures who would if asked *bear witness* to his influence (Ap. 34a). The second instance is when Socrates, in suggesting his own penalty, notes that if the jury will not accept his recommendation of a single *mina* fine there are others 'prepared' *to pay*: Plato being one (Ap. 38b). Of course what makes these self-citings worth mentioning is precisely this: that Plato puts himself there in that context. He is concerned with the *life* of philosophy and will bear witness to that and that only. He is prepared to pay the price of this life. We need not labour this point. What we want to note is that the Platonic intervention, which amounts to recognising the Socratic event in all its singularity, is the first mark of the subject – this recognition establishes the subject of an education by truths. The full extent of this intervention is the corpus itself and not Plato, as Plato himself insists (L.VII. 341c). Thus the Platonic intervention, which in its initial stage is to recognise the Socratic encounter as an event, of which Plato himself makes us aware, is recognisable in the body of thought it initiates. As we said, it marks the first 'stage' in the complex of the subject. But just as with the event, the same trajectory is played out within the dialogues as well. That is, in each dialogue we are confronted with the state, the event and the intervention, and the complex of the subject to which they give rise. Plato has no choice but to double up on the names, as we will see.

FIVE FEATURES OF THE INTERVENTION

The exposition of the intervention extends across three meditations in *Being and Event.* To deal with this we propose to divide it into five sections after the manner in which Badiou introduces this notion into his meditation on Pascal (BE, 212–22/235–46). What we will do in these sections is provide an analysis and immediately flesh it out in its Platonic context. Our five categories of the intervention are the following:

1. the event as one multiple;
2. that it belongs to itself;
3. the notion of the originary Two;
4. the state form of this two;
5. recurrence;
6. time.

So, we begin with the event as one multiple.

THE EVENT AS A ONE-MULTIPLE

This time it is from the perspective of the intervention and thus we presume that something has happened. As one multiple it collects and presents the elements of its site. The encounters of the dialogues force together all the elements of the sophistic position – its teaching for money, the force of opinion, the relations between demagogue and sophist and also the youth, the non-sophist, and the elements of the non-sophistic, non-presented position such as the unknown declarations 'I know nothing' and 'I am not a teacher', the conviction of truth, the free address, the injunction to know thyself and so on. In this sense, the encounter organises the void place of a division: a division which makes no sense to the state and therefore whose consequences must be tested.

THAT IT BELONGS TO ITSELF

Badiou notes that the multiple form of the event as shown in (1) and its nominal expression are 'impossible to separate' (BE, 203/225). This is to say that to recognise the form-multiple of the event is already to name it as such. If we refer back to the matheme $e_x = \{x \in X, e_x\}$ we can see that its signification *ex* is included in its form$\{x \in X, e_x\}$. Thus if (1) is recognised as event, the event is simultaneously signified as such. We noted this above in the example of the clicking fingers. In a way it forces its own nomination from the intervention. To nominate then is not, as with a constructive logic, to 'constitute' its reality but to mark its *belonging to* the situation as a *separation from* this 'reality'.

As Badiou says:

> The essence of the intervention consists – within the field opened up by an interpretative hypothesis, whose *presented* object is the site (a multiple on the edge of the void), and which concerns the 'there is' of an event – in naming this 'there is' and in unfolding the consequences of this nomination in the space of the situation to which the site belongs. (BE, 203/225)

The encounter in the dialogues can only have one name, albeit a complex one, and that is 'Socrates'. In straightforward terms it is this *figure* alone who attends every encounter. This raises a couple of questions that requires us to step outside the text for a moment. The relation between Socrates and Plato has been a vexed one for the history of scholarship and we will deal with this in Chapter 5. What we note here is that Plato intervenes in the evental occurrence with this name 'Socrates'. This nomination forever marks the irruptive constitution of the dis-relation between the non-sophistic figure and the sophistic figure and every articulation, every renewal of this encounter concerns education as its site. What is singularly at stake between these two figures of the encounter, regardless of 'who' issues in their place, is the fundamental question of any education by truths, that is: 'How are we to live?' What we are suggesting is that the name 'Socrates' functions in the dialogues to mark that 'the only education', effectively made up by the elements of the site gathered in their disassembly by the event, is named by this figure of Socrates. Badiou says, 'this name like every evental name is the index of a central void in the earlier situation' of the sophistic state – namely, the lack of a non-sophistic education (HB, 13, trans. modified). What Plato does by naming the event 'Socrates' is establish that education is that which must *take place*: it is not an assumed function of the state but belongs to the situation of its site, which is to say 'to all' and not to the determinations of sophistic interest. However, the question of the genesis of this name is important. If the name already circulates within the state and is as such a recognised term of the situation then it cannot serve to name a new multiple, let alone one that presents what is unpresented and belongs to itself: 'No presented term of the situation can furnish what we require, because the effect of homonymy would immediately efface everything unpresentable contained in the event; moreover, one would be introducing an ambiguity into the situation in which all interventional capacity would be abolished' (BE, 203/ 225). How, then, can Plato use the name Socrates to signify the evental irruption of an education by truths? As the Athenian jury found, the name Socrates does not circulate within the state for education. This name names only what is *not* an education in the Athenian state. Consequently, the name can only come from the void itself – in this situation, from what is *not* sophistry. In regard to the state, Socrates is the name of that which is unpresented for the situation. The name is an element of the site whose sole referent is the event (and as we will see that which is 'to come'). Plato deploys the name post-eventally – Socrates is not *the* event. As we saw, each dialogue emphasises the centrality of the event that brings this name to bear. Therefore it is not Socrates who determines the encounter he names but the encounter that determines that its name be found. As we have seen, the state can never recognise such a nomination. For the state, Socrates *is not an educator* (and for Plato, not 'after their pattern'), and the name circulates therefore 'illegally' – which is why each attempt to extend the reach of this nomination to test others in terms of their belonging to the event confronts the reactive figure of the state. In this sense we can see that the name Socrates 'convokes the void' of the sophistic situation. That is, it confronts and exposes the universal lack of a non-sophistic education.

The notion of the originary two

To present the elements of the site and to present itself makes the 'Socrates' event an ultra-one in Badiou's terms. This seems a vague determination, but its dimensions are clear. In the first place, not being a term recognised by the situation means that both the name and what it names are not one insofar as the state is concerned. Yet, as we saw, the event is a one multiple made up of the elements of the site and itself. What distinguishes the event is that it is not a term of the situation. It is not represented. The name functions only *for* the event. There is the event *and* its name. The latter represents the former, which is 'without representation'. As a form of representation the name (of its event) is one, while the event ultimately is a non-one of the one which is the representative situation. There is then the one of the name which signifies and the one which is not-one for any type of representation. Thus the event is two ones or ultra-one or just Two. 'The Two thereby invoked is not the reduplication of the one of the count, the repetition of the effects of the law. It is an originary Two, an interval of suspense, the divided effect of a decision' (BE, 206–7/229). In relation to the dialogues the implication is straightforward: the only education is (post-)Socratic. As much as this is a specific Two of the Platonic situation, produced by its situational effects, it is also a generic Two in that it convokes the form for any such procedure. What it denotes is the immanent division of a single point which splits the lack of a non-sophistic education and an education by truths. The name Socrates as name-of-the-event marks the passage between the evental occurrence at the site and an education by truths (this being the set of all the enquiries to come subject to this name Socrates). This Two allows no room for the state which knows neither the site nor can tolerate any such enquiry.

The state form of this Two

This Two, however, is recognised by the state *in its state form*. The inexorable laws of metastructure affect whatever presents, no matter how abnormal. What essentially circulates of the event is the name. The decision that it belongs to the situation is just that, a decision. The veracity of the decision will be determined by the consequences of the subjective enquiry. This means that the belonging of the event to the situation remains undecidable and so not presentable. The truth of the event, in the sense of its taking place, is always uncertain except for those who intervene. On this we can recall how Socrates named only a few who could speak for him at the trial and the dialogues themselves show only a few more (Theaetetus, Hermogenes, Plato) who would take up the Socratic form. Insofar as this name is concerned, if it circulates due to the intervention it can be represented by the state in a pair with what the event itself presents. What the name presents is itself and what the evental occurrence presents is the site. So the state 'knows' this couple as the represented term $\{X, \{e_x\}\}$. For the state, this is the 'canonical form of the event' (BE, 207/230). As Badiou argues, the state certainly captures the event in the form of a Two but for the state there is no relation between the two terms it represents. It recognises a certain juxtaposition in its representation but as we have seen all along with Socrates and education, from the perspective of the state there is simply no intrinsic, established or even implicative relation between them. Certainly, the trial recognises the juxtaposition of the two, but only insofar as it is established that it is the void that separates them. What the state knows of this juxtaposition is its essential irrationality whose 'lawless' 'incoherence', its unknowability, must be re-secured. In terms that might have been written with our Athenian situation in mind Badiou notes that:

> This is a classic enigma. Every time that a site is the theatre of a real event, the state – in the political sense, for example – recognizes that a designation must be found for the couple of the site (the factory, the street, the university) and the singleton of the event (strike, riot, disorder), but it cannot succeed in fixing the rationality of the link. This is why it is a law of the state to detect in the anomaly of this Two – and this is an avowal of the dysfunction of the count – the *hand of a stranger* (the foreign agitator, the terrorist, the perverse professor). It is not important whether the agents of the state believe in what they say or not. What counts is the necessity of the statement. For this metaphor is in reality that of the void itself: something unpresented is *at work* – this is what the state is declaring, in the end, in its designation of an external cause. The state blocks the apparition of the immanence of the void by the transcendence of the guilty. (BE, 208/230–1, emphasis in original)

In relation to the corpus this quote needs no glossing. To say something unpresented is at work is to sum the procedure that Socrates names with regard to the sophistic state – there is 'no one like me' Socrates asserts at the trial (a point reiterated across the dialogues). Suffice to say that in his meditation on Pascal Badiou notes that in regard to the Christian event the Romans, despite not recognising what is at stake, nevertheless detect that it would 'prove a lasting embarrassment for the State' (BE, 213/236). The very invention of the dialogues has the effect to this day of ensuring the latter (though it is too often considered as past history rather than historical present) but ultimately to embarrass the state is neither here nor there. To take one's leave of its determination is the intent and the event offers the chance of such a separation by invention.

Recurrence

Here we hit upon the curious fact that the implicative structure of the event and the intervention seems to become circular and thus the intervention is a function with no legitimacy outside the event whose existence as such it guarantees by its intervention.[9] This is a question that again reminds us of the debate concerning the relation between Plato (who intervenes) and Socrates (the name of the event). Which dialogues are Socratic and which Platonic? Does Plato speak for Socrates, or does he put words into his mouth? If Socrates never wrote, then how can the dialogues be Socratic at all as it is only through Plato, who did write, that the voice of Socrates is heard? So it goes. There is a real question here, one that Badiou addresses but in language which requires some interpretation. We will give an explanation we think satisfactory as far as it goes. Ultimately, the difficulty hinges on his notion of time.

What is at stake is the form of the intervention. First let's recount the problem as Badiou states it:

> Because the referent of the intervention is the void, such as attested by the fracture of its border – the site –, and because its choice is illegal – representative without representation –, it cannot be grasped as a one-effect, or structure. Yet given that what is a-non-one is precisely the event itself, there appears to be a circle. It seems that the event, as interventional placement-in-circulation of its name, can only be authorised on the basis of that other event, equally void for structure, which is the intervention itself. (BE, 209/231)

Quite simply the logic is in danger of being circular. Thus what Badiou does is 'split the circle' at the point where the intervention itself would become another event, an event for the first event, and thus we would have the problem all over again. Instead, he notes that any intervention presents one event for another. What does this mean? Here we note that Badiou takes the very logic of intervention, whose singular function is to decide, from the axiom of choice. Without going into detail, this 'occasional' axiom works at the level of function or operation. Like the intervention it operates on an existence which it simultaneously guarantees. However, it is not the operation per se which can provide the guarantee of presentation. In the case of the intervention, nothing of the situation guarantees its existence beyond its function. It cannot ultimately secure the existence whose existence it has decided into being. It requires another existence beyond and consequent upon itself. Badiou puts it this way, 'an intervention is what presents an event for the occurrence of another. It is an evental between-two' (BE, 209/232). What Badiou is suggesting is that the event (pre-its *own* intervention) is in some way equivalent to an Idea. That is to say, it is the Idea of another event that makes it possible to think the presentation of the intervention even as it is nowhere presented. The existence of the intervention as a presented multiple is subtended to the event to come. For Badiou, this 'evental recurrence' is essentially the name for history as discontinuity. There is no History, just as there is no Nature. At any given point 'in time' there are interventions on events on the one hand, and the Idea (of the event) which will have presented the form of the intervention. At the same time as the event to come stands guarantor for the existence of the function of intervention, the current situation, being infinite and historical, also carries within it traces of past events. Incredibly, Plato gestures toward just such a historicity of the encounter (such is what is at stake here) between 'discursive thought' or *dianoia* (Badiou glosses this as 'the thought that links and traverses') and *eikon*[10] ('affirmation and delectation', a poetic form that 'dwells on the threshold' (HB, 17)) when he says in the *Republic* 'there is a long-standing quarrel between poetry and philosophy' (R. 607b).[11] This recursion to the subject of poetry, the 'secret, esoteric dimension of sophistry' (MP, 22), occurs in the context of Socrates pointing out to Glaucon that when he meets admirers of Homer who claim that the latter is the educator to all Hellas whose works should be taken up as a guide to manage and educate people and that 'one should arrange one's life in accordance with his teachings', you must 'listen to them kindly but must be adamant that they cannot be admitted to our commonwealth' (R. 606e).

Time

In this way, Badiou says, intervention 'forms the kernel of any theory of time'. Intervention is Time itself. Time is 'thought as the gap between the two events' (BE, 210/232). Between two events intervention *takes place* and thus to identify the old quarrel as Plato does is to allude to the subjective struggle that produces this *time of truth*. Clearly this time is not subject to chronology or measure as such. While the subject itself might form a finite instance, as Badiou says, truth, understood as post-evental unfolding of the pre-evental situation's void – its lack of a non-sophistic education – has no such constraints. The 'measure' of this Time established by intervention is between event and exhaustion. In the dialogues Time is the production of Plato, for as the author and the actor of the intervention he speculates on this time by grounding his intervention on the situational 'circulation' of Socrates as name of the event. The work the intervention institutes is simply the production of a new time, the latter being simply the unmeasured distance between events, and, as such, an evental time – the time of philosophy, the time of an education by truths, 'bounded' by the material occurrence and the institution of the Idea (cf. Tht.172c+). Despite the various and numerous attempts to cure us of the 'Plato disease', perhaps the time inaugurated by the Platonic intervention upon the discursive rule of the sophistic state has not yet been exhausted. 'In terms of recurrence', Badiou says, 'beginnings will be measured by the re-beginnings they authorise' (LS, 147). In this context what is most critical to note is that 'intervention generates a discipline' (BE, 207/229).

The Cave event

To finish this chapter and illustrate the interaction of event and intervention we will present a reading of the famous story of the cave. We will focus strictly on the evental aspect of the story. It is fairly uncontroversial to say that the story of the cave is a metaphor for the entire procedure that the Platonic corpus enacts: the movement from the determinative regime of opinion to the subjective and thus educative production of truths. As we go, we will note the concentration Plato focuses on the event and suggest how the intervention functions in turn. In truth, as we said, the intervention draws its real legitimacy from the consequences it engenders or the time it institutes. Some of these will be mapped out in the chapters to come.

We will recount the outline of the story. Socrates proposes to Glaucon that there are men living deep underground in a cave. From the surface runs a long passage down to where these men, from childhood, have been bound hand and foot facing a wall of the cave. Behind and above them burns a fire. Between the prisoners and the fire is a parapet as at a puppet show, Plato says. Other men, using various 'things of stone and wood', project shadows onto the wall in front of the prisoners. The bound prisoners cannot turn around and so all they have ever seen are these 'shadows'. We can expect, Plato adds that any conversation they may have between them is about these shadows. Further, the wall carries the echo of the other men's voices and so, to the prisoners, it is as if the shadows speak. This is their whole and only reality. 'It's a strange image', Glaucon says, 'and strange prisoners you're telling of.' 'They are like us,' Socrates replies (R. 515a). We are then to imagine a prisoner is somehow freed from his bonds. He is walked toward the firelight. Every movement is painful and his eyes, accustomed to shadow, cannot properly make out the things of stone and wood exposed by the fire. Someone tells him that all he was used to seeing is merely illusion. Now, they say, he has a chance to come closer to the truth. Plato says that at first the 'escapee' would be perplexed and would wonder if the things of stone and wood were actually less real than the shadows. The light from the fire would hurt his eyes and he would prefer the comfort of the shadows and his old certainties. But before he could return to his bonds someone forces him up the long passageway on the arduous journey out into the sunlight. On arriving outside the cave he would see nothing at first – the radiance would be too blinding. He would need to grow accustomed to the new conditions, shadows first, then reflections in water and finally the things themselves. Then he would see the heavens at night and lastly the sun itself as the source of all light and the movements of life itself. He would then recognise that what he took for wisdom in the cave was nothing of the sort and would feel sorry for his comrades. These cave dwellers, Plato says, had their own practice of honouring those among them with a good memory for the order in which, and the association by which, the shadows appeared. The escapee, he says, would be unlikely to covet these prizes now. Feeling this way, the escapee goes back down to his former comrades hoping in turn to liberate and compel them to know their ignorance of what there is to know. They find him imposing and ridiculous; they laugh at him, tell him his sight is ruined, and finally, Plato says, they kill him (R. 514–17a).

Now, what is of primary interest is simply the point at which the prisoner is 'turned'. Cornford's translation says, 'Suppose one of them is set free and forced suddenly to stand up [and] turn his head'. Lee says, 'suppose one of them was let loose and suddenly compelled to stand up and turn his head . . .' Grube/Reeve say, '. . . one of them was freed and suddenly compelled to stand up and turn . . .' Jowett says, '. . . at first when any of them is liberated and compelled to stand up and turn his neck . . .' and the English translation of Heidegger's own translation says 'whenever any of them was unchained and forced to stand up suddenly, to turn around . . .' (R. 515c).[12] The turning is conditioned by an apparent contradiction: compulsion and freedom.[13] The logic at work here is this: to be freed is to be compelled to turn. This is certainly the prototype for Rousseau's famous claim that the 'general will' forces us to be free. Badiou himself shows a similar logic in regard to the event. The subject is both seized by and decides for the event – he is compelled by the occurring and decides for the 'truth' of the compulsion, this truth being the sum of the subject's 'education'. Liberation and compulsion again work an implicative force upon the becoming subject of the event. We will return to this below.

The prisoner is to turn from image to reality, from what appears as such to what is (we know from our discussion so far that 'what is' is what insists in its absence to sense). Plato gives no reason for this liberation of the prisoner. As we have seen, the *abstract form* of an event 'can be known' – it will happen at its site and be situated. It will mobilise the multiples of this site and will belong to itself. Its occurring, however, and its being taken up as something rather than nothing, is a matter of chance insofar as the encyclo-paideia is concerned.

Yet the centrality of this event to this story of education is clear and this is what makes this compulsion to turn non-trivial. To reiterate, the event is not a necessity in terms of its occurring – nothing of the cave-site can determine that it necessarily takes place. Plato certainly gives no indication either way. It is certain, however, that without this intervention event the prisoners would have persisted in their reality. The event is a necessary contingency, similar to that which we elaborated above concerning the staged encounters.[14] *As an author*, Plato has to necessitate a contingency which in turn necessitates an enquiry. But this is to affirm the point with regard to the event. It is what establishes a beginning on the basis of chance. Yet it is firmly of its situation and attached to its site. It draws on what the situation does not present and this alone is what makes it unknown or incalculable for the state. In truth any notion of the miraculous should be reserved for the work of the subject. For if they re-collect the terms of the situation in such a manner that it no longer takes its rule from casual ascription, the reign of opinion, the apparatus of repression or relative measure, then by all appearances that would be a truly miraculous occurrence, a true education.

So, that the event happens is necessary to the re-collection of terms (generic procedure) which the prisoner will undertake, yet there is simply nothing which can compel an event to be an event. The prisoner is freed by the force of contingency alone. Why him? Why now? Why at all? In normal circumstances people can organise, rise up, revolt, etc., an artist can invent an unheard of work. But to be unique, strange, aleatory unheard of and so on in terms of the situation is not enough to ensure that what happened becomes an event. What we can say, based on our previous explanations, is that the event of liberation/compulsion is in a precise sense an effect of the fundamental conditions of the cave-site. The inhabitant's world of shadows, *as a world of shadows*, no matter how well organised, how well celebrated, taught, known and reproduced, nevertheless presents within itself a singular (in)existence. For the prisoners, reality consists entirely of the sounds and images coming from the wall. This constituted the sum of their knowledge. The notion 'to be freed' did not exist to them. Liberation, in the sense that it refers to a place other than that present to their knowledge, was void to the prisoners. The site of this liberation/compulsion is knowledge or education. It is this that 'the turn' in turn refers to: the void buried in the excess of the prisoner's knowledge of their world.

As Plato unfolds the story we of course come to see that what was void to this cave situation was that its truth was other than what appeared as reality to the prisoners. The event of the liberation/compulsion exposes this void: that there was *something* which was non-apparent. The turn, which the event compels, is the first movement toward drawing the consequences of there being a 'hole' in this reality, in the knowledge determinative of the prisoner's situation. We should stress, with Plato, that the cave-dwellers revel in their knowledge or *memories*. They accord honours to those who excel in this. Plato is alluding to the fact that for the cave-dwellers their knowledge accounts for what there is to account for. They have a false conceit which, as we know, constitutes a rule of excess. They fail to know that they do not know precisely because they share the lack of a non-sophistic education. This conceit forecloses the void that wanders about there and whose appearance offers both liberation and compulsion. Such is its indifference.

What we can say is that the conditions of the cave are such that the insistent lack of truth presented there, at some point in its history, will have forced itself to the surface. If the insistence of this void is to be marked it requires its encounter. 'The event', Badiou remarks, is attached, in its very definition, to the place, to the point, in which the historicity of the situation is concentrated' (BE, 178/199). This is what the event is, the conditional imposition of its existence at a site. The event is the mark of this insistent void. What happens must assert itself as that which happened. Plato simply could not tell his tale without the founding event at its centre. The prisoner must be made such that he can *turn*. What turns a prisoner, an inhabitant of such a situation, any situation? Simply, as Plato shows, a chance encounter. Again, thinking of the situation and not the authorial force of the narrative, 'why this prisoner, why now, why at all?' The questions are not answerable, essentially because the event is indifferent to these definitions. As we saw, *every* 'prisoner' partakes of the lack of a non-sophistic education and, as such, the event at this cave-site addresses itself to anyone at all. Certainly, not every prisoner will submit to the demands of the turn and in this sense we can say that what answers these unanswerable questions is the extent or the effectiveness of the subjective process initiated in the turn.

The event of the cave is the essential move in the subject's being 'unbound' from the cave. The act of liberation, Plato reminds us, is only the beginning. The chains are removed but their reality is still compelling. Faced with what has happened he is perplexed, undecided. No knowledge supports his predicament. Plato suggests the prisoner is overwhelmed by what he doesn't know and would seek to go back to the *state* of not knowing that he didn't know, even though to do so given what he now 'knows' is strictly speaking impossible at risk of severe pathology. Essentially, the prisoner now *knows* nothing (he *knows* he *knows nothing*): nothing in regard to what happened – to be freed is an unheard of thing – and nothing in regard to what this event means given that it has happened, and most importantly, that what he did know was all the time conditioned by this 'nothing'. It is the latter which will supply the subject with the discipline to go on and to address what else he does not know.

Plato says that the prisoner must be dragged out of the cave itself into the light. This is to say the event forces upon the subject the pursuit of its consequences. He must investigate the logic of the turn. For this becoming subject, compelled to be so by the chance of an event, the consequences lead up and out of the reality of the cave and ultimately back down again. Plato's pessimism, won by his experience with Socrates, intervenes here and he imagines the prisoner killed in his attempt to illuminate the connection between his comrades and the event of the turn toward freedom. But this doesn't preclude an analysis of the return. The *return* is a necessary part of the same enquiry predicated by the turn. The prisoner's return is a metaphor for the necessity the subject has of working for the event through the state. The subject cannot retreat to the mountain top but like Zarathustra must go down again. The difference is that where Zarathustra sought *his* equals – and of course could not find them – the prisoner is an example of the insistence of equality itself.[15] As we said, nothing in the cave story distinguishes this prisoner from any other. As an event is addressed to all insofar as it happens, then the attempt by the prisoner to free his comrades is an aspect of the universalism inherent to the event insofar as it convokes the void of the situation. As we saw, that it was *this* prisoner and not another cannot be a matter of calculation or identity but only chance. As such, the void convoked in this event must as with any situation be everywhere included; thus every prisoner shares the lack of 'liberation' which the event exposed with regard to the first prisoner. Justice demands that the universal address inherent to the event be the condition of the pursuit of its consequences. Education is therefore 'not what it is said to be by some, who profess to put knowledge into a soul which does not possess it, as if they could put sight into blind eyes' (R. 518bc). Rather the education of the first prisoner – occurring to him only by chance – *is* the education of all – as 'all men possess the power of learning the truth and the organ to see it with' – or it is not an education at all (R. 518c). We can see that this is axiomatic for Plato. The subject and the state stake out their rivalry over this. For the former, even death is no event in the life of the truth it stakes out while the latter, 'having no single mark before their eye at which they must aim', confuse truth with its place of annunciation and are compelled thereby to reproduce its place at whatever cost (R. 519bc).

Conclusion

The event 'summons the void' of the previous situation – it is its index. The name Socrates designates that what is void to the sophistic state is a non-sophistic education. This is to say, what every element of the sophistic state shares is the 'lack of a non-sophistic education'. The encounter with the sophistic figure of the state institutes the existence of this lack. The event is the irruptive insistence of this lack. This lack named by the event is in anticipation of what is to come. In the trial the Socratic figure insisted that he was not a sophist. The sophistic state insisted that in being the only one who was not, he therefore did not educate. In putting this figure on trial the state necessarily invoked its own limit. It recognised that there was 'something unpresented at work' – a stranger, a terrorist or a perverse professor – an orator 'not after their pattern' (Ap. 17a). In sentencing him to death, necessarily, as Anytus noted, it sought to codify this limit as external to it. Socrates was not *of the state* and so he must not be and more particularly Socrates as the name of the event, the name of the figure which encountered sophistry at its limit, must not *be thought*. What the sophistic state sees in the death of Socrates is the death of his being thought – which is to say, the death of his thought being practised. Plato stages a great reversal here of the Parmenidean maxim, as Socrates is literally that being which 'must *not* be thought'.[16]

In Socratic terms the height of ignorance is to profess to know what cannot be thought. Such ignorance prefers to do harm rather than receive it. Rather than know its lack, the state excises the possibility of its thought. Yet this lack will insist. It is of the very being of the Athens of the dialogues that it does. This name, Socrates, stands within the dialogues as the figure around which what-is-not-sophistic-knowledge might gather. Potentially, every element of the situation, every inhabitant of the sophistic state of the Athenian situation can be connected to this name by the share it has in the void. Of course the void is not subject to knowledge, and so identification with the Socratic figure, or more accurately an 'association' with this figure is not possible without an enquiry of some sort. Each inhabitant must be tested. Not in terms of their belonging to the situation nor to its state. We know the latter is the case but in terms of whether they can be connected to the event and thus can come to be separated from the state as elements of the situation to come. To demonstrate this possibility we turn to what we call Socrates' 'implicative or prescriptive statements'. These, we will argue, serve to both confirm the measure the Socratic figure takes of sophistic excess, in other words to pierce a hole in its knowledge, and to operate a faithful enquiry into this situation for those who might have their heads turned, as it were, by the Socratic event. To paraphrase Plato, the 'equality of minds is a duty, not a matter of fact' (R. 519e). In Badiou's terms applicable to this 'poet'- intervener, 'the imperative is voiced: fidelity is required' (BE, 261/289).

Notes

1. J.-J. Rousseau, *The Social Contract*, p. 22.
2. In *Anabasis* Xenephon depicts him as enormously eager for wealth, self-interested, lacking affection for anyone, and says he made use of those who were 'pious and practiced truth' for his own material benefit (2.6.21–7). See also Nails, *The People of Plato*, pp. 204–5.
3. The *Symposium* is unique in that it stages a series of encounters. There is an implied encounter when it opens with Apollodaurus recounting to a friend a *chance encounter* he had with Glaucon in the street. The story of the *Symposium* proper, as Apollodorous tells it, begins with another encounter in turn. Aristodemus runs into Socrates who is

heading to Agathon's for the dinner (Plato doesn't miss the pun on the names here either, using a proverb to capture Socrates as being between two good men). The next series of encounters are more interruptions. Socrates does not enter with Aristodemus but stays outside thinking. When he does come in, he interrupts the meal. When the speeches start the order is interrupted by Aristophanes having a bad case of hiccoughs (as well he might) and finally, the gathering is altered completely by the arrival of a drunken Alcibiades. The event-Idea is present throughout. What is interesting to note is that there are seven identifiable encounters which effect the telling of the *Symposium*: as many as there are speeches. The commentaries on Aristophanes' hiccoughs are legion. See, for example, Chiesa, 'Le resort de l'amour: Lacan's theory of love in his reading of Plato's Symposium', pp. 61–80 and Mladen Dolar, *A Voice and Nothing More*, pp. 24–6. Dolar calls these hiccups 'the most famous in the history of philosophy'.

4. After returning from battle at Potidea, Socrates seeks out his friends. In their company he meets the beautiful youth Charmides. As the discussion progresses Charmides, the physical object of attention, gives way to his guardian Critias – 'later' the well-known leader of the Thirty. That Socrates is noted to be just home from battle is to establish his credibility as a fighter against the tyranny – a *polemos*.
5. Socrates encounters a friend who asks him if he's been off chasing Alcibiades. Socrates says, 'yes', he has seen him but there is something more interesting to talk about. He proceeds to recount to him the story of meeting Protagoras –'the wisest man alive' (Pr. 309d). In this story he and Hippocrates are discussing the status of sophistry (Prt. 313cd). Hippocrates is eager to meet Protagoras and so they head to Callias' house where Protagoras is staying. The scene is well worth repeating. Socrates and Hippocrates, arrive at Callias' door (recall Ap.20a; Callias has spent more on sophists than all others combined). The doorman, 'a eunuch', overhears them from inside. He opens the door, sees them, and says 'Ha! More sophists' and slams the door shut in their face. They knock again and Socrates appeals to the doorman, 'we are not Sophists' (Prt. 314de). Once they are inside, they are confronted by a veritable who's who of sophistry and we, the readers, by a who's who of the dialogues. It is a true 'historic' comic moment told with reference to Homer's depiction of Odysseus' descent into the underworld. The gathering includes Prodicus, Protagoras, Hippias, Pericles' sons Paralus and Xanthippus, Protagoras' star pupil Antimoerus and also Eryximachus, Phaedrus, Tantalus, the sons of Adeimantus, Pausanias and Agathon, and Alcibiades and Critias, to name almost all of them. The depiction of the sophists set up in separate rooms of the house discoursing to their various bands of followers is given great comedy by Plato's description of their movements. Essentially they are 'on stage':

Protagoras paces and turns and his whole band turns on his turn, creating a great whirl around the room. Hippias, the polymath, is depicted on a high seat with followers arrayed on benches around answering questions on the various subjects on which he was expert. Prodicus too, the grammatician, whom Socrates compares to Tantalus, after Homer, is, as is fitting for the thief and stockpiler of divine wisdom, set up in an old storeroom where he remains in bed. The allusion is analogical and particular – particular, as Prodicus is the sophist concerned with tracking down the true meaning of words, a task whose fruition forever escapes him but which is lucrative nonetheless (see Cr. 384bc). More generally, Socrates is telling Hippocrates, this is what sophistic teaching amounts to – it is an ever retreating and circling hermeneutics whose promise no amount of the 'general equivalent' can achieve. Although it has all the power of the best comic scene the depiction also has its geometrical design and the ultimate point as ever is philosophical. 'When he turned around with his flanking group, the audience to the rear would split into two in a very orderly way and then circle around to either side and form up again behind him. It was quite lovely' (Prt. 315b). The sophists are spatially distributed (just as they come from all Hellas and beyond to 'form up' in Athens) and are seen to move within a series of defined points. Plato carefully matches the movement and the siting of the sophists to the conceptual content or intent of their discourse. Socrates, as Odysseus, is the aleatory figure. One should note also that the sophists, while gathered under the same roof, occupy separate rooms with distinct followers. It is a non-gathering in our sense insofar as what is included is so after the rule which renders them distinct.

6. Cf. Parmenides' Proem, which Sextus Empiricus recounts and comments on: 'In these words Parmenides is saying that the "mares" that carry him are the non-rational impulses and desires of the soul, and that it is reflection in line with philosophical reason that is conveyed along "the famed road of the goddess". This reason, like a divine escort, leads the way to the knowledge of all things. His "girls" that lead him forward are the senses. And of these, he hints at the ears in saying "for it was being pressed forward by two rounded wheels," that is the round part of the ears, through which they receive sound. And he calls the eyes "daughters of Night," leaving the "house of Night," "pushed into the light" because there is no use for them without light. And coming upon "much-punishing" Justice that "holds the corresponding keys" is coming upon thought, which holds safe the apprehensions of objects. And she receives him and then promises to teach the following two things: "both the stable heart of persuasive Truth," which is the immovable stage of knowledge, and also "the opinions of mortals, in which there is no true trust" that is, everything that rests on

opinion, because it is insecure. And at the end he explains further the necessity of not paying attention to the senses but to reason. For he says that you must not "let habit, product of much experience, force you along this road to direct an unseeing eye and echoing ear and tongue, but judge by reason the argument, product of much experience, that is spoken by me." ' Sextus continues: 'So he too, as is evident from what has been said, proclaimed knowledgeable reason as the standard of truth in the things that there are, and withdrew from attention to the senses.' (Empiricus, *Against the Logicians*, pp. 24–5, VII, 111; verses 29–30.)

7. In *The Emergence of Social Space: Rimbaud and the Paris Commune*, Kristin Ross recounts how Verlaine and Delahaye refer to Rimbaud as *l'Oestre* or gadfly. In the context of describing the discursive and sexual relations between the members of the *Cercle du Zutisme* Ross says, '*L'oestre* is included in the vocabulary of sexuality as well: *oestre vénérien* means an ardent or immoderate desire for the pleasures of love; while the Greek *oestrus* signifies a prophetic or poetic delirium' (p. 135). In the same text Ross recounts Rimbaud's relation to 'Vagabondage'. As the quote above suggests, and his way of life illustrates, Socrates is himself something of a vagabond. Ross says that for the state 'what is particularly disquieting about vagabondage is its ambiguous status: technically, vagabonds have not violated any laws (except the laws against vagabondage), they have not committed any crimes. But their 'way of life' places them in a state that supposes the *eventual* violation of laws: vagabonds are always virtual, anticipatory. She quotes a writer of the nineteenth century: 'You can't say to a vagabond . . ., "Don't do it again"; instead, you would have to say, "Change your way of life, take up the habits of work" ' (p. 57).
8. Cf. Parmenides speaking about the moon: 'Bright in the night, wandering about the world, a light from elsewhere' (in Barnes, *Early Greek Philosophy*, p. 88). Cf. Badiou speaking of 'revolutionary thought' and alluding to Mallarmé, '*Nous-sommes lampadophores*' (TS, 126).
9. Cf. *Logiqueṣ des Mondes*, where intervention and nomination are collapsed in favour of a topology of intensity.
10. See Cornford's gloss in his commentary on the *Republic*, p. 222. He says *eikon*, to which *eikasia* is linked etymologically, the latter being the lowest form of cognition, amounts to likeness or representation, comparison or conjecture. Badiou does not say that poetry is any of these, though Plato does. There is little doubt that for both, sophistry, as that educational form which inherits and extends the poetic tradition, is what is at stake. See R. 509d–511b.
11. Παλια τις διαφορα φιλοσοφία τε καί ποιητική. Badiou renders this as '*ancien est le discord de la philosophie et du poétique*'. Badiou, *Petit manuel d'inaethétique*, p. 33.

12. Cornford, *The Republic of Plato*; Grube/Reeve, *Plato: Complete Works*; Desmond Lee, *The Republic*. See also Jowett's Introduction to his translation of the *Republic* at http://www.gutenberg.org/files/1497/1497-h/1497-h.htm; Heidegger, 'Plato's doctrine of truth', in *Pathmarks*, p. 159.
13. The term 'turn' has a great post-Platonic heritage. Many have taken up this notion. Heidegger uses it against Plato as does Nietzsche and Deleuze, and Vlastos invokes the terrors of the 'mathematical turn'. But both Nietzsche and Heidegger do see an inherent link between truth, education and liberation. For Nietzsche's view see 'Schopenhauer as educator'; for Deleuze see *The Logic of Sense*. Heidegger sees the essence of this turn in the essential link between truth and education and thus for him Plato's turn is something like a founding negation. According to Heidegger, Plato's *paideia* has turned beings away from the hidden origins of unhiddeness and toward the idea which is, thus, only representable in the forms of reason, thinking, logos and so on, all the names by which Plato proceeds in the dialogues to *present* a thought of truths. See Heidegger, Plato's 'Doctrine of Truth,' pp. 155–82. On this last point, cf. Deleuze, LoS, 257.
14. For a radical reappraisal of the contingency/necessity 'relation' see Quentin Meillassoux, *After Finitude: An Essay on the Necessity of Contingency*, and see also Meillassoux, 'Potentiality and virtuality', *Collapse: Journal of Philosophical Research and Development*, pp. 55–81. In the same issue see Ray Brassier, 'Enigma of realism' (pp. 15–54) where he discusses Meillassoux's project. See also Brassier, *Nihil Unbound*.
15. There is a similarity of a sort. Zarathustra is of course constrained to be the bridge to the 'new man'. For Badiou, the pass of the subject through the situation is the manifest realisation of the 'new man'. For Nietzsche's Zarathustra, this new man was *imminent* but not *immanent*.
16. Here we have the 'obscene', as Žižek might say, underside of the Parmenidean maxim 'it is the same to think as to be' for as that which must not be thought Socrates must therefore not be.

CHAPTER 4

Fidelity

> 'Intervention generates a discipline: it does not deliver any originality.' (BE, 207/229)
>
> 'The name subsequently circulates within the situation according to the regulated consequences of interventional decision.' (BE, 206/228)

The retrial of Socrates

In naming the event (Socrates), the intervention (of Plato) not only decides that the event (encounter) exists, that it belongs to the (Athenian) situation of its site (education), but it simultaneously initiates the *trial* of its consequences.

It is illuminating to think that the Platonic corpus enacts the retrial of Socrates. With the successive enquiries of each dialogue, the questioning of those suspected of sophistry and those who bear witness to it, the determined differentiation of the knowledge of opinion from the truth of such knowledge, Plato certainly seems to be concerned to establish a new verdict. However, it is not a new verdict on Socrates Plato seeks. It seems to us that the retrial enacted through the corpus does indeed find Socrates guilty of corruption. But what Socrates corrupts is a corrupt state – one that does not know what it claims to know (CCT, 245 and D, 96). This, as Plato notes, is the worst of all corruptions and one should be grateful to be delivered of it (Grg. 458a). In order to find Socrates guilty of what amounts to the instigation of an education by truths – which *is* the 'lack of a sophistic education' – Plato has to conduct a distinct form of trial with parameters, means and methods which mean nothing in terms of the sophistic state (cf. Phd. 69e). We have seen above that the state knows nothing of the make-up of the site, that it knows nothing of the event or rather the immanent relation of the event to its site, and that it knows nothing about the intervention that establishes the belonging of the event to the situation of its site by giving it a name. We have seen that this name does not name education in the sophistic state. However, the event/encounter, by its very occurrence, establishes that sophistic knowledge, despite itself, is not-all. If the encounter 'takes place', then there is something besides the encyclopaedia. For Plato, it is *by* this point that education *is* possible. What the Platonic intervention establishes as possible is the reality of this possibility and this reality is that of the subjective enquiries which readdress or retry the situation from the point of the encounter. *This* patently illegal trial, which Plato enacts as a singular series of enquiries, is what Badiou names fidelity (BE, 394/432).

Faithful enquiries

In itself, this fidelity is neither 'a capacity, a subjective quality, [n]or a virtue' (BE, 233/258). Nor is it a knowledge. In Badiou's terms, it is an operation. As such, it exists *ideally* by virtue of an intervention and *materially* by virtue of its results. Operationally, and taking the name of the event as its point of orientation, a fidelity is a series of situated, particular and yet random *enquiries* among the 'inhabitants of the Athenian situation'. These disparate enquiries realise a single, yet ever incomplete, result: to divide rigorously this situation in two and, as such, to establish there, as consistent, what has hitherto been ruled impossible. On one side of this division there will be elements of this situation tested as *positively* connected to the name of Socrates – these we might call *associates* – and on the other, those tested as *not-connected* to the name of Socrates and as such to that which the name refers: these, in Badiou's terms, remain *inhabitants*. Unlike the trial in the *Apology*, however, the faithful, thus Platonic, retrial of Socrates is not regulated by the finitude of death but by the infinitude of 'his' address. The Socratic trial of sophistry, constructing as it does what Badiou calls a 'generic subset', is ever incomplete.

There are two essential and mutually implicated 'components' of this fidelity: 'the operator of faithful connection' and 'enquiry'. The first provides the rule of the latter and it is by the latter that the result is attested. These two features of 'fidelity' will be our focus. Our argument will be that Socrates' absurd claim to ignorance, that he 'knows nothing', a claim heard across the entire corpus and as such not regulated by the 'Socratic problem', functions therein as the 'operator of faithful connection'. In short, it connects (or it does not) the Athenian inhabitants encountered across the dialogues to their 'unknown' (indiscernible) universal condition signified by the event encounter: namely, their lack of a non-sophistic education. Through this 'operation of connection' is established a new orientation to one's situation and, thus, the basis for a new thinking of the situation entirely. The second term of fidelity, enquiry, will be understood to be the procedure of investigation undertaken within any given dialogue. The operator of faithful connection thus serves as the rule of enquiry. For Plato, enquiry, and more specifically enquiry with others, establishes, or as we will see in the final chapter, *forces* the result of 'Socratic ignorance': a result incommensurable with the sophistic state.

The operation of fidelity

Before turning to the specifics of enquiry subject to the rule of connection it is beneficial to provide an overview of what pertains to the operation of fidelity. This will set this rule within the context of the categories so far discussed and will also establish the parameters of the links between them. Moreover, it will leave us with a clear path to talk about the operator of faithful connection as the critical component in establishing the shape of the subjective or generic education Plato has in mind when he distinguishes education from the practice of the sophist.

(a) *Fidelity is a 'situated operation' specific to its founding event.* (BE, 233/258)

We can take the fact that a fidelity operates within the parameters of the situation as given. There is no outside for a fidelity. However, what specifies the fidelity is not the situation per se but the event. In the context of a faithful procedure of enquiry an inhabitant of the situation is *connected* or not to the event. Connection is not coincident with the operations of structure: belonging or inclusion. The inhabitant belongs only to the situation, which counts it as a one existent of the situation that includes it. Recall, nothing can belong to the event except the event itself, insofar as what happens forms a one with its own name. Socrates is and signifies the encounter between non-sophistry and sophistry. As this suggests, the rule or the criterion of connection establishes something like an in-principle relation to the event. Without ready knowledge or, more accurately, without being able to partake of the knowledge of the state, the mode of the subjective enquiry must proceed by a different 'logic'.

We could say that an 'ignorance' subtends the *re-collection* which enquiry provides.[1] For Badiou, this procedural 'lack of knowledge' takes the form of militancy. The militant functions by conviction or, as Badiou says, by a 'knowing belief' or confidence. One 'believes' in the *eventality* of the event: *but* every stage of the enquiry is a test of the veracity of the conviction. Conviction or fidelity is no right. The militant is not privileged with some knowledge or insight. A militant is simply one who enquires into what it is he does not know, predicated on the confidence that, to quote Mao, 'we will come to know all that we do not know'.[2] In Badiou's words, knowing belief means that 'by means of finite enquiries, the operator of faithful connection locally discerns the connections and disconnections between multiples of the situation and the name of the event. This discernment is an *approximative truth*, because the positively investigated terms are *to come* in a truth' (BE, 397/435, emphasis added). Fidelity is not a virtue precisely because without the event/intervention *there is no subject*. It is not a quality pertaining to the individual, group or work that partakes of a militant function; it denotes the *formal* relation of the subject to the name of the event. In referring to the concept of the avant-garde, Badiou says 'by its existence alone, [it] imposes choice, but not *its* choice' (BE, 221/244). As he notes, no inhabitant is constrained to suffer the effects of the event, nor subscribe to a militant procedure. Nevertheless, regardless of any one's opinion on the matter what is true for this situation – and it is in fact inscribed within the situational form itself – will remain so, which is also to say 'become' true for all. Knowledge is not predicative of truth. In the last instance, it is the existence of the operator of faithful connection which determines both that a fidelity carry out its enquiries and determines also the character of the resulting division.

(b) *Fidelity* is not. *What exists are the groupings that it constitutes of one-multiples which are* marked, *in one way or another, by the evental happening*. (BE, 233/258)

A fidelity is essentially constituted by its results in the straightforward and retroactive sense that the result testifies to the prior enquiry by which they are established. There are only two results: either an enquiry finds an element positively connected to the name of the event (written $a \square e_x$) or it does not (written $\sim (a \square e_x)$). It is similar in this respect to the initial count-as-one whose result is a structured multiplicity or situation. By virtue of presentation, a one-multiple 'exists'. What is not presented is not one. As we saw, the operation of the count cannot itself be caught up in the one of its result. Thus, not being an element of the situation, it cannot be represented. In ontological terms it cannot correspond or be 'numbered by an ordinal'. As not counted, and given that all 'historical situations' are infinite, it can only be commensurate with the infinity of the situation and not its state (BE, 235/260). A fidelity is therefore formally infinite insofar as the operation that it designates cannot be circumscribed by the state qua encyclopaedia, while its results, the sole record of its being as such, are finite. This is easy to see in the Platonic corpus: if every dialogue is an enquiry into the being-faithful-to-the-Socratic-event then we see that, formally, fidelity continues despite the finitude that each dialogue marks. Fidelity *traverses* this series. Again, whether the finite dialogue (the written text qua corpus) concerns justice, courage or love, it nevertheless supports a fidelity to the Socratic event insofar as it registers within it connections to and not to Socrates solely on the basis of the encounter his name inscribes as having 'taken place'. We have already said that the same operator of faithful connection is operable in all dialogues and consequently there is 'in principle' no limit to the extent of a fidelity even as the sole mark of its existence is constituted by the finitude of its enquiries. One could still enter into such a 'Socratic' fidelity today – provided one adopt the subjective position of subtracting oneself from what today passes as the knowledge of Platonic philosophy!

The non-connection with the state amounts to the fact that, although the state can represent what the fidelity establishes *as its result*, the state cannot 'get between' the multiple and its connection to the event. This is to say, *it cannot determine nor recognise the rule of connection between these multiples*. The *results* of faithful connection are subject to knowledge – such is why *interpretations* of Plato abound – but the extent of a fidelity's capacity to establish connections is not. The latter are, very literally, a matter of truth – such is why fidelities to Plato are rare. The existence of a fidelity depends solely on the 'name of the event' (which is itself a multiple), on the operator of faithful connection, on the multiple therein encountered, and finally, on the situation and the position of its evental-site . . .' (BE, 329–30/363–4).

(c) *Fidelity operates, to a certain extent, on the terrain of the state.* (BE, 233/258)

Insofar as it works with already presented multiples (an event is so for *a* situation), a fidelity 'counts the parts of a situation'. With regard to the post-evental situation the subject constitutes a rivalry with the state. Badiou notes that 'there is always something institutional in a fidelity' – in the sense that in counting parts it organises inclusions and not belongings (BE, 233/258). Yet these inclusions operate under the injunction of the event and the operator of faithful connection and not in reference to the determinations of the state. As such it is more provocative than helpful to say that a fidelity organises inclusion. It is true, if we devalue the statist connotation with knowledge. As we saw, a fidelity organises *another mode of discernment* – a militant mode (BE, 329/363). It is institutive rather than constructive. To say fidelity acts as a 'counter state' as Badiou does at one point, despite the ambiguity it conjures, actually serves one of our interests in this work and that, as we mentioned, is to regard the Republic or the so called 'Good state' as an ideal non-state. At risk of paradox we might call this a subject state even as there are no state subjects. We say this because, while a fidelity might operate on the terrain of the state, what it recollects by doing so is a 'set' or collection, dominated or better still constituted by non-statist determinations. This is what Badiou calls the generic set, the set made from that which was indiscernible to the existing situation – what we have been referring to as the 'lack of a non-sophistic education'. What this simply means is that while, as mere procedure, fidelity may take an objectively state form, and thus has available to it 'all presented multiples', it is not submitted to the *rule of the state*. It is subject to the unknown named event, the indiscernible multiple it exposes and the operator of connection drawn from the former alone. In other words, the post-event procedure of fidelity treats the same excess as the state – the problem of knowledge – but it is not subject to the same rule as the state in doing so. It is not by the particularities of *interest* that a fidelity marks its connection.

The resulting re-collection avoids state determination insofar as a single element shows itself to be connected. This single instance of 'truth' – of that which is *to come* – constitutes the distinction between the subject and the state. What a faithful subject signifies is the *existent* possibility of a new *way* of life. Again, we can see that everything depends on the operator of connection, the formal link between the evental name and the situation, for it is by this criterion that the enquiring of the subject *avoids* being determined by the state. What a fidelity achieves, if it achieves anything, and which the enquiries establish as its results is the in-different recollection of the inhabitants of the situation relative to their connection to the event. In this manner it does organise and thus help to institute – though not constitute per se – a *new* and *generic* part of the situation, and as we know, this *is* a nonsensical and illegal part in that it is made up of those who are connected to the absurd figure of Socrates, the only Athenian who does not educate. This generic part, for which Socrates is the ultimate name and the lack of a non-sophistic education its ultimate condition, is precisely what Plato, through the dialogues, adds to his Athenian situation.

The militant logic of enquiry

Having established the general form of fidelity it is clear that it is by enquiry that the rule of connection or operator of fidelity affects its results. It is relatively clear that Badiou uses enquiry in a very Platonic sense. Quite simply, an enquiry seeks what it does not know on the basis that one can come to know. This is the great question of the *Meno* and below we will draw the connection between fidelity and the question of how one might search for what one doesn't know.

Because an enquiry lacks knowledge, it must be a militant procedure. It is not by knowledge but by decision and conviction relative to an event that the enquiry takes place. This is the rule of enquiry. It is certainly ridiculous to claim that the enquirer knows *absolutely* nothing – is simply *tabula rasa*. Badiou himself notes that it is beneficial to be knowledgeable, to *know* one's ignorance – that is to say that one 'has ignorance'. Rather, the enquirer is *without* the 'encyclopaedia' in its effort to discern what the event signifies as such. Socrates acknowledges this duality when he says that a 'wise and disciplined soul follows its guide and is not ignorant of his surroundings' (Phd. 108a). For Socrates knowledge exists, despite the state: this is his conviction. What is needed is the means to know this existence and thus to establish this existence as known. An enquiry therefore proceeds by a rule of the event – sophistic knowledge is not-all – that such knowledge is a conceit. We will discuss below how this rule is 'of this event'. It suffices for now to see that it is not a rule known to the state. Rather, it is a mode of the subject: the post-evental, and in this regard irrational, traversing of the situation, testing connections relevant to a conviction, thus opening up and splitting the situation at the point of the event's site. The disjunction, to which the Socratic trial attests, between the education proper to Athens and that which Socrates signified is established through enquiry as a real, significant and consequent break with and through the state of the situation. It is the realisation of an anomaly without precedent. The encyclopaedic order is broken with and broken down – bit by bit, enquiry by enquiry and dialogue by dialogue. The enquiry is a test of that conviction subject to a rule of connection. Importantly, the need for enquiry establishes, retroactively, that an event is the mere evanescence of a truth and not its instantiation. The truth of this situation remains that which must be 'made manifest'. The work of the faithful subject is to *turn* the void-part of all, in our terms, 'the knowing of nothing', into an 'education by truths' – inhabitant by inhabitant.

One can see that this is the typical Platonic inversion. Note, the subject does not coincide with either the results of its enquiries *nor* with the place wherein this education by truths is supposed established. The faithful subject neither precedes the event nor constitutes its truth, it denotes the procedure of its invention. Fidelity is essentially a free discipline, opposed to that (in)discipline one submits to under the rule of the state. Plato names the latter a 'cowardly sort' of discipline in that one submits to a rule of interest in order to avoid the demand inherent to the pursuit of wisdom (Phd. 254+). At some point this pursuit, whose form, as Plato consistently reminds us, is always that of an enquiry, will involve a confrontation with the rule of interest. Fidelity, thus, is Badiou's word for courage – the courage to continue through enquiry, to subtract this truth from this state and to turn it to universal account.

Recollection as militant enquiry: the case of the slave-boy

As we noted, the concept of the militant enquiry seems to resonate with Socrates' answer to Meno's question. It is worth examining therefore the function of recollection in Plato's *Meno*. The intent here is to suggest that Plato's efforts to establish the conditions of possibility of new knowledge lead him – not without mathematical support – to speculate on the rationality of that which cannot be expressed: in other words, that which is indiscernible. To achieve this, Plato has recourse to a variant of apagogic reasoning wherein an absurd statement functions to open any such enquiry, thus organising an entire reorientation on its basis.

Re-collection has three linked senses:

- It denotes a specific operation: that of forming a *new* gathering of elements.

- As a noun it denotes the gathered form of the new collection – that it is a 'recollection'.
- It suggests that something intrinsic to the elements so gathered has been recollected in and through the specificities of their re-collection.

That is to say, the elements recollected on the basis of the event and relevant to the 'operator of faithful connection' therein recollect, in Plato's sense, that which under the conditions of the state, remain void. Being thought here is the place of the inexistent as immanent to the situation – precisely what the diagonal, and so literally incommensurable, trajectory of the faithful subjective procedure provides for through the dual operations of 'the operator of faithful connection' and 'enquiry'.

In the *Meno*, Meno presents Socrates with what has become known as a paradox. Namely, that if to learn is to learn what one does *not* know, how should one learn it, can one know one has learned it given one doesn't know what it is (Men. 80e)? Socrates, far from dignifying it with the term paradox, dismisses it as a 'debater's argument' – in effect something belonging to the eristic brothers of the *Euthydemus* and sophistics in general (cf. Phd. 101e). Nevertheless, as is typical, the sophistic premise is investigated and the known conditions 'worked through'. In order to refute the 'paradox' Socrates elaborates the theory of recollection:

> As the whole of nature is akin, and the soul has learned everything, nothing prevents a man, after recalling one thing only – a process men call learning – discovering everything else for himself, if he is brave and does not tire of the search, for searching and learning are, as a whole, recollection. (Men. 81d)

As is well known, Socrates goes on to engage with a slave to provide a demonstration of recollection. That Socrates, the strange citizen par excellence, works with the slave, the non-citizen par excellence, thus suggesting to us that both the slave and Socrates share a void link with the sophistic state of the Athenian situation, is one thing. That the demonstration involves the incommensurable or the irrational or 'that which cannot be expressed' is another.[3] Ostensibly, being-immortal, a soul knows everything there is to know. Any man therefore, in order to learn, need only recall one thing (establish one *point*) and from there, with effort, he can come to know anything at all. As we saw with the Cave an encounter of some sort *founds* this recollection. In the *Meno* the slave is turned toward recollection by the Socratic question – a question which does not contain any aspect of the answer returned to it. If the learner comes to know then what is prior to the initial recall can be understood to be constituted by an undifferentiated and infinite store of prior-knowledge. We need to understand this term 'prior-knowledge' very specifically. It is not knowledge that the learner has, but the learner qua inhabitant of a situation is always already capable of knowledge.

For Plato, throughout the corpus, and given that he claims that any man can *come to* reason, what is prior to knowledge is conceived as ignorance. In this sense, ignorance denotes the lack of knowledge. However, ignorance, understood as the lack of knowledge, suggests an ambiguity upon which Plato most certainly plays. There is ignorance and there is ignorance of ignorance. When Socrates claims ignorance, it is ignorance of a specific type of knowledge which, for him, *is not knowledge*. Recall Socrates' claim against sophistic Athens that *he* is 'neither wise with *their* wisdom nor stupid with *their* stupidity' (Ap. 22e, emphasis added). Yet when he accuses sophistry itself of ignorance, it is ignorance of its own non-knowledge that he is referring to.[4] This is its conceit, the rule it brings to excess. And excess in the *Meno* is the *place* of the incommensurable. Contrary to what the conceit of the 'crude' (Tht. 156a) sophists insist, we know already that ignorance does exist in the sense that 'what is not' known, what is not 'of the situation', partakes of being nonetheless and is therefore available to representation: albeit without thought. Which is to say also, that as being pervades this lack it too is a Form and as such can be the subject of the 'philosophers' discourse.[5] What is needed to specify the existence of this lack is an encounter. On the basis of this encounter which opens up the situation to its lack or properly its 'void', Socrates claims that proper association, which is to say the right form of enquiry, will induce a recollection of this prior-knowledge such that 'bit by bit' it becomes knowable.[6] Extrapolating a little and playing with the terms, what we can propose is that knowledge is here the supposed, and already existent, *result* of the re-collection – a recollection that works out the subset of the generic condition of sophistic Athens, that the lack of a non-sophistic education is for all. In this sense, what the learner learns by re-collection 'will have been' new in the specific sense that it has never before been collected in such a form and by such a practice and subject to such a condition. As Socrates notes, it suffices to 'recall one thing only' in order to begin to 'discover everything else for himself' and this, we suggest, is precisely what the encounter provokes. The encounter disjoins the state from knowledge, opening the situation to the possibility of recalling this disjunction and thus discovering a new 'world of knowledge' on its basis.

However, as we have argued, ignorance as that which subtends the general regime of the Athenian state has therefore a state form. This is sophistry. However, sophistry does not constitute a re-collection. The distinction between sophistic knowledge and 'Socratic' wisdom is axiomatic for Plato. As an operation sophistry is the 'false conceit' of recollection. This is why Badiou designates knowledge (as opposed to truth), the encyclopaedia, the state and inclusion as *representation* (BE, 102/119). For Badiou, as for Plato, representation is a third-order operation: three removes from truth (R. 602a), and 'its creations are poor things by the standard of truth and reality' and as such 'stimulate and strengthen elements which threaten to undermine reason' (R. 605b)

As the general regime of the state what sophistry amounts to is the *insistence of ignorance*. Or, to put it in more Platonic terms, ignorance is *constitutive* of such a state. In effect, Plato insists that sophistry represents the *error* of ignorance insofar as its clever debating procedures *imitate* those of recollection. Whereas, in Plato's estimation, the 'non-sophist', from the point of 'ignorance' – that *there is some*-(no)thing rather than *no*-(some)thing at all – re-collects, that is, seeks the truth which is to be had by enquiry, the sophist, more anxious on the account of the void which it disavows, *represents* such truth, which is to say, that which is indiscernible, as nothing. What Socratic recollection constitutes is precisely 'another form of discernment' one which treats the situation from the standpoint of the event and not the state (neither Gorgias or Anytus, sophist or demagogue) (BE, 328/363). Thus, given all we have said about the site, the event and the name, re-collection cannot be subject to the rules of discernment deployed by the state. Re-collection is in no way representation and it is such an obtuse notion (it remains a central problem in Platonic scholarship) precisely because it has no currency in the state. It is predicated on the existence of the 'irrational' – that which 'cannot (or *must* not) be expressed, which, in Badiou's language is that which is indiscernible (diagonal) to the state. As Szabó points out, the indiscernible is the condition of 'that which cannot be expressed' in the *language of the current situation*.[7]

Given that we have established the incommensurability of the event and the illegality of the name put into circulation by the intervention, what is necessary to orient a new thought of the situation is a statement equally absurd to the state but that, as an affirmation (of that which is already subtracted) realises, within the situation, positive connections. In this sense the combining of the incommensurable mathematical problem of the doubling of the square with the absurd statement that all knowledge is recollection is an exemplary instance of the rigours associated with a non-sophistic education. Every conceit, which presumes to rule, individuals or states, must be tested.

In sum, the key points are:

1. Plato invokes an indiscernible yet collective capacity for truth.
2. A singular instance is enough to precipitate enquiry.
3. Once begun, it (recollection) has no intrinsic end and no intrinsic trajectory.
4. It is a committed process. In order to draw its full consequences one must refuse to be put off.
5. By continuing, one establishes or *forces* a generic recollection of the indiscernible – one learns *without knowledge* the form of what is to come.

What we need to establish now is the non-connection between the rule of connection and the knowledge of the state. This is the question of how the operator of faithful connection is really an evental statement for a generic condition. Education is the site for this non-connection but the question is how a non-sophistic education, the only education, actively avoids state determination.

The operator of faithful connection

There are two things that bear upon our analysis. Firstly, if subjectivisation, the procedure precisely of turning the event toward the situation, is a Two – that is to say, *there is* the event *and* the procedure of relating it to its 'situation' – then the intervention having taken place must necessarily *imply* the existence of the 'operator of faithful connection' as within this complex (BE, 393/430–1). This is to say we might profitably understand the operator of faithful connection as *implicated* in the decision for and recognition of the event itself. Badiou suggests as much when he says 'the operator of connection, □, has no *a priori* tie to belonging or inclusion [situation or its state]. It is, itself, *sui generis*: particular to the fidelity, and by consequence, attached to the evental singularity [encounter and its name]' (BE, 236/262). Secondly, what is significant about this operator of faithful connection is that through the mode of enquiry it is precisely what does the work of arranging 'the forms of knowledge in such a way that some [indiscernible] truth might come to pierce a hole in them' (HB, 9).

In *Being and Event* Badiou does not address the 'logic' of the connection between the evental-intervention and the operator of connection insofar as the former provides the latter with its only referent. Rather, he argues that knowledge, insofar as we understand it to act as an encyclopaedic determinant, cannot recognise an event given that its connection to the site and the name drawn from it does not belong within the strictures of the encyclopaedia. We have seen how the name Socrates does not fit education as understood by the sophistic state and, as such, this remains an 'illegal nomination'. Given this, the connection of multiples or inhabitants of a situation to an evental name via a connection whose sole existence depends on the prior existence and 'sense' of the latter cannot be based on the encyclopaedia. This is to say the state has no criterion for assigning such connections. However, to say that the state cannot do it is not to say how the event/intervention does it. It is to say only that the evental intervention at the site must do it. It seems to us that Badiou approaches this question when he notes that, '[o]ne of the most profound questions of philosophy concerns knowing in what measure the evental constitution itself – the Two of the anonymous void bordered by the site and the name circulated by the intervention – *prescribes* the type of connection in which a fidelity is regulated' (BE, 238/263). Thus the question is the measure of prescription between the site-event-name, taken together or singularly, and the regulation of a fidelity. This is to ask 'how faithful will the subject be, and how will this faith be measured?' Again, however, this is not quite our question. Our question pertains to the manner in which the site-event-name prescribes the criterion for the operation of connection which establishes the shape of fidelity. In *Being and Event* it is broadly *assumed* that, as the latter's connection to the event is established in the intervention, it must draw its rule from what is given there. This *is* the case, but we need to explore how this is so. In other words, we need to ask how the intervention induces a statement ('I know nothing') that directs a militant enquiry. We have to address ourselves to the connections that are internal to the complex of the subject. What we suggest is that the logical force of implication grasps the immanent movement between the axiomatic, anticipatory interventions induced by the event and the prescriptive divisions a process of fidelity institutes on behalf of this anticipation. Ultimately, we trace the movement from an event to what it prescribes of itself for the subject.

The logic of connection

Our elaboration follows Badiou's preliminary study of implication in *Court traité d'ontologie transitoire*.[8] In terms of implication, to name the event – which is not – is the first order of (subjective) logic.[9] Its particularity is that the event has no referent but itself and 'itself' *has* disappeared. It is our claim that the nominative decision, which marks the being of the subject, acknowledges that, from the decision for the event, let's say A, certain steps ensue, B (A→B). Thus, as Badiou has already joined the decision A to the subject (the former being the very founding gesture of the latter), it seems that A→B has been deduced given that B, as subjective enquiry (next steps), is part of the *complex of the subject*. This is not to say the enquiry will necessarily ensue – subjectivisation, as the term suggests, is procedural – just that, if it does its being as such belongs to this complex. We can see that if A has been deduced, which it clearly has in *Being and Event*, then B has been too. This is to say that nothing is certain except that, *if A then B* means anything, it is that steps (enquiries) must be taken which ensure, ultimately, the veridicality of this junction (cf. CM, 59).

There is, if we adopt some terminology from Badiou's use of category theory, an isomorphism here. Between the decision and these 'next steps', there is an identity that is only determined to exist from an 'extrinsic' view (CT, 170–1). An isomorphism is roughly equal to saying 'there is an event if and only if a subject ensues which names it as such and demonstrates its consequences by faithful enquiry', and 'there is a subject if and only if there is an event for that subject' (A←→B). An isomorphism, roughly speaking, is a complex of arrows wherein a source is a target and a target a source.[10] Ontologically, which is to say intrinsically, the site, the event, the decision and the fidelity remain distinct or at least conceptually separable, but under the conjunctive (or re-collective) concept of subject (our *complex of the subject*), their connections are logically specifiable, in terms of implication. What we are saying is that from the perspective of what Badiou calls the 'generic extension', 'the presumed finished form of the subjective process of liaison between the event (thus the intervention) and the procedure of fidelity (operator of connection)' (BE,

239/264), the *decision* and this *work of the subject*, which includes its operational prescriptions, are formally 'identical' (CT, 171). If we understand the concept of subject in terms of a 'group', and we have repeatedly said the subject names a 'complex' of operations whose specifications are only retroactively qualified, then no aspect of the group 'subject' determines the relation itself (CT, 172).[11] It is important to note implication is formally neutral. In essence, and this is its importance in terms of stabilising an operation, it says nothing other than *there is* some '*associativity*' (CT, 169).[12] Let us note again the importance of association to a Socratic education wherein there is no teacher.

Importantly, the distinction between these two, the decision and the 'next steps', is realised logically if it is possible to cancel out the inversion or the isomorphism. Any cancellation of the subjective procedure on Badiou's terms is a failure to insist on (to continue to institute) the real of the connection between the name, trace of evanescence and inhabitants encountered in enquiry. Such a failure renders the in-distinction between the source and its target (the logical reciprocity of decision and its consequences) a reality. (State) knowledge thereby can and will insist on this in-distinction. In the last chapter we saw that *this is* how the state configures the Two of the name and the event whose name it is, and the same holds for the event and subject. This insistence on identifying non-identity for exclusion can be summed up in Leibniz's postulate: 'every non-contradictory multiple desires to exist' (BE, 316/350). Badiou counters this in terms of subtraction by saying: 'nothing can be granted existence – by which I mean the existence a truth grants at its origin – without undergoing the trial of its subtraction' (TW, 103).

The logic of its connections is not, thereby, pre-formed but is an immanent fact of the chance encounter which establishes its possibility. The failure, then, to take the next steps *implied* in A (the event) is a failure of subjectivity alone and not of the implicative structure that underpins its possibility – nor does it prove the lack of an event. In fact, this failure of subjectivity is the 'success' that Alcibiades refers to when he notes that as soon as he breaks his association with Socrates he returns to the polis and to the service of goods under the condition of interest. Alcibiades has the virtue of understanding that it is not the interest of the polis which causes this 'shameful' neglect. Rather, *an interest in the polis* is the effect of the neglect of a faithful association with 'Socrates'. As Aeschines has Socrates say, regarding Alcibiades, 'if I thought it was by some craft (*technē*) that I was able to benefit him, I would find myself guilty of great folly'.[13] If Alcibiades is made conscious of anything at all by being ashamed it is that he gives up on the Socratic Form. As he says, I am doing nothing about my 'way of life' (Smp. 216c).

In sum, if 'subject' is the name for a complex of operations, which is to say a group (supported by a body or *corpus*), then the subject names a set of operations whose existence as such is dependent on this purely implicative structure founded in decision. The point which returns us to the categories and concepts of *Being and Event* is again the retroactive form upon which Badiou insists. In this case, the consequence of the decision, which is to say the step-by-step deployment of the faithful procedure, establishes the truth of the decision. So, mixing our logical and metaontological terms of reference, our assumption is that the decision, as part of the group 'subject', is isomorphic with the 'next steps'. The 'subject', in this sense, cannot simply be the image of the event, its 'inert identity' so to speak, but as 'other to its image' the subject is the very form of the *eventality* of the event itself (CT, 173–6). The operator of faithful connection therefore, being central to the subjective procedure of fidelity, which we will also call a statement or prescription given that it institutes an enquiry, can be said to draw its legitimacy only from the event-encounter. It is not and cannot be a prescription dependent on, nor conforming to, the encyclopaedic rule of the state. Socrates' claim to ignorance is, in short, nonsense. In rejecting both a *spontaneist* reading of fidelity, wherein only those who made an event can take part in it, and a *dogmatic* reading, which states that every inhabitant of the situation is determined by the event Badiou says, 'a fidelity is definitively distinct from the state if, in some manner, it is *unassignable* to a defined function of the state; if, from the standpoint of the state, its result is a particularly nonsensical part' (BE, 237/262–3).[14] Keeping in mind that, for sophistry, Socrates is a poor copy of an Athenian man, a false citizen unable to properly or 'knowledgeably' attend the polis, whose claims to 'know nothing' and to 'not teach' are *conceits* – 'grandstanding and crowd pleasing vulgarisms' for Callicles (Grg. 482c), 'an imbecilic sham' for Thrasymachus (R. 336bc) – and thus he circulates as a nonsensical figure in general, it is hardly possible that the procedure the Socratic encounter initiates would be either amenable too, or a function of, the state. In general, then, fidelity names the practical and prescriptive operational form of the subject in relation to the name of the event. In our terms, fidelity is the relation – understood solely as operation rather than identity per se – the Platonic corpus establishes 'historically' to Socrates, while internally it is the relation of Socrates to a 'non-sophistic way of life'.

What we need to keep in mind about this operator of faithful connection are three related things:

1. It is an *implied* statement of the event. That is to say, the recognition of the event by the intervention necessarily includes whatever pertains to the event-site and so to a non-sophistic education. In this sense the claim to ignorance is a militant claim at once against the state and indifferent to it. This statement has no referent within the situation as it is.
2. The statement is *prescriptive* in terms of orientation. That is to say, it organises and orders a trajectory of determined enquiry, other than that of the state. It is not a statement of knowledge but a prescription drawn from the event alone.
3. It is *subtractive* in its effects. That is to say, as the operator of a division it subtracts from the existing situation elements connected to the event. It is subtractive precisely because this new set of elements, elements connected for a fidelity, is recollected from the 'fullness of presentation' itself – albeit on the basis of its void. We could say that the operator of faithful connection is born in a decision for that which is undecidable and borne by the faithful subjective (post-evental) insistence as to the existence of the indiscernible. What the statement signifies for the subject is that 'there is not', no consequences of an event.

In sum, the operator of faithful connection is implicative in terms of the event, prescriptive in terms of orientation and subtractive in terms of operation. It supports the possibility of the subject in its faithful procedure of thinking the truth of the event.

SOCRATES' PRESCRIPTIVE STATEMENTS

We can now return to the dialogues. What is very interesting about subjective work under a single rule of connection as it is played out in the dialogues is that Plato organises it around three different statements. These statements are ubiquitous, and help to both punctuate and structure each enquiry undertaken therein. Even if we did not conceive of these in the way we do the force of the statements registers in the quantity of Platonic scholarship dedicated to their investigation.[15] These are, in their most straightforward manifestation: I know nothing; I am not a teacher; what is X? What these statements refer to are elements indiscernible to the knowledge of the sophistic state. In this way they carry the form of a double negation or reversal and, as such, could properly or perhaps popularly be understood as impious statements verging on corrupt practice.[16] What we are proposing is that what the evental decision implies is expressed in the form of these implicative-cum-prescriptive statements. These statements have prescriptive force in the dialogues, opening the situation at the point of the encounter to the enquiries that follow. These statements do not belong to the order of knowledge but are possible only as a consequence of the event. By these statements the subject maintains its distance from the order of knowledge, the *encyclopaedia*. The statements give the enquiring subject(s) the means to orient themselves in this distance. The state, as we know, exists as a prohibition on unbinding – particularly, in this case, the unbinding which association with Socrates threatens – and works to foreclose such a possibility. Obviously, these statements are anathema to the sophistic state in the sense that to utter them in the context of 'education' makes no sense. These statements are applicable to Socrates, the 'differentiated proper name', and no one else (BE, 92/107).

These first two, to 'know nothing' and to 'not teach', are not statements available to the sophists whose whole *raison d'être* is caught up in the positive correlation of these to each other via the logic of exchange. These statements immediately put the fullness of sophistic knowledge at a distance and instigate a separation between the utterer and the state. Quite obviously, these can be said only in the context of a militancy which, using our terms, seeks to institute the subjective consequences of the evental – thus absurd – name. In a similar fashion, the 'what is X?' question – what is justice, what is love, what is knowledge, what is courage, and so on (again, ubiquitous across the dialogues and in the scholarship) – displaces the sophistic ethic concerning the measure of all things. It asks something, or rather *addresses* something, which is never reducible to interest or perspective or to power. In fact, it functions in the dialogues more like an axiom than a question, an 'idea-statement' (to corrupt Heidegger), insofar as, following Aristotle, it is 'that which is necessary in order to learn something else'. In this sense it is not a demand for a definition but its principle. What matters here is that each statement announces in the specific space of its deployment the necessity of division and the condition of re-collection. Where an inhabitant of the corpus stands in relation to this operator of connection is ultimately where one stands in relation to the state and all that implies.

One divides into three

It is our contention that these three statements can be reduced to one: the claim to ignorance. A summary sketch of the scholarship on these statements, to which there is much addressed –their use and their function are a matter for continued debate – helps to show the legitimacy of this reduction.[17] Some scholars consider Socrates dishonest in his use of the first two claims. It is too evident, they claim, that he has knowledge and so there is the assumption of some expediency or knowing dissembling going on. Some commentators seize on his claim in the *Symposium* (and *Phaedrus*) that he *knows* about love; others, that 'to *know* he knows nothing' is an admission of knowledge (as we noted above this is better described as conviction rather than knowledge); still others retreat to the well worn trope of irony, a trope which is itself open to several divisions.[18] Interestingly, the general division on Socratic 'knowledge' is formed along constructivist and non-constructivist lines, although none, as far as I know, investigates its Liebnizean or Gödelian orientation.[19] Rather, they regard Socratic *elenchus* in terms of what it may or may not construct in the way of a knowledge. The void or indiscernible dimension of this – its lack of place or inexistence within the Athenian state and the generic character of this lack – is not taken into account and Socrates is reduced to yet one mere competitor in the knowledge stakes. This latter retreat allows the all too common notion to flourish that the masses are incommensurable to thought, given that it is they who have consented to the 'death of knowledge'. Corresponding to this politically is the notion that the trial was some sort of mistake or anomaly: this in turn leads to attempts to excuse the 'democracy' and agree in the condemnation of philosophy. Richard Rorty, for example, ultimately prefers democratic conversation to the perils of thought. The rehabilitation of the sophist from 'imitator of the wise' to 'one wise man among many, for better or worse' follows from such a 'retreat'.

Whether Socrates' disavowal of teaching is serious and in what way is also widely discussed, but as Socrates points out in the *Meno* (and elsewhere), if one teaches this already presupposes one possesses knowledge. In the *Apology* he notes that this would be a fine thing and that if one was a teacher one should be well paid. For Socrates, as he does not know he therefore cannot teach. So the question of where one stands on his being a teacher depends pretty much on where one stands in regard to his knowledge.[20] We should remember that in the *Apology*, the only 'public' dialogue, he forcefully rejects the notion that he is a teacher, saying, 'I have never promised or imparted teaching to anybody; and if anyone asserts that he has ever learned or heard from me privately *anything which was not open to everyone else*, you may be quite sure that he is not telling the truth' (Ap. 33b, emphasis added).[21] The implication here should be marked. Teaching, insofar as it is conceived within Platonic Athens, is an exclusive pursuit open only to those who have already decided for state knowledge. This is really to say teaching concerns those who already profess to know (their product) – one way or another – whereas what Socrates 'has to say' is open to all. Socrates pursues a practice which *any* one may take up. 'Knowing thyself' is not for him alone. Precisely, finding the means of address 'for all', or better for *any* one, is the subjective task Plato sets out as the Corpus. As Socrates notes in the *Theaetetus*, the common complaint against him is that he asks questions but never gives his own view (Tht. 150c and R. 336b). This is because, he says, 'I am barren of wisdom'. The god has 'forbidden him to procreate. So that I am not in any sense a wise man. I cannot claim as the child of my own soul any discovery worthy of the name wisdom' (Tht. 150c). Socrates invokes here the distinction between association, where one shares in the pursuit of wisdom with 'others', and teaching where one is subject to the professions of another's 'knowledge' – and this can be through questioning or through the various types of rhetoric and oratory. Socrates says that association with him might see the student/subject deliver 'fertile truths'. But these truths are *offspring* of the subject's own and are not furnished by Socrates and are never subject therefore to the established norms of teaching or exchange (Tht. 150b and R. 518bc).

For the most part the 'what is X?' question is examined on the premise it seeks a definition. It is argued that for Socrates, ultimately, definition is essential in order for the discussion to be at all productive.[22] It is assumed also to have some methodological import. Infamously, Geach, after Wittgenstein, investigated the (mis)use of this question in the dialogues and 'found' it so ubiquitous that he was able to name it the 'Socratic fallacy'.[23] What makes the use of the question fallacious, Geach argues, is that the definition is only ever approached using examples, and so the knowledge of examples seems to precede the very definition that gives (supposedly) the latter currency. Things, on this reading, are back to front. To wit, 'if you cannot recognise cases of piety without knowing what piety is, then how can you appeal to such cases in order to arrive at that knowledge.'[24] Apart from this throwing the status of knowledge in general into question, the 'fallacy' also has the problem of linking what are considered different types of knowledge – the propositional and the expert (one who can both 'do something' and explain how or why it is done). If both require a definitional foundation, they are somehow equated by their difference. Other considerations find that this question is the basis for the constant aporias to which the dialogues succumb. The consequences of this can go either way. It can be seen as an intrinsic ethic of philosophical discussion in that the failure it induces is the subsequent matter for further discussion, or it can be understood to reveal an inherent flaw in philosophy itself – that it cannot really tell us anything and its presumption of being a discourse that pursues truths is simply cover for its inability to tell us anything of the world that matters to our living in it.[25]

This sketch by no means exhausts the variations on the theme of the statements. It is not our goal, our task or of much interest to rehearse or *directly* refute them. Our own assessment provides the latter. In our conception 'Socrates', understood with regard to the intervention, cannot be understood in terms of knowledge. The encyclopaedia cannot evaluate the content of his statements nor situate their place of enunciation – such is why, perhaps, they cause so much trouble still to constructivist, language-oriented scholars.

'I KNOW NOTHING': A FORMAL PRESCRIPTION

What Plato seems to have done here is construct a *set* of 'obscure' yet formal prescriptions. We can call them obscure because they attach only to Socrates 'itself', and yet have a visible and obvious linguistic sense (if not a referent) within the Athens of the dialogues – teaching, knowledge and X (justice, virtue, the good, etc.). For example, when Polus (a figure who, as a youth, is shown in the dialogues to be capable of going either way – to stay with sophistry or to connect with Socrates) answers Chaeraphon's question concerning what it is his master Gorgias 'is' by describing him as the 'teacher best at teaching a certain expertise', Socrates intervenes saying, 'but *what is it* that his art consists in' (Grg. 447d–448e)? What we see here, by drama *and* content, is that it is an interventionist statement rather than a demand for a definition per se, especially given that the definition almost never comes. It breaks into the conversation too bogged down in sophistic circles (Polus has been mockingly 'praised' for the well rehearsed rhetorical style of his answer) and reissues a challenge to the discussants to renew again the investigation in discursive, enquiring or 'evental' terms. What Plato is gesturing toward when he deploys this obscure and axiomatic statement is surely the Form of whatever is under enquiry. With this intervention Plato wants to provoke a reanimation of the discussion. The Form is that which is not subject to becoming and, as such, its definition per se, as opposed to its manifestation, is not a matter of enquiry, being as it is always the same. Rather, the subject of definition is what this Form conditions and, as such, is the name of. This is why for Plato's Parmenides the Forms are the reason all discourse and knowledge is possible (Parm. 135bc).[26] It is not the definition of the concept which is at stake but rather the knowledge of its Form. As such, this question seeks to illuminate the existence for discourse of that which animates and conditions its appearance. For example, the discussion of justice in the early stages of the *Republic* certainly takes the 'corporeal' dimension as primary – justice, as noted, is associated by the three early interlocutors as either traditional to a people, a matter of the current majority opinion or a matter of strength. Socrates will intervene with this question, 'yes, but what is justice?' to point out that the discussion is lost in opinion and sophistry. He will insist that it is the Form of justice which is at stake in a philosophical conversation and that the universality of the Form is subtracted from all claims of interest – such as those of Cephalus, Polemarchus or Thrasymachus. The upshot is that for Plato the eye of all discussants must be again turned to its Form which can be its only 'definition'. A Form as Plato notes in *Theaetetus*, by its very consistency is that alone which supports a transformation (Tht. 247e+). From *this* re-intervention which promises a transformation by association certain figures retreat (Callicles, Thrasymachus, Polus, Gorgias, Protagoras, to name a few) and a certain few figures continue to participate with Socrates in enquiry (Theaetetus, Glaucon, Adeimantus) (cf. Tht. 148e). In relation to Plato's decided avoidance of sophistry, it is the Forms alone which allow for shared enquiry: without Forms no discourse; discourse addressed to all.[27] These statements, reduced to the one 'operator of faithful connection', are not presented by Plato with regard to sophistic knowledge, but with regard to the void-site of this knowledge. Armed with this anomalous statement 'I know nothing', Plato's Socrates confronts the (non-)knowing of sophistry with that which it is not. If the sophists profess to know, Socrates cannot know that knowing, as that knowing is itself an imitation of what it is to (truly) know. If the imitators teach then Socrates cannot teach as both the form and the method imitate a form and a method and subject both to a concept (interest) to which truth is indifferent. When sophistic knowledge and teaching contrive a result from the combination of these two which satisfies the order and the repetition of the state and not truth itself then Socrates' statements are such that they 'pierce a hole in this knowledge'. He declares, 'what is the truth (X) of your knowledge?' To the state, this is tautology and, as such, without answer. For Plato, by contrast, it is the beginning of the recommencement of what must continue, which is to say, it is the beginning of the recommencement of participation. The upshot is that 'Socrates' can only be fruitfully encountered as 'a way of thinking'. His statements help to construct that thought.

Some remarks on the operator of faithful connection in the *Cratylus*

In the *Cratylus* the declaration of ignorance occurs four times. Each has a distinct context but is set to achieve the same effect in that it institutes a separation and conditions a recommencement thus beginning again the procedure of indiscerning terms connected to the evental name. The first instance of the statement is truly splendid: Socrates encounters Cratylus and Hermogenes[28] discussing the 'correctness of names'. They invite him to join in. Hermogenes complains that Cratylus is evasive and 'oracular' and is suggesting he has some *private* knowledge to which Hermognes should submit. Socrates replies:

> Hermogenes, son of Hipponicus, there is an ancient proverb that 'fine things are very difficult' to know about, and it certainly isn't easy to get to know about names. To be sure, if I'd attended Prodicus' fifty drachma lecture course, which advertises as an exhaustive treatment of the topic, there'd be nothing to prevent you from learning the precise truth about the correctness of names straightaway. But as I've heard only the one drachma course I don't know the truth of it. (Crt. 384bc)

Here, Plato incorporates several themes. He refers explicitly to the dialectal exercise of thinking, which he elsewhere refers to as the 'long detour' and whose difficulty he elaborates in the *Republic*. This is an explicitly educational reference which speaks to the discipline involved in the pursuit of truth or wisdom. This is immediately offset against the ability to buy knowledge – an ability he does not 'have'. We know that this statement is both ironic and makes a point seriously held for Plato. In Jowett's alternative translation, Socrates has not simply chosen not to attend such a class but notes he was 'too poor to', thus referring again to the immediate relation between money, knowledge and position within the polis whose conceptual and practical linking Plato utterly rejects. We need to note that this statement comes in the very first speech Socrates makes in the dialogue. It is directly consequent on his encounter with the two figures: one, the assured figure of Cratylus – a Heraclitian we soon learn – and Hermogenes – separated from money and sincere in his desire *to* know. This statement *re*opens the discussion. It establishes *there* a new orientation to the question. It splits Hermogenes and Cratylus – from each other at first. Indeed, as is consistent with its use throughout, Socrates uses this statement to put himself between the youth and the sophist. However, it is not just Hermognes he seeks to disjoin from the sophistic method of enquiry: ultimately, he wants to separate the sophist (Cratylus here) from wisdom itself. As in the *Sophist*, this is both the real work being undertaken – of which the initial separation is then the true consequence – and the most truly difficult task of all. This is one reason why the statement must be reintroduced more than once. This task is always, in effect, to 'resume again'.

The statement is repeated for the second time shortly thereafter. Hermogenes is at the point of being convinced that names are not 'inconsequential', but is reluctant to change his opinion until Socrates makes known to him the 'natural correctness of names' that Cratylus asserts as true. Socrates reminds him he has no position of his own on this. He says, 'I told you a while ago [t]hat I didn't know about names but that I would investigate them with you' (Crt. 391a). Here Socrates reiterates his separation from sophistic knowledge and reaffirms the commitment to discovering the *truth* of this knowledge relative to the procedure of discernment it demands. The statement both halts a certain form of dissemination, in this case Hermogenes' acceptance of Cratylus' position, a position Socrates also finds sophistic, and reorients the conversation toward its goal but does so through yet another sophistic position. The exhaustion of one aspect of the investigation has not exhausted the possible sophistries regarding the topic under discussion. Indeed, sophistry is constituted by the diversity of opinions and the defeat of one opinion only clears the way for further offspring. Socrates and Hermogenes, committed to the long detour, must dutifully rebegin at the point of encountering this next sophistry. This next encounter implies the operator of faithful connection once more. One cannot overlook that directly subsequent to this second use of the statement Plato has both Hermogenes and Socrates reject a series of sophistic claims concerning names precisely by naming various features of sophistry. Callias is again *named* as the buyer of sophists and Protagoras is named in this same context. The latter's *Truth*, which contains his famous relativist maxim, is also brought up to again be dismissed by Hermogenes. The latter mocks Socrates' suggestion that he follow his brother Callias and seek out Protagoras' wisdom. He says 'as if I desire the things contained in it [*Truth* – note the pun and reversal] and thought them worthwhile, when I totally reject them' (Crt. 391c). The sophists are put aside and the poets – from Homer to Heraclitus (Crt. 391d–402a+) are yet again named and addressed and subjected to discussion under the orientation of not knowing what it is 'they (profess) to know'. Note again, however, that Socrates and his interlocutor *work through* the diversity of opinions as the 'hard but worth doing' path of truth.[19] The latter is singular, in the sense that it cannot be one among others equal to it – such is the diversity of opinion – but also universal, precisely because it is the only thing that can be for all. The universality of truth quite simply subverts the global diversity of opinion. Again, we see our immanent division subtending the trajectory of the dialogue.

The third instance is at 428b where the enquiry with Hermogenes comes to an end. Hermogenes (like Theaetetus) is one who subject to this enquiry has been connected to the Socratic event. Indeed, it is because he has been so connected that Cratylus re-enters the discussion, and he does so we must note by subversively aligning his own idea on the subject with Socrates. He effectively accuses Socrates of making inspired 'oracular utterances' – precisely what Hermognes accused Cratylus of doing in the very first exchange of the dialogue – and these he says 'are as if spoken after my own mind' (Cra. 428c). The dialogue effectively rebegins here, ostensibly at the same point at which Socrates had originally encountered the two 'friends' except that now Hermogenes recognises his connection to that which sophistry cannot know. Again, the dialogue rebegins under the condition of the evental statement. Socrates gently separates himself from Cratylus' 'will to association' by saying that he is not sure of his own wisdom. He manages to suggest by implication that Cratylus' wisdom is also not certain and thus they should reinvestigate because 'self deception is the worst of all things' (Crt. 428d). Again we see that the operator of faithful connection conditions the enquiry which will separate out the sophistic from the non-sophistic. And again we need to note that it is on the basis of another encounter, for Cratylus has essentially reappeared to Socrates and to the dialogue at this point. He is *encountered* again, this time as himself. We should not overlook Plato's own point, which is that Hermogenes – whose own name we have seen discussed in regard to its lack of appropriateness given his character – has been speaking 'as Cratylus'. Thus he was misnamed as Hermogenes given that who spoke was Cratylus. This, as we have noted, is a constant of the dialogues, for we are often presented with figures who really speak for one sophist or another or from the perspective of one sophistic position or another. Self-deception or conceit is the very excess of state knowledge. Cratylus' attempt to align Socrates with his own claims to wisdom is part of the effort to reinstitute its rule. In contrast, Socrates insists that we begin again from the only truly subjective point that is without deception, from the point of *not knowing*. Critically for our claim that the operator of faithful connection turns the event to the situation and thus the inhabitant of the situation toward the event – and crucially what it signifies of that which is 'to come' – Socrates says that from *this point of ignorance* we must test our claims 'looking both forwards [to the generic set] and backward [from the site] simultaneously' (Crt. 428d).

The last instance of the statement occurs at the end of the dialogue where Socrates is taking leave of Cratylus, literally and intellectually. Cratylus remains a Heraclitean, and for Socrates, as we have seen elsewhere, this position is that of the 'insistence on ignorance'. For if all things are passing on, 'no one could know anything and nothing could be known'. There is no truth in the doctrine of the flux – in both senses. We do not need to revisit the links between Heraclitus, Protagoras and Homer. What is notable in this last instance is that the dialogue ends on the necessity of rebeginning. This is fully aporetic. This is to say, aporia is so often assumed a kind of defeat, when literally all that it means is that here and now the resources are lacking to go any further. Far from nothing being discovered or even resolved, what has taken place is the new orientation to the situation which will be the starting point for further enquiries at this site. We need not labour this point further but we should note the two final remarks Socrates directs to Cratylus.

Socrates tells Cratylus that he should go on to the country and that Hermogenes will see him on his way. This signifies that by seeing Cratylus off Hermogenes inhabits the truth of his name. As the son of Hermes and a good son at that (as Plato is to Socrates?), it is his duty to conduct souls to the land of the dead. The pun here (which is much more than a pun) is that Cratylus is not dead as such – even though his ideas may be – but is to be conducted by Hermogenes *into the country*. In the *Republic* it was suggested that all persons over ten, all who had already been subject to a 'sophistic education' under the current state, should be rusticated. In the country they might lose the trappings of sophistication and be able to then come back as new souls ready to constitute a new body, a new polis (cf. Phd. 67e).

Conclusion

In the dialogues the operator of faithful connection is the Socratic statement 'I know nothing', of which the other two are strategic variants. With this statement Socrates divides the situation in two. Given that the state of the situation is traversed, ordered and bound by sophistic rule and that the pursuit of knowledge equates simply to the pursuit of interest, to prescribe that in order to be truly educated one must 'not know' puts one at an immediate distance from this state. The sense of this prescription can only come through the conviction that what the state determines to be knowledge is not all and that inherent to it, subject to its rule under the constraint of its disavowal, is a lack or void which gives the lie to the sophist's profession. That the event, the encounter between the sophistic and Socratic figures, has *taken place* – which is to say that what is constitutively unknowable has happened – induces the subject to invest its effort in pursuing the consequences – all the way to the *Republic*. If such an encounter is possible what it opens to the situation is hitherto unknown enquiries. The situation itself becomes the matter for all enquiries. What these enquiries stake out is a divided set of connections – some connected to the evental name of Socrates, others not connected. The fundamental price of a connection is the avowed realisation that 'I know nothing'. As the *Apology* confirms, to associate oneself with such a claim is to subtract oneself from the regime of interest that binds the state. To be bound to the state in this way, by this knowledge, is what links the poets, the professional men and politicians and the orators of all types (Ap. 23e). In short, all the good men of Athens are bound by and to this knowledge such that to be a good man is to be so bound. It is not a coincidence that in the two dialogues that 'succeed' the *Apology*, *Crito* and the *Phaedo*, Socrates is eager to demonstrate to his followers the necessity of being connected for a fidelity to an education by truths precisely in order that this regime of interests be undone.

As we argued, the (Athenian) situation is structured wholly in relation to the elements (inhabitants) that make it up and *these* elements are indiscernible to the state in the sense that no knowledge at all predicates their collection within the situation for which they provide the matter. They simply belong and are as such equal in their presentation. For Plato, this Form must condition the constitution of the ideal, non-sophistic city. In other words, this thought of the city – being 'just' *as such* – must pervade the invention of the 'new place' the enquiries seek to produce. The faithful procedure, under the condition 'I know nothing', seeks to think through the presentation of this form. The immediate and procedural consequence is the avoidance of any representation. This is the serious and singular effort of the Platonic dialogues when conceived (as they most often are not) as the very *invention* of such a discourse – which is *by truths* and thus not *of the state*. If the state is the foreclosure of the unbinding which Platonic invention (under the sign of Socrates) seeks to manifest, the separation intrinsic to decision and the operation of faithful connection is a productive in-separation. From within the repetition of foreclosure, a repetition paradoxically necessary because the state is separated from the situation by the excess it inscribes, the faithful enquiry must produce this new form of separation. In reality, it is a separation from separation which Plato inscribes, but it is not a return to an origin but to the *new situation* of 'his' site – education. What this separation by evental supplement entails is the Real of its production. This separation must produce its own consistency; there is nothing already there which can be presented in the situation, apart from an illegitimate name and a series of absurd statements. The subject separates from the state to return to the indifferent equality or 'Form' of the situation via the evental-site. The idea has become subject. For Plato, this is the only education.

Notes

1. '. . . nothing prevents a man, after recalling one thing only – a process men call learning – discovering everything else for himself, if he is brave and does not tire of the search, for searching and learning are, as a

whole, recollection' (Men. 81d). Cf. Wahl in his Preface to *Conditions*, 'Le soustractif', pp. vii–xliv.

2. Mao is a great Platonist. The following is straight out of the *Theaetetus* (150b+): 'Investigation may be likened to the long months of pregnancy, and solving a problem to the day of birth. To investigate a problem is, indeed, to solve it' (Mao Tse-Tung, *Oppose Book Worship*, p. 2). In *May '68 and Its Afterlives*, Kristin Ross relates the story of the Maoist *enquête* or 'investigations'. This is a Socratic practice par excellence and Ross without mentioning it, and quite naturally, tells it in a Platonic language (p. 110). She quotes Georges, a Citroën worker: the Trotskyist would come to the factory armed with a tract, with quotes, page numbers, etc. The 'Maoist on the other hand, took their point of departure from what we told them. They *didn't know anything* before we talked to them. They listened to what we said and made a tract out of that. We were really struck by that' (p. 111, emphasis added). As Georges confirms, these encounters take the form of 'an enquiry *with* you'. In the overall sweep of educational history but particularly the contemporary educational situation it is interesting to note that with a well established state school system, teaching state knowledge, that this basic form of Platonist enquiry, which is to say learning, was discovered by workers only due to the intervention of Maoist political action. *The Platonic form of education is still a non-state form.*
3. The context should be kept in mind. Note: (a) Socrates engages in demonstration with a slave; (b) the demonstration involves the existence of the incommensurable, the irrational or that which cannot be expressed; (c) the demonstration has universal implications. The ruse of using the slave boy is of course no accident: the proof of the incommensurable is attained by two figures already decidedly 'incommensurable' – the slave and the (becoming) philosopher – who, to the state, is nothing. Both are 'without' a polis and yet together Plato has them enact the truth of this very 'incommensurability' whose application, it is demonstrated, can be equally applied to all. Cf. R. (534d) for Plato's critical reversal. The fact that Plato is talking of incommensurables is barely noticed in the more contemporary scholarship. Leibniz, interestingly, doesn't miss this (Leibniz, *Selections*, Ch III 'Knowledge and Metaphysics' XXVI, esp. pp. 327–8). According to Kerferd, the term diagonal – the incommensurable line marking the division of the square between two opposing angles – was used in *Meno* for only the second time in the Greek language. The first was in Aristophanes *The Frogs*. 'It is probable' (see Men. 85b) 'that the word was a relatively new and unfamiliar technical term. 'Indeed' he continues, 'it is not impossible that the word was invented by the sophists' (Kerferd, *The Sophistic Movement*, p. 39). Szabó attributed it to the mathematicians going back to Pythagoras (Árpád Szabó, *The Beginnings of Greek Mathematics*, pp. 86–8).

4. Note that in this way there is room for the sophist to have knowledge in relation to specific things (see, for example, Tht. 151ac). The caveat is that one should not assume one then has wisdom.
5. We refer here to the discussion in the *Republic* concerning the distinction between traversing and pervading. For Plato, being pervades all Forms – this is what makes them the same. Yet, relative to one another, they are different and thus all forms are traversed by difference. It is a very intriguing distinction, and one played out in the history of philosophy and most emphatically over the last century or so. Cf. Sph. (251d–256e) and Parmenides, *Way of Truth*, Fragment 6.
6. Cf. Aristotle, *Nicomachean Ethics*, Book VI and Heidegger, *Plato's Sophist*, pp. 21–6.
7. Szabó, *The Beginning of Greek Mathematics*, pp. 86–8.
8. The way I am setting things out here diverges from the context of Badiou's discussion in the essay 'Group, Category and Subject' but the substantive point is the same. Badiou asks the rhetorical question, 'what is an algebraic [logical] structure if not that which fixes a definition for an operational possibility' (CT, 169).
9. Hallward, *Badiou: A Subject to Truth*, p. 124.
10. 'Lin Piao – someone barely mentioned these days – once said, at the height of the Cultural Revolution, that the essential thing was to be, at a revolutionary conjunction, both its actor and its target. I quite like this formula. Yes, we are actors, but in such a way that we are targeted by, carried away by, and struck by [*atteint par*] the event. In this sense there can undoubtedly be collective events' (quoted in Hallward, *Badiou: A Subject to Truth*, p. 123).
11. See Chapter 6: '. . . the participating and the participated in are not, in last analysis, essentially different from each other, but are basically the same entity *in two different modes of being*' (Samuel Scolnicov, 'Two faces of Platonic knowledge', p. 7).
12. For the French word *associativité* I have adopted the literal translation used by Madarasz in his translation of *Court traité d'ontologie transitoire*. See Badiou, *Briefings on Existence: A Short Treatise on Transitory Ontology*, p. 146.
13. Nehamas, *Virtues of Authenticity*, p. 116.
14. The references Badiou makes at this point in BE recall David Hilbert's seminal paper 'On the Foundations of Logic and Arithmetic', where he sets out the positions ostensibly opposed to his own axiomatic procedure as the 'dogmatist' (Kronecker is named here – the same fellow who considered Cantor a corruptor), the 'empiricist', the 'opportunist' and the 'transcendentalist'. Frege escapes this classification – he is not given a categorical name – and Cantor is noted to have properly recognised the distinction between consistent and inconsistent sets but to have left open the door to a subjective approach. (For Hilbert and Frege,

see Jean van Heijenoort (ed.), *From Frege to Gödel: A Source Book in Mathematical Logic, 1879–1931*, pp. 129–38.)

15. The debate over their place in the dialogues goes on. This suggests that these statements have an element of incitement that continues to force itself on sophists, philosophers, enquirers of all types.
16. In traditional Greek religion to evoke the irrational was to commit impiety and was punishable by death. Szabó notes this tradition, which records that Hippasus who was 'the first to disclose the anomalous properties of the "diagonal" perished at sea for his irreligious act' (Szabó, *The Beginning of Greek Mathematics*, p. 34). Plato, without necessarily buying into the sacredness of the tradition, plays on this and ultimately inverts its logic, for mathematics has discovered that irrationals (incommensurables) *exist* and thus to be *impious* post-Plato is to deny their existence.
17. For an overview of the scholarship, see Thomas C. Brickhouse and Nicholas D. Smith, *The Philosophy of Socrates*.
18. For the first see, for example, Norman Gulley in Brickhouse and Smith, *Philosophy of Socrates*, p. 4; for the second, see Terence Irwin who supposes that Socrates does 'know nothing' and thus makes do with true belief for the sake of enquiry. For us Irwin is still too haunted by the logic of the constructivist (Irwin, *Plato's Moral Theory*). With regard to the third, Gregory Vlastos argues that many commentators mistake the types of irony at play in the dialogues. He makes a case for Socratic irony over a sophistic variant, traces the etymology of the terms, and finds a split in its use into function and meaning (see Vlastos, 'Socratic irony', *Socrates, Ironist and Moral Philosopher*, pp. 21–44, esp. pp. 23–4). John Sellars, by contrast, argues that the ascription of irony is little more than a vague truism unthinkingly repeated by almost all commentators. Sellars adds – and on this I agree – that 'when Socrates proclaims his ignorance in the *Apology* there is no trace of irony whatsoever' (Sellars, '"The problem of Socrates": review of Sarah Kofman, *Socrates: Fictions of a Philosopher*', pp. 267–75, at p. 275).
19. Cf. LM, 165 where Badiou cites Russell's paradox and notes that it is 'a *real* obstacle to the sovereignty of language'.
20. Brickhouse and Smith quite rightly point out that most people who profess to 'teach the Socratic method' do no such thing, that is unless they really *do not know* the answers to the questions they posit to their students (class after class, year after year) (Brickhouse and Smith, *The Philosophy of Socrates*, p. 54).
21. There is some ambiguity here no doubt. The key is the distinction between state and situation. As we will see, these statements are directed *at the situation* thus teaching here refers to the sophistic manner – privately, and for money. On this topic see Nehamas, 'What did Socrates teach?', in *The Virtues of Authenticity*, pp. 59–82, esp.

67–9, where Nehemas outlines (against Vlastos) what Socrates did not know as the basis for not teaching.

22. In Letter VII Plato provides an order of discourse: name, definition, image, knowledge, Idea (342be). Definition is *not* the founding term and the first four must be grasped before one 'has knowledge of the fifth'.
23. P. T. Geach, 'Plato's *Euthyphro*: an analysis and commentary', pp. 369–82. The technical exposition is at p. 371. See also Nehamas, 'Socratic intellectualism', in *The Virtues of Authenticity*, pp. 28–9, who dismisses this claim, in regard to *Euthryphro* anyway (where Geach claimed to find it most pronounced).
24. Nehamas, 'Socratic intellectualism', in *The Virtues of Authenticity*, p. 28.
25. Brickhouse and Smith, *The Philosophy of Socrates*, pp. 113–20.
26. Cf. Sph. (259e–260) and BE (8/14).
27. W. K. C. Guthrie, *Socrates and Plato*, p. 38.
28. As always with Plato names are used to trigger associations. Here, Hermogenes the 'son of . . .' alerts us to Hermes, the god of profit. Hermogenes' father, Hipponicus, was son of Callias II who made his fortune using slaves to exploit the silver mines at Laurium. Hipponicus, dubbed the 'richest man in Greece', married an ex-wife of Pericles (never far from Plato's sights) and had a son Callias – who Plato repeatedly notes is the 'son' who has spent more than anyone on sophists. Here, Socrates defines the meaning of the name Hermes. In essence, Hermes means speech, interpretation, the clever use of words. He is a deceiver and a wheeler-dealer (so this translation puts it) and a contriver through speech of gain. Socrates pointedly tells Hermogenes that he is no son of Hermes and thus no son of profiting through false conceit (407d–408a). That he is not like Callias suggests he is a youth connected for a fidelity to the Socratic event. See Debra Nails, *The People of Plato: A Prosopography of Plato and other Socratics*, p. 173.
29. We should note that Socrates in the *Cratylus* defines *alēthia* as a 'wandering that is divine' (Crt. 421a). This, as well as being a punning reference to Heraclitus' river, seems to us to be an allusion to the Socratic figure, the stranger who wanders about the city constrained to test the divine sign. See also Silvia Montiglio, 'Wandering philosophers in classical Greece', pp. 86–105: 'Since Homer, the wanderer was perceived as an uncanny figure, whose identity it was difficult to "locate". Wanderers are unknowable, unclassifiable. They could be anything because they appear to be from everywhere and nowhere. A wanderer may look like a beggar, but he could be a god' (p. 86). The difference for Plato is that Socrates is *within* the city, traversing what is there.

CHAPTER 5

Subject

> 'There is always a suspicion that the operator of faithful connection is itself unfaithful to the event out of which it has made so much.' (BE, 392/430)

> 'No writing of Plato exists or ever will exist, but those now said to be his are those of a Socrates become beautiful and new.' (L.VII. 341c)

> 'Well, then, can't I step up to a man and say "this is your name?" ' (Cra. 430d)

In this chapter we will work our way through Gregory Vlastos' reading of the 'Socratic problem' in order to establish Plato's *subjective* credentials. We are not arguing that Plato is the subject, but that the Platonic invention, the series of works, the faithful enquiries that result in the 'corpus', is precisely that which is so, subject to the Socratic event – the encounter so extensively and symptomatically played out in the *Apology* and 'resolved' by Plato in the *Republic*. In proceeding this way, we deal with the most determinate and active approach of analytic philosophy to the Platonic corpus and we at the same time are able, step by step as it were, to establish a new comprehension of the Two which animates the corpus. The premise of the analytic tradition is that there is a *relation* between the two figures. What if, instead of the determination of a *relation* whose intricacies must then be judged, classified and categorised, we assume that what exists of 'Socrates' (name of the event-encounter with sophistry) and of 'Plato' is 'merely' the composition of a corpus – the body wherein the recollection of the disjunctive procedure is supported and made available for transmission?

By elaborating a distance from the dominant Anglo-analytic tradition we can establish that, rather than denoting any known relation between 'Plato' and 'Socrates', what the corpus establishes is the composition of a truth of this Two which, as we have seen, must be subtracted from any statist determination and thus from any law of relation given as sense. Given that we have seen already some of what makes up Badiou's definition of the subject and thus illustrated some of its 'basic operations', and that in Chapter 6 we will trace what else occurs in the process of subjectivising the event *within the dialogues*, our method here is somewhat distinct from the chapters so far. We will not be arguing a positive case as such. Instead, we concentrate on two things: firstly, an extensive critique of Vlastos' separation of Socrates and Plato. Our opposition to Vlastos' position allows us to draw out several critical instances which support our theorisation of the corpus as subject. Secondly, making use of some of these instances, we give a reading of the *Phaedo* which shows this dialogue to be a meditation on the proper *course* a subject faithful to the production of truths must take in order to realise the 'place of a non-sophistic education'. Although we work through the 'Vlastos corpus', the ultimate focus of this chapter is the attempt to articulate the Plato–Socrates juncture consistent with Badiou's thought and thus to situate this juncture within the trajectory of an 'education by truths' – a *way of life* rather than an 'academic quibble'.

Gregory Vlastos' developmental distinction

The reason we turn to Vlastos is that, as Debra Nails says, his work on the 'Socratic problem' has influenced several generations of Plato scholars in the analytic tradition. Further, as Nehamas shows, almost all scholars post-Vlastos have accepted the logic of this distinction whether they agree or disagree with the conclusions.[1] We will draw our analysis from two of Vlastos' seminal essays and we will critique these positions as we proceed, in line with the *subtractive* development of the 'subject'.[2]

Vlastos' singular and 'large claim' is that unless Socrates was 'schizophrenic' (an unfortunate choice of terms) the historical Socrates and the Platonic Socrates, to adopt the shorthand, could not be the same thinker (SS, 46). Now, on the one hand, our argument maintains the obviousness of the distinction between a historical Socrates and a historical Plato – which is what the Platonic Socrates (or Socrates_{M} – $_{M}$ denoting 'middle period') amounts to (SS, 76). What makes the analytic distinction important for our purposes is two things: firstly, that they maintain an irreconcilable distinction between the two points to the existence of the Two as a critical point of departure in thinking the Platonic corpus; secondly, that several of the grounds Vlastos establishes for the irreducibility of the division are those which for us attest to a subjective fidelity, which is to say that the very affirmation of a division is the truth of a procedure. For example, where Vlastos portrays Plato's mathematical turn as, essentially, a betrayal of Socrates, we contend that it is on this point, the disjunction between the moral and the mathematical, that Plato shows his greatest fidelity.

In reading these studies it is not always easy to discern whether Vlastos was undertaking a primarily philosophical, political, even historical task. He begins his essay 'Socrates Contra Socrates in Plato', with the admission that he cannot leave the historical question to one side in his examination of the Platonic corpus. Vlastos says he is dogged by the question 'who are you talking about – Socrates or *a* "Socrates"?' So at first glance Vlastos posits his question as a historical one. He posits that it is through *a* Socrates in Plato that one can come to know *the* Socrates. In another essay 'The Historical Socrates and the Athenian Constitution', we see Vlastos portray Socrates, the Socrates of the non-Platonic dialogues mind you, positively as nothing less than a fifth-century BC version of a bourgeois-democrat, a reserved scholar, handing out liberal pieties to one and all in the name of the 'true' constitution of Athens,[3] although in doing so he overlooks a philosophic dimension which seems critical to the Socratic and Platonic approaches.[4] Yet it must be remarked that he does this via an encyclopaedic knowledge of the dialogues and a manifest knowledge of the ancient and modern sources. There is an assured virtuosity at work in these readings which both intimidates and repels, but his grasp of the philosophic texts is not in doubt. It appears to be this very virtuosity that permits Vlastos to have no qualms about treating Plato as a historian.[5] What we glean from this analysis are some points where *what is particular to Socrates is universal in Plato* and thus we can argue that the Platonic body (corpus) supports the truth of the Socratic event.

In 'Socrates contra Socrates in Plato' Vlastos' distinction revolves around ten theses advanced in a double form and dependent on a tripartite division of the corpus into early, middle and late dialogues.[6] Vlastos wants to concentrate attention on early and middle as it is between these two that the transition from historical Socrates to 'mouthpiece of Plato' allegedly takes place. Obviously, the later dialogues only reaffirm the disjunction put into play by the transition. The ten theses turn around ten 'contradictions'.[7] We say contradictions a little peremptorily but in essence this is the purpose they serve for Vlastos because, as we said, he does want to assert their logical irreconcilability.[8]

In this chapter Vlastos addresses himself to T2 predominantly, although it touches on some of the more minor theses. He considers T1 too obvious to bother with on its own – though the distinction seems *weak* as the analytics love to say. The complete argument is too large to summarise with any justice and the references too vast to contend with in this chapter. We will concentrate on two thesis and do so in two different ways. We will address thesis 5 regarding the mathematics by assessing the claims Vlastos makes with regard to the mathematical turn in a companion chapter of this collection, 'Elenchus and Mathematics'. This focus on the mathematical turn will incorporate T10 on method. We will address the theses on the Forms (T2) by a reading of the *Phaedo* in which we contend that, far from being a lesson on the metaphysics of the soul, Socrates is bequeathing to his followers a form of thought necessary for the way of life demanded by philosophy. This Form is that which the Platonic corpus presents qua subject body of thought, and of which the *Republic* is the exemplar. It is not our claim that Vlastos is wrong, per se, in his analysis; he provides ample evidence for his claims, although the politics is certainly questionable. What is problematic in the end is that Vlastos' division leaves little room for thinking the Corpus itself as the invention of a form able to think the Two of Plato/Socrates. As we will see, any move to formalisation is rejected by Vlastos on interpretive and methodological grounds as anti-Socratic. Vlastos' standard bearer is (his) Socrates; for Vlastos he is event *and* subject whose philosophical import reduces to the very pious, very average claim that 'you hold the secret of your happiness in your hands. Nothing the world can do to you can make you unhappy'.[9] Perhaps it is such contentions that prompt Jacques-Alain Miller to name Vlastos a great 'theologian'. There is a powerful irony at work here, for Vlastos all but accuses Plato of staging a metaphysical coup and instituting a mathematical tyranny on its basis.[10]

Vlastos builds a certain portrait of Plato as disciple. He contends that Plato does not write biography. He says that Plato writes what he thinks Socrates would have said depending on time and context. The relation between writing and saying is not touched on here. He states that Plato is always concerned with the philosophical, with affirming truths, defending the Socratic arguments that are true for all (SS, 50–1). Thus Plato is not memorialising Socrates, nor reproducing his words (SS, 50). The dialogues are a production in themselves. Plato, Vlastos contends, even as he masters the literary art of dialogue writing, is, 'we must assume', concerned first and foremost with 'philosophical inquiry' (SS, 52). Vlastos imagines a father/son relationship wherein the son continues to harmonise with and be bonded to the father even 'when he finds compelling reason to strike out along new paths' (SS, 53). 'And when these lead him to new un-Socratic and anti-Socratic conclusions, as they visibly do by the time he comes to write the *Meno*, the dramatist's attachment to his protagonists, replicating the man's love for the friend and teacher of his youth, survives the ideological separation' (SS, 53). As Plato the individual 'matures', then so too do the convictions of the protagonist. What remains is the philosophical commitment. Except for the developmental assumptions, for which he provides the unfortunate mixed metaphor of *patēr familias* versus *Bildungsroman*, what Vlastos elaborates here is not essentially opposed to our thesis although Vlastos' humanist-identitarian bent is anathema to the procedure of truths as conceived by Badiou. However, there are two points in this little tale that are telling, for they already hint at the primacy of the political in Vlastos' reading. The first is the notion of the 'compelled change'. This is simply what we have referred to as the mathematical turn: in Vlastos' terms the 'Platonic turn'. Structurally, it can be compared to our analysis of the Cave in Chapter 3. The second is Vlastos' contention that such a change amounts to an ideological commitment. We have no idea from this work what Vlastos might understand by ideology, but as a good liberal-democrat we suspect there is a hint of the pejorative in this usage, and certainly some of the rhetoric unleashed to describe Plato once he dares to deploy signs of this 'ideological commitment' through the mouth of Socrates would back this up. This, then, must cut both ways, for the Socrates Vlastos is most keen to defend with the term 'historical' is the moral philosopher in the guise of 'man of action'. Are we to assume this is nothing more or nothing less than an ideological commitment? I doubt that Vlastos would allow that. But as Lazarus suggests, history is at once predicated on the political and proceeds on the basis of its disavowal,[11] and Vlastos certainly seems to confirm this by saying that the Socrates of history is the one who 'made history, taught Plato and others, changed their thinking and their lives and through them changed the course of western thought' (SS, 45). Curiously, by acknowledging the transformative power of Socrates, Vlastos presupposes continuity where he wants to insist on contradiction. On the one hand, there is the Socrates of immediate effect, the teacher of Plato and others. This Socrates, who conversed in the street, the market, with all comers, who had no otherworldly (SS, 80) 'far-flung metaphysics'[12] as Vlastos does not tire of repeating, is obviously the historical Socrates told to us by all sources and insisted on as the true philosopher in Vlastos' texts. The Socrates who 'changed the course of western thought', however, is a more complex arrangement. Unless Vlastos wants to claim that only the early dialogues (*written* by Plato) have had this impact then he must count the Socrates of the Platonic turn in his latter contention. This means of course that the Socrates who is contra Socrates (which is Plato) is as responsible for this transformation as the anti-Plato Socrates. Obviously, the Platonic subject-body supports this irreducible and extensive Two. The individual body of the master could do no such thing (Euthd. 307bc).

The movement from T1 to T2, for Vlastos, is ultimately a matter not just of method, from elenchus to hypothesis (and thus demonstration and ultimately dialectic), but is also epistemological. This shift concerns one's 'knowing position' in terms of one's ontology. For Vlastos, Socrates assumes certain ontological commitments – both in himself and in his interlocutors. Vlastos argues that Socrates never reveals himself to have these ontological commitments in any theorised form. He gets away with this depending on the calibre of his interlocutor. With Laches or Euthyphro, for example, their professions determine their position on this. Both share the Socratic consensus; just like the 'man in the street', neither is an ontologist. It is not the same with Protagoras, for he *has* an ontological commitment –'man being the measure of all things'. Vlastos claims that this accounts for why, with Protagoras, Socrates never asks his 'what is X' question; to do so would reveal his ontological commitment and thus he would be forced to defend it, something he *prefers* not to do (in the early dialogues) according to Vlastos (SS, 58–61).[13] This is how Vlastos accounts for the lack of a theory of Forms in the early dialogues. Socrates believes in them but he doesn't tell anyone and if no one questions him then the (unsaid) morally based consensus stands. Thus there is some form of agreement, however arrived at, which allows discussion to take place. This is obviously a linguistic consensus rooted in a historical language and shared tradition which informs it. Regardless of where this shared knowledge comes from, it is there and so Socrates makes use of it. Such is Vlastos' claim. One may wonder in what sense the term 'philosopher' is being used if to think one's ontological commitments is off limits. It is true that in *Theaetetus* Socrates tells the youth that his divine sign forbids him from association with certain figures (Tht. 151a). But these are figures that have already associated with Socrates, figures that have been subject to enquiry as it were, and left him to return to their interests. There are others still that he finds are not pregnant with anything at all. These he recommends to whatever sophist seems appropriate (perhaps for in-semination), thus partaking of that other maiuetic skill, matchmaking. Nevertheless, these too have been tested in discussion (Tht. 151b). There is nothing a priori about it and no assumption as to anyone's untested commitment or capacity. Still, for Vlastos, the *Theaetetus* is neither an early nor a transitional dialogue, and so falls outside the parameters of discussion.

If one were to enlist the *Cratylus* as evidence of a Socratic attempt to address this untheorised moral consensus concerning language and the unstable history which records its use, we would again be rebuffed by the dialogue order which supports Vlastos' thesis. Being a middle-period dialogue, we cannot count it in Socrates' favour. Instead, for Vlastos, it is an example of Plato critiquing his master in service to his new commitments and it ends, of course, at the point where the very question of the foundation of knowledge can find no consensus (Crt. 440b–e). The problem for Vlastos appears to be that the *Cratylus* shows Plato putting into question the very un-thought ontological commitments that serve as ground for any elenctic and thus Socratic discussion. The first rule of the elenchus, 'say what you believe', is violated, Vlastos says, when one applies the form of reasoning by hypothesis. The elenchus, in Vlastos' words, is thereby 'scuttled' (EM, 123), presumably because everyone is now forced to think not just about what it is they know but the conditions of thought itself! The consequence of this change in method, of Plato's new found penchant for formalisation, which Vlastos narrows down to a single sentence in the *Meno*, is the leaving behind of the mythical 'man in the street', the measure of all things. For Vlastos, the break within sophistry, which he simply accounts for in terms of method (refutation) and form (as irony – not *eirōnes*), is literally the last word of Socrates.[14] For us, this is a matter of the Platonic formalisation of the Socratic break with the sophistic position. For Vlastos, anything after aporia is Platonic. We agree.[15]

Let's look more closely at the essay 'Elenchus and Mathematics' and therefore at T5 for it is here that Vlastos truly comes to mark Socrates from Plato and all talk of the faithful son is forgotten. We are not long into this chapter when Vlastos aligns the mathematical turn in Plato to the latter's thought on politics. Politics is the real theme of the chapter because for Vlastos the 'idea' of moral autonomy is paramount. This is not to say this is an illegitimate move. However, there is no reflection on the politics of *this* politics for Vlastos at all. After remarking that Plato's Socrates and Glaucon have decided that mathematics need be taught, he refers to how this claim features as a corollary to the decision instigated by the moral of the Cave. He says, speaking 'as' Plato, this means 'that only those redeemed from the ontological bemusement which is the common lot of unregenerate humanity, only those privileged few may be trusted with *absolute* power' (EM, 109, my emphasis). Yet the end of the Cave allegory is summed up by Plato like this: 'Yes, my friend; for the truth is that you can have a well governed society only if you can discover for your future rulers a better way of life than being in office . . . all goes wrong when . . . they set about fighting for power . . .' (R. 521d). The ruler will be one who disdains the pettiness of power in favour of a nobler life and yet is himself bound by the city (R. 52a).[16] Whatever we think 'noble' might mean, Plato makes explicit it has nothing to do with 'absolute power'. The argument here is not important but it is the first instance in the escalating rhetoric (the rest of the passage takes flight) of Vlastos' division of the corpus into non-reconcilable halves.

This passage is instructive for another reason. Vlastos wants to hit us over the head with this notion of the coming of the absolute rule of an elite. He wants to mark off a real split between Plato and the demos as he has done with Plato and Socrates. As we saw, he was able to reconcile Socrates with the demos and so the logic is clear: if Socrates is with the demos and Socrates is not Plato, then Plato is against the demos. This is a part of Vlastos' strategy and a mark of his consistency. The claim is that, for Plato, only those who are no longer bewildered and thus have their 'ontological commitments' sorted out can rule. This may be so, but for us, this is so only in the *Republic* qua ideal non-state. In the Athens of the dialogues such a figure comes to nothing. Indeed, in the state of the Athens of the dialogues it is the 'common lot of unregenerate humanity' as Vlastos calls them (Plato, in the allegory of the cave calls them 'other citizens', 'fellow prisoners', the' ignorant')[17] who are not at all bewildered. It is the population at large, as both Socrates and Plato charge, who rule with a clear conscience, using number as their form of right, persuasion as their means and interest as their 'ontological commitment'. The problem is, that know it or not, they have *this* 'ontological commitment'. The masses may not be 'in their right minds', true, but they think they are and that's what works in the polis.[18] Indeed, we saw above that Vlastos praises Socrates for sharing these untheorised commitments with the populace as the ground of all discussion. Is this not what is praised in other contexts? Is not the great Socratic victory the knowledge of ignorance? Vlastos is certainly one to praise the elenchus in these terms. It seems that Vlastos rejects the hypothetical method of the 'elites' because they dare to assert the existence of that which they do not know – as the *Meno* assuredly attests. They mark what is not known as real, by hypothesis. Whereas for Vlastos, as for the 'constructivist' analytic tradition as a whole, and as for the mystics of all centuries, the better rule is to leave the unknown unsaid, what goes unsaid in this rule is that this can only be done because they have established the means by which the unsaid is known. We are back at the problem of a false conceit. The point is that the populace act as though they have their commitments 'sorted out' while Plato's becoming-philosopher-kings (should they ever) have at least ten years mathematics, five of dialectic, fifteen back in the cave in state service, and only then the chance to rule without profit – or in sophistic terms, without interest.[19] Vlastos' reading here, on the one hand, is symptomatic to my mind of reading the *Republic* as seamless with the other dialogues when in fact the *Republic* is Athens turned on its head (or, perhaps, put right way up) and must be thought as such. Adopting the Lacanian register we should emphasise that Socrates was 'cut out' of Athens; he is the castrated figure who, as such, marks but does not know the truth of the sophistic situation. The power of truth is impotent. What Plato does in the *Republic*, as a faithful subject of this impotent truth, is not install the Socratic figure in power, but formalise the impotent power of the Socratic figure. Power is ever subordinate to truth and if the state *is* the 'good state', the true state (it cannot be any other way, truth is for all or not at all and if the state is ideally good there is no way it is in error – unless one wants to return to relativism), those who 'rule' by truths and thus, for all, are already subordinate to the situation in which they 'rule'. Absolute power indeed!

Continuing with the same rhetoric, Vlastos claims that Plato's restriction of the discussion of morality, right and wrong, to those who have made the mathematical study is the extreme antithesis to the Socrates of the Socratic dialogues. He contends that nowhere else in western philosophy is it so resisted. Here he ratchets up the Socrates as street-philosopher-pugilistic-democrat rhetoric: 'Not only does [Socrates] allow question *breeding* argument about good and evil to all and sundry, he positively *thrusts* it on them. He draws into his search for the right way to live the people he runs into on the street, in the market place, in gymnasia, convinced that this outreach to them is a god given mission' (EM, 110, emphasis added). We have mentioned the truth and falseness of this notion of Socrates speaking *to* all as opposed to the more strictly accurate *addressing all*, but what is more perplexing is that Vlastos skips over the early dialogue *Apology* wherein we find Socrates raising the possibility that it is his youthful imitators who have helped turn the people against him. These 'young men with wealthy fathers and plenty of leisure' *copy* Socrates and presume to test their elders. The victims then blame Socrates, their supposed *model* (Ap. 23c).[20] Recalling the anti-developmental work of Thesleff,[21] this passage has the merit of supporting both Vlastos and us. On the one hand, Socrates affirms that the method, even in untrained hands, does find men who claim to know what they do not and as such these untrained youth do therefore partake of the elenchus, method and content. On the other hand, it is their imitative practices which play a part as evidence in the trial of Plato's master and which play an even bigger part in his conviction. One must recall that in the *Republic* Plato seeks the place of non-sophistry precisely because it has no place and in such a place the youth must not form part of its destruction but of its proper constitution. This is the genesis of Plato's attempt here; it is not to forge a conspiracy of elites – the philosopher turns his back on any such position. In this, surely, Plato remains faithful to his master. Unlike Vlastos, who finds Socrates very much at home in Athens, we have seen in dialogue after dialogue that the singular virtue of the Socratic figure is that he has no place *in the sophistic state:* he is in fact an exile of the as yet inexistent Republic.

Although Vlastos identifies the *Gorgias* as the 'turning point' (EM,115, fn. 39) insofar as it is the last dialogue to employ the Socratic elenchus as the legitimate method of seeking (moral) truth, he argues that it is at 81d in the *Meno* that the elenchus is essentially abandoned in the face of the geometric paradigm (EM, 119). This is the point at which the axiomatic (or *prescriptive*) method begins to take hold. Axioms, he tells us, citing Euclid and contra Aristotle, are the *terminus* of all enquiry, something unconscionable in the Socratic elenchus, wherein, as we have seen, all matters are up for contest no matter how absurd – as long as they are the 'true' opinion of the holder.[22] This latter demand is rigorously un-axiomatic, we are to assume, even though if it is not held too, the conversation breaks down. And we should really observe that none of the opinions expressed within the knowledge of the dialogue situation is truly out of place within this situation despite what Vlastos wishes. To his cause, for example, he quotes Thrasymachus' 'perversely eccentric' thesis that 'justice is of the interest of the stronger' (EM, 114). As noted, if Thucydides is to be believed this thesis is far from perverse but is *the* thesis of Athens itself and all 'properly' constituted states.[23] But this would put Vlastos' Socrates qua democrat in a bind (all of a sudden he is a supporter of Athenian empire and tyranny) – as would the placing of the *Republic* in the period of the middle dialogues which is so often the case in the scholarship. Vlastos has solved this by splitting the *Republic* itself into early and middle periods (Book I early, II to X middle).[24]

The introduction of the axiomatic, prescriptive form, geometry, is coupled with the introduction of what Vlastos refers to as the doctrine of the transmigrating soul at 81a in the *Meno*. This enters along with the theory of anamnesis. Together these, which come to stay and 'saturate the *Phaedo*',[25] constitute what he has already referred to as Plato's 'far-flung metaphysics'. He identifies the critical line of this 'all-too Platonic Socrates': 'For *all* inquiring and learning is recollection' (EM, 120 and Men. 81d; Phd. 76a). One can surely ask here whether it is pure coincidence that Vlastos leaves off the crucial context of this claim, that 'once one has recalled a single piece of knowledge, *learned* it, in ordinary language there is no reason why he should not find out all the rest, if he keeps a stout heart and does not grow weary of the search; *for seeking and learning are in fact nothing but recollection.*' This 'all the rest' is the central concern. The desire to deduce the method by which enquiry can be available to all is surely the true mark of Plato's 'Socratism' and not its 'betrayal'. Further, is the theory of recollection the same in *Phaedo* as in *Meno*? Does Plato revise, alter or rethink its deployment and its content and form? If he does, what does this mean in relation to the fixed notion of axiomatic method that Vlastos determines puts an end to all 'free inquiry' – whatever that might be?

For Vlastos this post-*Gorgias* move marks the beginning of the end for the 'Socratic' dialogues. Such mathematics and the consequences its thought demands, the existence, no less, of the irrational and thus that thought must be established on the basis of 'non-thought', is 'beyond the reach of the layman', Vlastos contends (EM, 127). If this were to form the basis for 'moral philosophy', knowledge of good and evil would be forever foreclosed to the masses.[26] This last claim, leaving aside for now its assumption as to the intellectual capacities of the layman and the underlying conceit of such 'knowledge', is again based on the un-argued for premise that once the axiomatic method is introduced it is incontestable. On the one hand, Vlastos seems to consider mathematics here only in terms of technique and instrumentality, in a way akin (perhaps) to Heidegger and maybe Hegel before him (even though these figures rate no mention in Vlastos), while on the other, it seems to be permanently sealed off from what is possible for a subject altogether. Plato is seen to make use of mathematics for *other* purposes. The result of this turn, for Vlastos, which is a turn away from the supposed liberalism of his master (is this not the false conceit of wisdom par excellence?), is a sort of Popperian totalitarian nightmare – 'the philosopher-king looms ahead' (EM, 125).[27]

The question of fallibility seems central here. For Vlastos, the virtue of the elenctic method is that it is inherently fallible. The interlocutors hold traditional opinions, opinions of the polis untested by the Socratic elenchus. The dialogue proceeds on their basis; it stalls, restarts with 'new' opinions and ends in uncertainty. Each argument can be revisited as the methodological premise ensures, Vlastos says, 'the insistence of incontinence'. For Vlastos, in a way not quite explained, mathematical prescription is contrasted as infallible and ergo anyone who thinks from this paradigm thinks, or will no doubt come to think, that they too are infallible. Whether any mathematician at all ever thought either one of these is unknown. But what we again see is that the mathematical-cum-Platonic turn is discredited by way of political inference which is to say, by way of preference. Vlastos offers no evidence either for the thesis of mathematical, or rather hypothetical, infallibility or for the thesis by extension that mathematical form will determine totalitarian politics. But it is intriguing, from the perspective of democracy, thought in its fullest extension and not as the ideological self-representation of the bourgeois state, to consider the context of Plato's geometrical turn. For it is the case that this turn, 'the most sustained stretch of geometrical reasoning in the whole of the corpus' (EM, 118) takes place in the dialogue in tandem with a slave and not with one of the privileged boys of Athens who 'act the tyrant as long as their youth lasts' (Men. 76b). If the geometrical reformulation subscribes to any politics it is surely the 'irrational' *doctrine of fair shares*. In *Gorgias*, Plato draws a distinctive link between Socrates' accusation against Callicles that because he refuses geometry he therefore practises the doctrine of unfair shares and the accusation of Callicles that if things are as Socrates insists the world will be turned upside down. We should note in passing that the doctrine of fair shares is the principle or Form of justice upon which the *Republic* is 'woven in discourse' (Sph. 259e). Such a paradigm does indeed subvert the 'ordinary infinity' of counting by number, which is to say counting by opinion, whose malleability and manipulability is obvious to all. What Vlastos misses here is a necessary shift away from the identification of truth with the figure(s) of enunciation – the strongest, the richest, the force of numbers and so on. In the *Phaedo*, Socrates says to Simmias and Cebes, 'if you take my advice, you will think very little of Socrates, and much more of the truth' (Phd. 91bc). Truth and the figure of enunciation can no longer be sutured together as is instanced in the poetic tradition of the heroic, though flawed (thus good *and* bad), examples, for to remain so puts the very truth of the Socratic displacement at stake.[28] By bringing the slave and Socrates together, two figures with no place in the polis, which is to say two figures with a void *and* anonymous address, Plato ensures that the thinking of truth which constitutes the finite work of the generic procedure, of its becoming true, is delinked from any finitude, from any state and from any identity. It is anti-elitist and anti-totalitarian in that it thoroughly displaces the place of the enunciation which any elitism depends upon. Plato is committed to the thought that one can come to think. Geometry, mathematics is the model form given that what it demonstrates as demonstrated is true and true for all, but it is not determinant. What it thinks or demonstrates, and here in the *Meno* it is the existence of the incommensurable, is the condition of thought itself. Recollection, after all, is the *thinking* of the *unknown* thought of which everyone is capable. As we will see in the *Phaedo*, what one comes to know in practice is that one can come to know – perhaps even mathematics.

Rather than go on listing Vlastos' contentions it might serve our purpose just as well to listen to the rhetoric. In EM he claims, with regard to mathematics, that 'Plato's new enthusiasm bubbles out at all over the text' (118), that his terminology is now 'ostentatiously technical' (123), that Plato is 'preening himself' on his own expertise' with these technicalities (123), that he indulges in 'mathematical pretension', exhibits a 'lordly insouciance' (127), and ultimately that he was 'susceptible to beauty' (130), such is why geometry carries the day: the result is the 'scuttling of the elenchus' (123). Plato *contra* Socrates: which is to say, Plato contra the demos – the 'for all'. Vlastos here sounds for all the world like Aristippus quoted by Aristotle: 'As Aristippus said in reply to Plato when he spoke somewhat too dogmatically, *as Aristippus thought*: "Well, anyhow, our friend", meaning Socrates, "never spoke like that".'[29] What we can contend is that there is a critical fault line at the point of the universal. What for us makes the composition of Plato/Socrates the truth of the Platonic corpus, that every enquiry supports the universal trajectory of an education by truths, is for Vlastos the very point at which one must retreat to particularity and interest, and the tending of one's own garden (cf. TC, 124–5). In terms of the Badiouean definition of philosophy, Vlastos, in searching out the logic of the historical *at the expense* of the truth of the philosophical would take his place with 'Rorty, and Vattimo among the lesser sophists' (C, 77). This fault line of the universal where Plato takes his leave of the Vlastosian Socrates is critical, for as Vlastos repeatedly contends, Socrates converses with any and all.

It is precisely on this very point that the notion of the corpus as subject matters most, for what is *declared* by the event is that which is for all, but it is not by the event itself that this address is made manifest. The fact remains that it is only the Platonic corpus, faithful support of this declaration in action, that makes this 'all' at all possible. That is to say, without the work of the faithful subject who, taken by the event, convinced of its significance and determined that it continue, the Socratic address remains particular to its place and constrained by the statist conditions to remain in place. What Vlastos recognises in the 'Socratic address' is that which Plato also recognised. The difference, ultimately, is that through the corpus we see realised time and again the effort to realise the universality inherent to the Socratic event of breaking with the state and its logic of interest – thus its particularity and exclusivity. The 'egalitarian' address of the Socratic encounter, that 'a non-sophistic education exists *indiscernibly* and yet *for all*, is what Plato seeks to found as real, extensive and for all time. The corpus makes it possible after all to re-intervene in the Socratic event and to realise the importance if not the necessity for such an intervention – for a *subject*. 'It is a question of night or day, to be determined not, as in the children's game, by spinning a shell, but by turning about of the soul from a day that is like night to the veritable day, that journey up to the real world which we shall call the true pursuit of wisdom' (R. 321c).

That Plato does not suture himself to the master but enquires *with* him in both senses is what makes impossible Vlastos' dream for Socrates: that Socrates *be* the 'philosopher' (*without* being the non-sophist) and Plato only his mouthpiece. However, despite the witnesses he calls to the stand, Xenophon, Aristotle, Aeschines, Socraticus, Aelius, and Cicero among others, in support of his trial of Plato, without the insistence of the break as immanent function *for the entirety of the corpus*, there is no corpus of any worth (SS, 105).[30] The subject-*body*, which *is* the Platonic corpus, is the *faithful* affirmation of this disjunction, not its history and not its contradiction, and at the same time it is the affirmation of its contingent necessity and of the form itself. Therefore there is a sense in which we are not opposed to Vlastos but are instead to the side of him. Plato and Socrates *are* irreducible, a *Platocrates* in fact, such is the point of thinking them as Two, but it is by this irreducibility, by what can be made or thought (it is the same thing) to circulate between them or *as them* as Deleuze[31] might say, that a truth is forced. They must in fact be the Two which the corpus divides into without at all dissipating. The measure of their distance is what is critical and we will test some of this measure by what Socrates says in the *Phaedo*. The point is that Vlastos' distinction is ingenious and rigorous but in its insistence on the particular *against* the universal, ultimately sophistic for all that.

Truths contra Vlastos

That 'there are truths', Vlastos notes, is what Plato affirms *in regard to* Socrates, but this is not the same as what we are insisting upon. When, in the essay 'Art and Philosophy', Badiou insists 'there must be truths', he means 'to *make* truths manifest,' to forcefully distinguish truths from the repetitious, circulating knowledge of the state. It is, in other words, to decide that there is 'something besides opinion', 'something besides our "democracies"' (HB, 14–15). If there are not truths we have only an 'academic quibble' (HB, 15). What Vlastos' rigorously logical and rigorously Lyceanic (?) division is dangerously close to doing in insisting on the truth of the anti-Platonic Socrates against the so called anti-Socratic Plato, is subverting the very possibility of there being truth here at all. Thought is thereby reduced to an academic quibble because the logic of infinite dissemination – measure without measure – admits no 'place of taking place', no void insists in its marked out spaces. One simply, and constructively, interprets anew within the confines of the a priori statically divided: Hegel's bad infinite returns as unmarked 'dissemination'. The truth that the faithful-subject affirms is rendered meaningless, absurd to even think it, in favour of the logical repetition of distinctions and judgment. The corpus thereby becomes object of analysis, a static entity, a body dead like its master rather than the living subject, subject *to* its master's life. In his 'ten theses' we see that Vlastos refers to the dialogues he calls Platonic as taken with 'speculations' and crass 'flights of metaphysical fancy'. If, then, the 'Socratic' dialogues are the truth of the Platonic corpus as separated from the body itself then what Vlastos effectively does is assign non-truth to the Platonic corpus. In fact, there is no corpus because the term only signifies division and not its composition. For Vlastos, effectively, there is no subject of this division per se. In order to save Socrates he purposefully conflates the enunciation with the enunciator thereby confining truth to the private or the particular in the manner Plato attributes to the poets of antiquity, 'the friends of the flux' and the followers of Protagoras. With the death of the Socratic body comes the production of the death of its thought for Vlastos, just as the sophistic state assumed. In this way Vlastos has essentially inverted the trajectory of the *Phaedo*; moreover, Plato is the executioner and 'democratic' Athens is saved. For Vlastos, the price of saving the latter must be paid at any cost. Truth, the fundamental basis of any enquiry *which is not sophistic*, and the 'educated' subject it alone induces, is the price to be paid for an edifying, liberal myopia.

Aporia

As we have stated, our concern is with what Socrates is to Plato (and Plato to Socrates) in terms of an education by truths. If we accept, for now, Vlastos' transcendental-cum-empiricist division – his essay is not an affirmation of the truth of the division but an interpretative thesis on its dysfunction – then the question might be asked 'what is the elenchus for Plato?' That is, what does Plato do with Socratic elenchus given that it exists only as long as its 'body' does? As a first pass we would offer that while the Socratic elenchus sought after truth in its fashion, for Plato, its failing was simply its inherent limit in regard to its extension. For Plato, this limit, rather than undermine the sophistic state, rather than subvert it, actually seemed to strengthen it. Socrates' avowed refusal – according to Vlastos – to take the next step, a step his method was already pregnant with, which, in shorthand, we can call its formalisation, insofar as such a move extends indefinitely the reach of its address, only fuelled the conceit of the sophistic state. Within the Socratic method itself, not less than in the results it produced, there remained something lacking. It lacked resources for the next step; it was inherently aporetic. As Samuel Scolnicov observes, aporia registers in two ways. In sophistic terms it registers as despair while for the philosopher it is an incitement.[32]

To conceive of aporia in terms of incitement demands that what is *shown* to be lacking be taken up. Of course one does not *know* what it *is* that is lacking, just that a certain lack insists. This, as we have seen, is what a fidelity alone can seize upon and, as such, for a fidelity aporia means little given that to be faithful is to continue to continue. An incitement recognised but not taken up can only be conceived in terms of potential and this is not something that can be considered Platonic. For Vlastos, his eye on the preferred politics and under an erroneous distinction between mathematical form and philosophical procedure, aporia is positive in the sense that each man is left not to actually decide for themselves but to take away whatever they will from the discussion, in essence no more than they brought. It seems that Vlastos sanctions a perverse form of relativism, which might be to say 'humanism'. In this conception we are confronted with entirely autonomous and as such already constituted subjects: the 'anyone' who may come forward and the 'anyone' who goes away subject to the equivalences denoted in *exchange*. In this understanding, where incitement plays the role of pure potentiality, it is as well if the conversation never took place. Indeed the formalities of discourse are unnecessary – a discussion would do, a conference, a debate, a seminar or a chat from which all go away 'unscathed' as it were? In Vlastos' Socrates (not unlike in Aristotle) no transformation is demanded, no consequences need taking up, because we already have morally autonomous subjects conversing only to confirm a priori commitments that are off limits to enquiry. Knowledge (qua truth of knowledge) is little more than information gathered, consensus confirmed. The immanent and indifferent force of such a knowledge, that to take it up is to become transformed, is precisely that from which Vlastos shrinks as he offers praise for its foreclosure. The *subject* who arrives in wonder goes in despair and the truth of the dialogue comes or goes in the same manner. The fetish for the pseudo-democracy trumps the philosophical pursuit of truth.

For us, *by contrast*, aporia marks a *real* point of failure. It is of a particular and necessary sort. It is in fact the point at which knowledge, in the form of opinion, a form Hegel reminds us 'implies thought but not pure thought' is taken to its furthest reaches. 'So in perplexing him and numbing him like the sting-ray, have we done him any harm? No, I think not' (Men. 84b; Sph. 230a–e). Knowledge as opinion, rigorously tested opinion at that, fails in terms of its truth. Platonic aporia, an aporia to which Socrates in the 'historical' dialogues readily submits, therefore stands, retroactively speaking only, as a 'necessary failure' which by implication demands that it be thought again. Whereas Vlastos defines Socratic virtue as accruing at this point of failure, we determine Platonic necessity to insist. Aporia is the coming full circle of the pre-*Meno* dialogue, to use Vlastos' division: from that which Socrates *does not* know as the foundational point of *all* dialogues to that which *can not* be known under *those* conditions of thought. The impasse lies in the disjunction between what Socrates does not know, which, as prescriptive, is under the sign of the universal, and that which cannot be known which is sophistic and under the sign of the particular. It is our contention that Plato, from the *Meno* on, seeks to have done with this impasse in favour of the universality of the Socratic prescription over sophistic despair, a despair entirely provoked by the void, a void Socrates insists *can be thought*.

What we propose in terms of the Platonic corpus is that, confronted with the Real of the impasse of Socrates, Plato was forced to force the consequences of the break with opinion that Socrates instigated each and every time. Vlastos is right to isolate the above passage from the *Meno*, for it is here evident that at the very point where the elenchus 'fails' or 'repeats', Plato is now determined, and this due to his new understandings of mathematics – particularly the proof of the existence of the incommensurable – 'that which cannot be expressed' – to take up the consequences incited by Socratic aporia. The irrational is the very impetus for thought qua what must be thought and not the site of its retreat.

THE LESSON OF THE *PHAEDO*

In reading the *Phaedo* our intention is to listen attentively to Socrates' instruction in regard to what he terms 'the world to come'. This world to come has two compatible forms: one extrinsic to the dialogues and one intrinsic to the dialogues. The former is the Platonic corpus and perhaps includes the Academy itself.[33] In an earlier chapter we noted the double structure of the corpus in relation to the event, and in this chapter, in taking our distance from Vlastos, we have seen the corpus in terms of the double structure of the subject. There is no conflict here. The dialogues are instances of the event-truth-subject structure of non-sophistic discourse and practice. As a corpus they are the subject which supports the Socratic intervention within the Athenian state and within each dialogue this trajectory is played out over and again. It is this trajectory which we conceive within the dialogue the *Phaedo* where Socrates sets out the praxis of non-sophistry for his immediate followers, Simmias and Cebes. The praxis he sets out is that of the subject. It is patently clear that this is the way of life of non-sophistry and he of course is the exemplary figure in this regard. But Socrates stresses it is not his way of life alone, it is not particular to him but is for anyone at all. When Plato has Socrates say to Simmias and Cebes to pay no attention to Socrates but to the way of life (Phd. 91bc) Plato is returning us to the *Apology* where Socrates notes that his name is used by the oracle only as a sign of what it is to live without the false conceit of wisdom (Ap. 23b). Plato also reminds us of the very same thing when Socrates tells Crito that, in considering the education of his sons, he ought not to listen to the tellers of tales concerning what a non-sophistic way of life consists in, but pay attention to the 'thing itself' (Euthd. 307bc). This is all to say that in the *Phaedo*, the 'world to come' is not conceived in terms of some 'far flung metaphysics', but is the anticipated result of a prescriptive, materialist doctrine for revolutionary transformation. For our purposes we draw from the *Phaedo* three central terminologies: soul, body and immortality, and one central concept: the 'to come'.[34] It is through these that Plato confronts the paradox of 'subjective truth', for the life of the non-sophist within the Athens of the dialogues results only in death, and yet, for Socrates, the result of being dead to Athens is the life which is 'to come'.

To put it in terms of the body and soul disjunction which animates this dialogue, Socrates, the exemplary non-sophist qua philosopher, is at every turn 'nailed down' to the body of sophistic Athens. The latter, the body of knowledge the former must traverse, hinders the coming philosopher's trajectory and threatens to spoil the pursuit of truth. The true philosopher, or the philosopher by truths, confined as he is to this life of the body politic, must practise a step-by-step subtraction from this body, from its effects as from its demands. The philosopher, as Socrates says, must *practise* dying *to* the state. This practice is the only path out of the confusion the body of sophistic knowledge renders upon the soul. 'By keeping ourselves uncontaminated by the follies of the body we shall probably reach the *company* of others like us' (Phd. 67b, emphasis added). This path of purgation and purification, one that is removed from the dialectic of courage and fear, Socrates contends, passes through a form of death.[35] The soul, however, never dies. It is imperishable and so immortal which is why it 'passes through'.[36] Having undergone the 'trial of its subtraction' from the state in this life, the soul of the philosopher finds its true place in what is the life 'to come', whereas the souls of those contaminated by too close a contact with the life of the body undergo theirs, so the concluding myth contends, in the afterlife. The 'philosopher', possessor of the 'good soul' let's call it, prepares for the death which clearly is not *its* death.

The *Phaedo*, far from being a meditation on life *after death*, is a meditation, or rather a lesson, on what it is *to live* philosophically, which is to say *by truths*. What then must not live in order for philosophy to live? This is the question of the *Phaedo* and it inverts (rather than reverses) that of the *Apology*. For in the latter the question (posed by the sophistic state) was 'what must die in order that sophistry continues to live?' In the *Phaedo* it is Socrates who is to die this day. In the *Apology* he defended his way of life to no avail before a jury, who on the strength of the numbers, considered it to be no way of life at all. In the *Phaedo* he not only defends it in front of a more critical jury (Phd. 63e), the philosophers, he hopes, 'to come', but he sets down this way of life, the way of life which *must not be*, as *the* 'way of life' to come. Clearly, for Socrates, 'death is no event'.[37] Never having discovered Truth in this form of life, nevertheless living *by truths* (participation) Socrates sets down what is to be thought here and now by *reference* to, or even by *virtue* of, that which is 'to come' (Phd. 66b). As we have said throughout, the Republic, the thought 'result' of the displacement of the sophistic state (the 'sophistic body' in the sense we are using it here) is that which is always 'to come' in the dialogues. The Republic is the Idea of the dialogues. It is the reasoned place that the *figure* of Socrates already inhabits, despite the 'fact' that it is within the Athens of the dialogues that he moves. We have noted that Socrates' strangeness to Athens is due to his being an internal exile of the non-existent Republic. He is an anticipatory figure. Correspondingly, as noted, the Republic is thought throughout as 'that which is in Athens more than Athens knows', to use the Lacanian formulation. It is retroactively situated thus. If the *Crito* were read in this way, it would cease to cause consternation to liberal-minded commentators. Put in positive terms, in each dialogue the Socratic encounter with the sophistic body/state induces the thought of the 'place of philosophy'. In effect that which is 'to come', and can only come through the life of philosophy practised in the here and now, is at the same time that which every non-sophistic thought thinks. It is the inherent aporia of such thought.

Time being of the essence (at least in one respect) the Socratic instruction concerning an education by truths becomes more explicit. 'Nothing new, Crito, just what I am always telling you . . . if you neglect yourselves and fail to follow the line of life as I have laid it down both now and in the past, however fervently you agree with me now, it will do no good at all' (Phd. 115c). The true philosopher, he contends, has been ever practising for death (of this life); which, for the non-sophist, following our notion of the inversion, is the practice of the life 'to come'. For Socrates, this practice, carried out by the soul living in the body of the state, is purification: a practised purging of the soul through reason and by reason of all bodily constraints.[38] The fancies, loves and fears of the body, desires from which all wars and demands for wealth and prestige and empire issue, are constraints, for Socrates, on the very possibility of thought (Phd. 66bcd). One cannot practise thought, which is to say submit to its prescriptions, pursue wisdom and know truth, when one is 'riveted' down to the body and so subject to its claims, its clamour and its laws. What Socrates has laid down, by example, by reason, is the practice of 'subtracting' oneself from the perversions, distractions and desires of the body (politic), and this in order 'to set out for the [other world] where there is prospect of attaining their lifelong desire' (Phd. 68c). As we have seen, 'subtraction', for Badiou, is the affirmative form of this desire for purification. What Plato describes is what Badiou calls a generic procedure. The subject lives only insofar as he thinks in the here and now the form of that which is 'to come'. The dialogues, wherein Socrates subtracts truth from within sophistic discourse – and this by rigorous and respectful discourse 'with them' – are the situational practice of the thought of the 'to come'. In the dialogues, Socrates has no recourse in the situation other than to orient his thought on that which *is not* but has 'happened'. To quote Badiou, glossing Malevich, subtraction is 'to invent content at the very place of the minimal difference, where there is almost nothing'. And so 'here must be, and there will be, a new act, a "new birth" . . .' (TC, 57). The 'philosopher' takes leave only insofar as he invents the world 'to come' of which *this* world is pregnant. In other words, the would-be philosopher is simply he/she who thinks the situation again under condition of what has remained unthought. In the *Phaedo* Socrates pursues this world 'to come' in a fantastical analogy: a labyrinth in which the pure are sorted from the impure in terms of their practice while alive. In this labyrinth souls undergo further sorting by means of being plunged into the depths, whirled about by force, risen to the surface to be tested and if failed plunged anew into the cavernous depths. The metaphor of the Cave is easily read here, as is the form of the Socratic practice, but as he tells Cebes and Simmias, 'no reasonable man ought to insist that the facts are exactly as I have described them'. But, he says, 'something similar is the case' (Phaedo, 114d). Considered from within the situation of the Athens of the dialogues wherein Socrates is condemned, sophistry is triumphant, where war and wealth are the very objects of all desire 'is not the Republic similarly fantastic?' Should any reasonable man believe that the Socratic way of life is ideal – just, true, courageous and wise?

Near the beginning of the dialogue Plato makes a point of situating Socrates: 'As he spoke he lowered his feet to the ground and sat like this for the rest of the conversation' (Phd. 61d). This may be a retort to Aristophanes, but it is also a set direction telling us that what is to be said here has material import.[39] This is no flight of fancy, no 'famous last words'. What Socrates sets out to elaborate is the indiscernible soul as the carrier or the nascent form of a truth. The soul is a part of every body. It is imperishable, immortal; it continues despite the exhaustion of particular bodies. It is a *part* of the body or is *attached* to the body – for Plato, as for Lacan, what constitutes the impossibility of their 'link' is love: a good soul will, by love, constitute a good body – but the soul is an infinite part and any body only its 'finite support'. The body, heavy with the sensuous world 'saturates' the soul, reducing its sense of pleasure and pain to that which the body commands. In this way, it 'makes the soul corporeal' (Phd. 83d) and so unlike that which, by negation, it has affinity. The demands of the body, registered as pleasures or pains, have great effect on the soul. 'When anyone feels a keen pleasure or pain it cannot help supposing that whatever causes the most violent emotions is the plainest and truest reality; which it is not. It is chiefly visible things which have this effect, isn't it?' (Phd. 83c). The good soul has intercourse not with that which is immediate to appearance, that which is already a resemblance, but with that which is indiscernible within that which appears to the body. The body, for Plato – replying to Simmias on 'attunement' and Cebes on 'perishibility' – deals in plausibility, in verisimilitude, and thought so based is an impostor. For Plato, *there are* other things than bodies and the languages which construct them.

For Socrates, the practices of the philosopher are eminently paradoxical in that really, they prepare the soul *for life*. Philosophy, in Socrates' terms, is lifelong preparation for *life*: a life which must pass through the mediation of death. But death is no end. What is the character of death, what dies at death and what cannot die? For Socrates, the 'good' soul, that which has spent its time in this finite body under the condition of a reasoned practice ever persuading the body from its demands toward that which is the 'desire of the soul', far from coming to perish, only truly lives in the 'world' that is 'to come'. That which forms the consistency of this world, that which constitutes its body and of which anybody is a part, forms the *prison house* of that which is 'to come'. The immortality of the soul, the infinity of a truth, is linked by Plato to the theory of Forms through the theory of recollection. The question of how the soul can practise a subtraction of itself from the body is a question of recollection. We return here to our argument from Chapter 4. What the soul recollects are the Forms. This is illustrated by Plato with the famous example of equal sticks. We see two sticks; they appear to be the same length; this recalls to our mind the idea of equality. Importantly, it does not matter, in this sense, whether they are actually measured as equal, for the point is that something like and something unlike can prompt a recollection of the Form which is always the same. Sticks are not 'equality' but their appearance together in a certain configuration recalls the Form. Upon measuring the sticks, after we have recollected the Form it presents, if we find them unequal this in no way diminishes the recollection of the Form which provides the stable of any measurement.

This is the Platonic trajectory: the indiscerning of that which appears in order to establish its truth. The Idea drives the enquiry; the enquiry does or does not establish the idea. 'It is thus legitimate to treat the enquiry, a finite series of minimal reports, as the veritable basic unit of the procedure of [subjective] fidelity, because it combines the one of discernment with the several of classification' (BE, 331/365). The Idea is what is re-collected in any confrontation with appearance, any generic enquiry, which is to say any participative procedure of indiscernment. This is Plato's point. Recollection of the Form is what allows the soul to live as if it were already dead to the body (politic) (cf. Phd. 64b). That there are Ideas which exist without appearance, that are 'generic' in secular terms, suggests that there is 'another world' both prior to – in that it is to be re-collected – and posterior to – in that through this recollection it is invented *as such* – life in the body (of the state). The good soul, which could be *any* soul, all being nothing but souls and thus partaking of a generic equality, orients its thought practice in the body (of the state) here and now, which is to say 'in life', to this idea of that which is 'to come'. The soul then, alive in the body but partaking of the 'world to come', the world wherein this 'fiction' will have been true, lives in this world as that which 'will have been'. 'Beauty is beautiful because it partakes of that absolute Beauty, and for no other reason. Do you accept this kind of causality?' (Phd. 100c). For Plato, the soul is the militant form whose enquiries produce 'here and now' that which is 'to come', which is to say it is its *immanent constitution*. In this sense, Socrates is the soul for which the Republic will have been the body. This 'transmigration', we say with tongue in cheek, is the basis of the final chapter.

As we saw in Chapter 3, Badiou contends that the event founds a discipline of time named the intervention. Intervention equates to what Plato calls 'participation'. This Time is the time 'between events', wherein the intervention qua series of inquiries into the truth of the event constitutes the life of the subject. With the death of the body whose life marks the finitude of time the soul undergoes the trial of its continuance. In his argument concerning opposites and the processes of generation Socrates determines that one becomes another via a starting point or, as one translation intriguingly has it, a 'deflection' (Phd. 71b).[40] It is this deflection which prevents the simple straight-line effect wherein one simply becomes the other. This, Socrates argues, would lead to all things becoming the same as ultimately all that is living would become dead, and as there would be nothing alive to become dead consequently only the dead would exist. Thus, for Socrates, there must be a point through which the soul passes, for it is this point, whatever it may be, which ensures the mutual generation of opposites. In Badiou's terms, being-qua-being passes into what-is-not-being-qua-being at the point of the (evental) void-site. Without the event, the site marks only the impasse of this passing.[41] The event therefore, marks the new time of what is 'to come' in the subject body that partakes of it. It marks the disjunction of what is, and what can be of what is.

Without elaborating too much on this point, what Socrates has marked in the dialogues is a point of discontinuity which ensures its very opposite: continuity, as a re-beginning. Subject to *deflection* it is not the reproduction of a repetition. Crucially, this point also ensures the impossibility of the approach of opposites, wherein the opposite would become opposite to itself: the odd, for example, never becomes even. In this way, Socrates points out the ultimate impossibility of identification between what *partakes* of one form and that which *partakes* of another in terms of this participation. We know that odd can never be even and that odd and even are opposites. Two is even and three is odd but two and three are not opposites; yet two, which partakes of even, retreats or disappears at the approach of three, which has odd in it. Further, anything at all thought together with two other things can count as three and thus partake of odd. Each of those same things may also count as two and partake of even. But odd will never be even and two never three. The stability and thus immortality of the Forms is argued for in this way.

If one thinks the context of the argument for the Forms, rather than the argument itself, one immediately sees that Socrates is assuring his auditors, as he attempted to at the trial, that although the sophistic state has counted the exemplary non-sophist as sophist precisely because it cannot count a non-sophist (this would recognise the existence of what is not), the non-sophist can never *be* other than what he is. As he says, in the face of the approach of the opposite 'the three will sooner cease to exist or suffer any other fate than submit to become even while it is still three' (Phd. 104bc). Socrates, who participates in truth, retreats or disappears at the approach of sophistry which, inasmuch as it identifies itself with the interests of the state denies the real effect of participation itself.[42] The reverse is also true: at the approach of non-sophistry, established not simply as true but as 'veridical', sophistry is constrained to retreat, to assume its proper place. Socrates is assuring his followers that truth is not destroyed in its retreat from sophistry even though, with his impending death, this may be what appears to take place. Sophistry, rule of opinion, can never be the discourse of truth no matter its ascendency, its strength, its force of numbers, within the body of the state. Rather, in its abeyance truth becomes 'obscure'. To cut this short, the non-sophistic form whose name in the corpus is Socrates awaits the new form of participation. As we have stressed, the Socratic lesson of the *Phaedo* does not concern death but the very possibility of a life lived by truths. The Platonic ethic is that of Badiou: continue! Continue, in the face of the triumph of sophistry to be the immortal that you also are.

The subject body, the Platonic corpus, the place of non-relation

So, what then of our body, the subject body, the Platonic corpus as that which affirms the non-relation between Socrates and Plato but nevertheless forms a generic Two and which we playfully name 'Platocrates' – the name of that which continues? Socrates, for sophistry, is the individual body, so singular that it must be and can be killed. Plato provides this dead Name – a name which marks the taking place of the encounter with sophistry (state and local) and so names as a consequence the set of all that which is not-sophistry – with a body: the Platonic *corpus*. It is a 'thought' body of work, a series of dialogues and a set of enquiries, which supports the immortality of this name. For Badiou, such a body of thought is a set of possibilities. Plato provides the thought of the dead Socrates with a body qua set of possibilities. What the Platonic corpus faithfully makes possible is that the address of that which is not-sophistry be to all and for all. Transformation is the form which transmission takes under the subjective procedure. The 'for all' to which a non-sophistic education is addressed (predicated entirely on the ontological fact that a non-sophistic education is lacking for all) is constituted in the very procedure itself. A step-by-step, connection-by-connection, generic re-collection of parts.

Our argument, finally, is that here in the *Phaedo*, as Socrates takes leave of his friends, the soul of the non-sophist takes leave of the squat, snub-nosed, barefoot Silensus (Smp. 215b). It takes its leave after a life of subtractive discipline, a discipline practised on the basis of the immanent existence of the Idea of that which is 'to come'. Every enquiry, every encounter with that which *appears* as wisdom, justice, courage and so on within the sophistic state body recollects the form of a non-sophistic discipline. Each recollection, against the demands of the body, which every subject feels and experiences, reinforces the desire for truth – a truth indiscernible in appearance precisely because it cannot be discerned by the knowledge and practices of the sophistic state body. In this sense, the indiscernible, as Plato knew it in the *Meno*, is subject to recollection, which is itself the very form of thought which disciplines that (non)state which is 'to come'. The subject works within the situation on the basis of that which is 'to come' subject to that event/deflection which (in)determined the form of the situation in which the subject practises his singular discipline. What is indiscerned, subject to the event, within the situation of this practice is precisely that which is verifiable only in terms of the world 'to come'. Therefore, as it is 'to come' it is, for the sophistic state, for the demanding body, *that which is not*. In the words of the non-philosopher, it is that which is already dead or deserves to die, which is really to say that this world to come, of which Socrates is the sole *marked* instance within the current state, can only be said as what 'will have been'.

The Platonic body, then, is the result of the Socratic practice of purification. It is Socrates' 'other side'. What each dialogue recounts from the encounter with sophistry is the Socratic practice of subtraction. We can only call it Socratic thanks to the Platonic corpus itself. Plato names the practice after the event that is initiated in the event of the break with sophistry induced by Socrates. Socrates is the name for the encounter; the subject-body is the (post-)Socratic practice of being faithful to that encounter. The Platonic corpus embodies the trace of that encounter and supports its practice.[43] 'The entire being of the subject,' Badiou says, 'resides in supporting the realisation of truth' (BE, 397/435). The *Phaedo*, in which Plato makes *his* absence known, is a dialogue that performs for us the movement of the philosophic soul from its Socratic embodiment to its eternal form within the Platonic corpus. The truth of the Socratic encounter with sophistry, who's *Form* is eternal, finds consistent yet finite support in the new subject-body, the Platonic corpus. At the same time, the immanent trajectory of the procedure of philosophic subtraction from the sophistic state at the point of the encounter sees the death of the body of Socrates as the freeing of the grip of the Athenian body. The soul is freed from this grip and makes its way, as Socrates vividly recounts, to the world posited here and now as that which is 'to come'. Plato can now construct a series of dialogues in which the consequences of the displacement can be thought in terms of their coming to be rather than as purely aporetic incitements. Here we can consider Plato's absence at the death a final and primary act of fidelity; for just as Socrates absents himself from the philosophical address, wisdom, as such, speaking through him, so with Plato. The Platonic corpus in which, Plato says, one will never find a word of Plato becomes that through which wisdom speaks, but as with Socrates, it is in the form of a dialogue 'with you', a philosophical praxis marked by a Two (Phd. 58e–59).[44] The *transformation* which is not a *transmigration* will have begun at the turning point of regeneration and 'we should leave nothing undone to attain during life some measure of goodness and wisdom: for the prize is glorious and the hope great' (Phd. 114c).

Conclusion

In the gap between nothing and something, despair and incitement, the 'portmanteau' word 'Platocrates' announces its function. The subjectivity affirmed by the Platonic corpus is that Plato wants to have done with the failure while at the same time acknowledging failure as part of what it means to continue as a subject. As long as Socrates remains within sophistic Athens he can only mark the conceptual point from which all new knowledge begins. That is to say, in Athens, to have no knowledge of sophistry, to not know what it knows – that there is no truth – is to remain vulnerable to its conceit. Socrates has a choice: either leave Athens or force Athens to not know itself. By proceeding in the way he does, Plato will bring to formalisation what Socrates, in the *Apology*, claims as his central virtue, a virtue he opposes to the *homo economicus* of the sophistic state. The virtue Socrates opposes to this is the *consciousness of non-possession*. Non-possession meets no exchange. The Platonic corpus is that which brings form to the Socratic non-place, to the lack that Socrates never tires of insisting is shared, unformed, by all. The Platonic corpus, as an existence 'for all', and for all time, stands as the *living* (thought) body *for* the dead *body* of the living master. In Badiou's terms, the Platonic corpus as subject to the Socratic event (the life not the death) amounts to the next step, which is to say Plato is faithful to (Socratic) fidelity, the educator to 'that which is to come'. After all, as Socrates readily admits, a wise man does not leave a good master (Phd. 62d). The Republic, in our reading, is the world 'to come', the *master* which Socrates commends to his disciples. Is it not that world generated from its opposite and passing through a 'counter-point'? 'We should use such accounts,' Socrates says, 'in order to inspire ourselves with confidence' (Phd. 114d). But as Plato's absence tells us, this world to come must be thought philosophically, which is to say it must be formally constructed faithful to the evental procedure which constitutes the life of philosophy. It is not, then, an after world, a heaven or a myth-ideal that Plato envisages but the living place of a displacement, a place of thought demanding its invention. What the Platonic corpus secures extrinsic to the dialogues, the imperishable of philosophy, the *Republic* is to secure immanently as the 'pure present' (LM, 537).

Notes

1. Nails, *Agora, Academy, and the Conduct of Philosophy*, p. 56. She notes, knowingly, that it is unsurprising that there is near unanimity in analytic circles regarding the chronological order of the dialogues and the accompanying thesis of developmentalism as 'apples do not

fall far from the tree'. See also Alexander Nehamas, *The Virtues of Authenticity*.

2. 'Socrates contra Socrates in Plato' (hereafter SS) and 'Elenchus and mathematics' (hereafter EM), in *Socrates, Ironist and Moral Philosopher*. These two essays form part of a longer and ongoing study in which Vlastos hoped to delimit the philosophy of Socrates.
3. Vlastos makes much of the final passages of the *Crito* where Socrates speaks as the voice of the Law (Cri. 50–54e) speaking to him. The problem is not that Socrates invokes the Law against man's use of it – this is a consistent theme after all, and one useful to the *Republic* let alone *Laws* – the question left begging by Vlastos is the relation between the Law that speaks through Socrates in this passage and democracy. Vlastos simply merges this voice of the Law and democracy such that Socrates obeying the Law equates to his being a good democrat. Elsewhere Vlastos affirms that Athens was 'the most extreme democracy of [Socrates'] world'. (What of Thrace? But one must remember that for the liberal, democracy is a *state form*.) Anyhow, as we of the twenty-first century know, this is not to say 'that much'. See 'The historical Socrates and Athenian democracy', *Socratic Studies*, p. 101. Cf. Badiou (C, 63).
4. We cannot pursue this here but Vlastos, in opting for Socrates as a good democrat, must still insist on a notion of the 'good' which the leader, who knows the good, can disseminate to the people who elect him. Indeed, Vlastos quotes Socrates telling Callicles that if he *improves* the masses he does 'good'. In this, Socrates is said to be subversive (Grg. 515a). This, for Vlastos, accounts for the charges against Socrates who was wronged by men and not by law (Crt. 54c). However, the question of the good remains. And the good no matter how it is construed is a matter of Form, an aspect of the corpus which Vlastos assigns to the anti-Socratic dialogues.
5. Nails, *Agora, Academy, and the Conduct of Philosophy*, p. 160.
6. Vlastos says that this division of the dialogues broadly conforms to that decided by stylistic analysis, except that he claims to have reached his division in terms of an analytic of method: the greater or lesser, better or worse use of the elenchus. Interestingly, he claims there is near consensus in this century and the last in terms of dialogue order. Not everyone shares this consensus on the consensus. John M. Cooper, for one, points out the reliance on interpretive method for these orders and remarks that that while there is near conformity ('unfortunate' he says) in referring to early, middle and late dialogues there is no unanimity in the determinations of what goes where (see Editor's 'Introduction' to *Plato: The Complete Works*, p. xii). Deborah Nails devotes Chapter 7 of her work to a study of Holger Thesleff's 'attack' on developmentalism. Nails says that one of the best arguments against the thesis of

developmentalism is Thesleff's discovery of the 132 dialogue sequences. Essentially, when 'the same dialogues are examined for the evolution of Plato's thought on different topics, different sequences are derived'. Further, it is possible that 'opposite sequences can be derived for the same dialogues on the same topic' (Nails, *Agora, Academy, and the Conduct of Philosophy*, p. 128).

7. In abbreviated form, with early dialogue characteristic presented first and Platonic dialogue features second: T1, moral philosopher/whole philosophical encyclopaedia is his domain; T2, no *theory* of forms but (axiomatic conviction)/grandiose metaphysical theory of separately existing forms, separable soul, learns by recollection; T3, elenctic method, disavowal of knowledge/seeks demonstrative knowledge, confident he finds it; T4, has no model of soul/has complex tripartite model of souls; T5, no mastery of mathematics and no expressed interest/mastery of mathematical science; T6, concept of philosophy populist/elitist; T7, prefers Athenian constitution/elaborate theory of political formation which place democracy low on rank; T8, conception of Eros without metaphysics/love is thought through Forms; T9, piety is deist (in essence) realised in action/communion with Forms, mystical, realised in contemplation; T10, method is elenctic, refutation of interlocutor's proposals/didactic, critical of earlier forms, maieutic.
8. This irreconcilability pertains equally to method. Taking his lead from Aristotle, Vlastos divides elenchus – what Aristotle calls *peirastic* and defines as 'a thesis is refuted when, and only when, its negation is derived', to which Vlastos adds, 'from one's own beliefs' – from *dialectic* and from *demonstration*. The latter, Vlastos contends, is best understood as coming from the 'axiomatised science of geometry'. Vlastos happily uses 'debate' as a synonym when talking of the elenctic method despite the crucial distinction made by Plato's Socrates between debaters and dialecticians. The latter debate yes, but subject to the decided 'existence' of truth; the former, for victory regardless of truth. This is simply what Plato wants to ensure remains inscribed in the future history of 'philosophy'. (Gregory Vlastos, 'Elenchus and mathematics', in *Socrates, Ironist and Moral Philosopher*, p. 12.) Richard McKim makes the point that too often the analytic tradition interprets the dialogues under the assumption that Plato was doing philosophy as they do it. He says, 'we are to rest assured that, had [Plato] not been born too soon to enjoy the blessings of Aristotelian and modern symbolic logic, he would have done much better' (McKim, 'Shame and truth in *Plato's Gorgias*', p. 34).
9. Vlastos, 'Epilogue', in *Socrates: Ironist and Moral Philosopher*, p. 235. One always despairs of the type of philosophy that makes true Marx's grand statement in Thesis 11. Cf. Badiou (TC, 93).
10. J. A. Miller, 'Philosophy <> psychoanalysis'.

11. Sylvain Lazarus, 'A propos de la politique et la terreur'.
12. Vlastos, 'The evidence of Aristotle and Xenophon', in *Socrates, Ironist and Moral Philosopher*, p. 80.
13. The obvious irony here, to use one of Vlastos' favourite designations, is that this Socrates has a knowledge which he withholds from his interlocutors. He knows what they are and he uses this knowledge against them. If one is deemed to be committed to the consensus then Socrates proceeds on that basis; if one is not, like Protagoras, then he proceeds on the basis of that knowledge. The very brush Vlastos hopes to tar Plato with, his own Socrates seems to deploy.
14. Vlastos, 'Socratic irony,' pp. 21–44, esp. pp. 23–4. Cf. Samuel Scolnicov, *Plato's Metaphysics of Education*, p. 50, where Scolnicov suggests that irony as a pedagogical device works only on the few. Kierkegaard, consistent – in a very particular sense – with Scolnicov, claims that 'irony is the very incitement of subjectivity' (Søren Kierkegaard, *The Concept of Irony: With Constant Reference to Socrates*, pp. 211–12).
15. G. W. F. Hegel, *Lectures on the History of Philosophy: Plato and the Platonists*, Vol. 2, p. 54. Hegel refers to this point in Plato where, he says, 'many turn away'. It is the point where the beautiful introductory sophistries give way to rigorous dialectics.
16. Such a ruler is akin to the position of *metaxu* – the position of both mathematics and love in the dialogues. One wonders if Aristotle's preference for the 'middle class' is not pre-empted here.
17. Cornford's translation. Grube/Reeve call them 'prisoners' or 'the uneducated'.
18. Cf. Phd. (64b). As Lacan says, 'man accommodates himself to non-truth perfectly well' (SEM III, 214). Is this what Vlastos endorses, finally, in his anti-Platonism? Are Socrates' gentlemen's agreements with rich Athenians enough to transform humanity?
19. Cf. Vlastos: 'What the passage [above R. 521c–523a which Vlastos has chopped] purports to disclose is how this soul-transforming change can come about – how creatures of time and sensuality may be liberated from the empire of the senses, translated into another form of life in which love for timeless truth will dwarf all other desires and ambitions' (EM, 109). The sarcasm, again, *not* irony, is obvious. Yet he never explains how ten years of study of mathematics *would not* change one's thinking. Obviously, the sensual creature will out for Vlastos.
20. Socrates doesn't blame the youth, however.
21. Nails, *Agora, Academy, and the Conduct of Philosophy*, p. 128.
22. The footnote Vlastos inserts to explain his conception of the axiom is interesting. He says he uses it to mean 'indemonstrables of a deductive system, be they definitions, postulates, or "common assumptions" (as the last are called in Euclid)' (EM, 112, fn. 26). Indeed, it is difficult to

see why Socrates' own method can't be said to be axiomatic, at least when Vlastos insists that each conversation start in the same way under the same conditions. Is this form itself not a postulate from which all can begin? Does not the conversation terminate when this condition is breached? Cf. Nails, *Agora, Academy, and the Conduct of Philosophy*, p. 224: '[I]n Plato, as in science, no first principle or theory is ever really free from the exchange of the phenomena, exempt from further probing.' And further, Plato was 'all along examining the assumptions as well as the implications of what we with marvellous hindsight and in the footsteps of Aristotle, identify as the theory of Forms.' She goes on to say that it matters not when the dialogues were written; what is of philosophical importance is that Plato contests and criticises his own theory over and over again (p. 225).

23. Vlastos does recognise the direct link between Thrasymachus and Thucydides' *Melian Dialogue* in 'Socrates contra Socrates' (p. 52). Perhaps rhetoric will out.
24. See EM (46–7 and fn. 2). This is not merely a Vlastosian idiosyncrasy. The books are sometime separated into periods but not always in *this* way, that is part in the period of the early dialogues and part in the middle. One would not accuse a scholar of Vlastos' ability of being disingenuous.
25. This is an interesting choice of terminology by Vlastos, for it is in the *Phaedo* that we see Plato express the very reverse sentiment. The soul is 'saturated with the body' when it by itself does not free itself from the latter's determinations by way of reason (Phd. 83d). Cf. CM (77).
26. As Jacques Rancière insists, it is the 'explicator pedagogues' who need that their pupils *not know*: 'Before being the act of a pedagogue explication is the myth of pedagogy, the parable of a world divided into knowing minds and ignorant ones, ripe minds and immature ones, the capable and the incapable, the intelligent and the stupid' (see *The Ignorant Schoolmaster: Five Lessons in Intellectual Emancipation*, pp. 5–6). Miles Burnyeat sees no problem with the concordance of mathematics and ethical thought. He claims that 'the content of mathematics is the constitutive part of ethical understanding', this because 'the goal of any mathematical understanding is knowledge of the Good.' If 'knowledge is virtue' is a central Socratic maxim (as Vlastos repeatedly insists) and mathematics may provide the best means for such 'knowledge', then Plato is 'in virtue' (Burnyeat, quoted in Michael J. White, 'Plato and mathematics', p. 235).
27. We should mention Vlastos' essay 'The paradox of Socrates' in *The Philosophy of Socrates*, wherein he makes space to elaborate some objections to the (historical) Socrates. His essential claims are three. The first is a sort of 'damning by faint praise' in that he claims that even if one does not agree with Socrates one must at least acknowledge his

consistency. Consistency is regarded as a secondary effect. His second objection is that Socrates cared nothing for facts, that, in fact, this lack of empiricism was due to his 'deductive' method. These two accusations, if I can put it this way, are consistent with Vlastos' displeasure with Plato's 'mathematical turn', yet here he is talking of the historical Socrates. Does Vlastos see here in the historical Socrates the seeds of his own undoing? Thirdly, Vlastos ascribes Socrates' 'failure' to a 'failure of love'. But it quickly becomes plain that Vlastos is conceiving love in terms of (a non-Greek) pathos. He praises Jesus' weeping for Jerusalem and in contrast he condemns Socrates in Nietzschean terms for his 'despotic logic'. The pattern in Vlastos' singular objection to the historical Socrates can be clearly seen: consistency, deduction and logic, thus *mathematics*. Vlastos is simply an anti-Platonist (see pp. 15–17).

28. Havelock, *Preface to Plato*, p. 234.
29. Aristotle, *Rhetoric*, 1398^b 30, *The Complete Works of Aristotle*, p. 2229.
30. In his 'The evidence of Aristotle and Xenophon', Vlastos gathers evidence from Xenophon, Aristotle and Plato himself (thus he is already *not* Socrates) to present his case of the division between Plato and Socrates. Whether Vlastos is employing historical evidence to divide the philosophy or philosophical evidence to affirm the history, we don't know. The former, in Kant's terms, would have Vlastos preferring the catechism over dialectic (Immanuel Kant, *Education*, pp. 81–2).
31. In *The Logic of Sense* Deleuze discusses the 'portmanteau word'. In Deleuze's terms this portmanteau word is the law of disjunction. It marks the introduction of disjunction or the ramification of divergence into a *series*.
32. Samuel Scolnicov, *Plato's Metaphysics of Education*, p. 50.
33. 'Let no one ignorant of geometry enter here'. Cf. R. (527c). In discussing the necessity of geometry, *the* 'knowledge of what always is', Socrates says that in terms of understanding 'there is a world of difference between someone who has grasped geometry and someone who hasn't'. Clearly, for Plato, to enter into the Academy is to enter into the infinite (to which Plato is surely gesturing here) composition of an 'other' world. In referring to Plato among others on this very point Badiou says, 'it still remains the case that the cold radicality of mathematics is the necessary exercise through which is forged a thinking subject adequate to the transformation he will be forced to undergo' (TW, 14), and further, 'as far as we are concerned, mathematics is always more or less equivalent to the bulldozer with which we remove the rubble that prevents us from constructing new edifices in the open air' (TW, 17). It is one of those anomalies of history that today the Academy is the safe harbour of a myriad of sophistries where the absolute last thing desired is an 'other world'. The Academy, at the absolute service of capital's

power, demands absolute subservience to what is – this *pensée unique*. The Academy today teaches exactly what the sophists of Plato's time did: how to make one's way in the world so that the world remains exactly as it is. One distinction is important. Whereas Protagoras could claim that he was a sophist, today, the Academy pushes its sophistry, without any hint of irony, under Plato's guise. Its *rhetoric* is 'of truth' while its *practice* is the determined denial of its very conditions of possibility. 'But since he imitates the wise man he'll obviously have a name derived from the wise man's name' (Sph. 268c).

34. In general analytic readings of the *Phaedo* they divide the arguments therein into four types: (a) the Cyclical argument deals with the generation of opposites – particular and general – sleep/awake, hot/cold, pleasure/pain, life/death; (b) the Recollection argument; (c) the Affinity argument, which addresses resemblance between the soul and categories such as the invisible, the unchanging, etc., as opposed to the visible, the mutable, etc.; (d) the Final argument, in which Plato considers cause and attributes it to the Forms. See, for example, David Bostock, 'The soul and immortality in the Phaedo', pp. 404–24.
35. Socrates is careful to mark off subtractive practice from any form of savings wherein one forgoes one thing to gain something else. In this sense, one is brave in battle because one fears retribution if one runs away. He regards this type of temperance as self-indulgence and he characterises it as a form of exchange. 'A system of morality based on relative emotional values [which is to say interest] is a mere illusion, a thoroughly vulgar conception' (Phd. 69bc). This suggests that Socrates is not an ascetic.
36. Again, there is an analytic distinction between these two – *imperishable* and *immortal*. But that the soul passes through both or participates in both unlike anything else in fact 'synthesises their disjunction'.
37. Badiou, 'Of an obscure disaster', p. 60.
38. Socrates is always careful to say things like 'as much as is possible' in this context.
39. Cf. Phd. (70c): 'I hardly think that anyone now – even a comic poet – would say that I am wasting my time and discoursing on subjects which don't concern me.'
40. This is Hugh Tredennick's translation. Cf. *Laws*, at 893e. The generation of all things occurs 'when a starting point *receives increase* and reaches the second stage, and from that the third, and so by three stages acquires perceptibility for percipients.'
41. It is the thought of the impasse inherent to ontology itself that forces the 'pass' of the subject – so Badiou contends.
42. In this sense, we can see that Socrates' claim that the good man must stay out of politics in the sophistic state is a genuinely subversive and not evasive act. Cf. Badiou: 'It is better to do nothing than to work

formally toward making visible what the West declares to exist' (P, 148).

43. The notion of the *trace* can be read at the beginning of the dialogue. The reason for the delay in Socrates' execution is that Athens every year sends a ship to Delos to commemorate Theseus saving the life of seven youths and seven maidens from the Minotaur. Theseus achieves this by following Ariadne's 'golden thread'. We have certainly argued that as the name of the event Socrates insists as the orienting trace of the subjective procedure. Here Plato gives us a clue that Socrates is laying down his own golden (or red) thread for others to take up (Phd. 58b).
44. Phaedo tells Echecrates that Socrates and his followers were engaged in a 'philosophical conversation' in the prison cell. Coupled with Plato's stated absence the inference we can draw is: (a) that this is not a historical recording of Socrates' actual last words and in this respect (among others) it is entirely consistent with the dialogues as a whole; (b) that all the dialogues are to be understood as being written down subject to the Socratic prescription for philosophical enquiry. It is Socrates 'to the letter' which Plato inscribes in the dialogue form and not 'biography'.

CHAPTER 6

Generic

> 'If, in the situation, there is such a relation between some conditions and the statement $\lambda(\mu_1)$, then the belonging of these conditions to the part ♀ implies, in the corresponding generic extension, the veracity of $\lambda(R_{♀}(\mu_1))$.' (BE, 411/450)

> 'The ultimate effect of an evental caesura, and of an intervention from which the introduction into circulation of a supernumerary name proceeds, would thus be that the truth of a situation, with this caesura as its principle, *forces the situation to accommodate it*: to extend itself to the point at which this truth – primitively no more than a part, a representation – attains belonging, thereby becoming a presentation.' (BE, 342/378)

THE SUBTLE DIALECTIC

A recurring theme of Plato scholarship is the relation between the *Republic* and the rest of the dialogues. There is a consensus that recognises the *Republic* to be the dialogue wherein Plato, in new ways, synthesises and restates his central ideas. This is another way of saying the *Republic* collects these ideas in a new form. Ferrari, commenting on the 'history' of such a consensus, notes, and I summarise, the *Republic* may not always be considered the most technically proficient or even the most philosophical of the dialogues and it may not be the most beautifully written: there may be disagreement over whether it's a political or moral work (however spurious this distinction may sometimes be), but in general there is agreement with Schleiermacher's remarks in the nineteenth century and subsequently Kahn[1] that the *Republic* is the culminating text that the many shorter works *anticipate*.[2]

Ferrari's comments expose a subtle dialectic, one that invites us to take a step beyond this consensus. The shorter, 'earlier' works anticipate the culminating text, but this anticipation is only visible once the longer work exists. In this sense the *Republic* exposes within the shorter texts something that was already there, so to speak, but would not be fully realised without the *Republic* to expose it. What is there in the early texts is not merely so 'in anticipation', but is that which the very ascription of anticipation is predicated upon. We would therefore posit that what is thought in the so-called early dialogues is the thought of the Republic. This dialectic, whose movement is immanent rather than applied let's say, is demonstrable whether we examine an individual text, say the *Apology* in relation to the *Republic*, as we have, or examine the 'shorter works' collectively.

Throughout these dialogues Socrates is effectively singular. He is the only *non*-sophist and as such inexists to the education of the state. In the *Republic* the Republic is thought into existence as a *non*-sophistic city and, as such, is unlike any other. It is almost impossible not to see the Republic as the conceptual result of all Socrates' work while at the same time we see that such a result animates the thought of this very work. Recall that in the *Cratylus*, Plato demands this double movement when Socrates says, 'we have to turn back frequently to what we've already said, in order to test it by looking at it backwards and forwards simultaneously *as the aforementioned poet put it* [Homer]' (Crt. 428d, emphasis added). In the *Republic* Socrates, from within this poetic encyclopaedia, will look forward to the just city in order to look back and discern what its just citizen must look like. In Plato's hands this movement has the spatial temporality of an equation. Regardless of the variables, they share the same Form.

Samuel Scolnicov illustrates this atemporal reciprocity with reference to Plato's understanding of 'participation'. Given that truths are exposed subjectively and remain unknown to the situation in which they originate the comparison is fitting. He says, '. . . that the *participating* and the *participated in* [emphasis added] are not, in the last analysis, essentially different from each other, but are basically the same entity *in two different modes of being*'.[3] If, therefore, we can identify a subjective or participatory procedure, then this procedure, in some way, is already that which it *participates in*. Conversely, what is *participated in*, in some way, is already a part of the *participating* procedure. The subject is one mode of this being 'true', while the 'result' let's call it, that which is *participated in*, is another mode of this same being-true. Formulaically, we have two modes and a single form.

Intriguingly, Scolnicov's analysis turns around the question of knowledge. He argues that there are three conditions for (the) knowledge (of Forms) in Plato: 'the Form must be (condition i) *for someone*, (condition ii) *in itself*, and (condition iii) *in relation to others*'. He concludes, 'Plato does not distinguish, so far as the Forms are concerned, between the presuppositions of condition (ii) and condition (iii)'. Ultimately, for Scolnicov, Plato denies both the Parmenidean ontology, in which there is no room for true discursive knowledge [and] a total Heraclitean-Protagorean relativism and subjectivism' which has 'no concept of truth'.[4] It is worth recalling that in the *Sophist*, Plato determines that as variable as they are – and despite, for example, Heraclitus's dislike of Homer – Homer, Hesiod, Heraclitus, Protagoras and Parmenides all participate in the same Form. As such, *they* – this 'many headed sophist' – *are* this Form (Sph. 240c). Significantly, Protagoras announces to Socrates and Hippocrates, with his eye fixed, Plato notes, on the company of sophists gathered at Callias' house, that he teaches only what the student comes for: 'sound deliberation, both in domestic matters – how to best manage one's household, and in public affairs – how to realise one's maximum potential for success in political debate' (Prt. 318e–319a). As the *Phaedo* illustrates, the analogy is clear: sophistry is the Form of the state while that which the state is not is the Form of non-sophistry. The subterfuge that subtends this dialogue between Socrates and Protagoras, as it subtends the corpus entirely, is that the Republic is already at work within the Athenian state (HB, 1).

In the *Republic* Socrates concludes one part of his enquiry (or starts another – it is the same thing in Plato who only 'concludes' so as to go on)[5] by asserting, '. . . then a just man shall not be any different from the just city with respect to the form itself of justice . . .' (R. 435a). Plato's method, as this indicates, is to hypothesis the just city to be able to identify the figure best suited to it. He moves from the 'fiction' of the result, insofar as this result does not exist other than in the discourse they are fashioning and so, conceptually, to the truth that founds it. The former is or will be, if we suppose such a just city to 'exist', the knowledge of the latter. In our terms this 'latter' has been that which the Socratic subject reveals to the Athenian situation of its 'unknown' event. In light of Scolnicov's points above, the indistinction of the *participating* and that which is *participated in*, this quote provides something of the key to this final chapter, for it seems to us that it is on the basis of the thought of the ideal city that Plato is able to show that the just man *has existed* in Athens. By thinking through the Republic Plato forces the recognition of this truth.

THE REPUBLIC IS THE WORK OF LOVE

We do not need to argue that Plato's 'just man' is Socrates, and we do not need to argue that Plato's Republic, the 'city in discourse', thought-through and declared to be 'the only city worthy of the name', is the just city. What we do need to account for is what makes 'Socrates' the name for that which *participates*, and the 'Republic' the name for that which is *participated in*, the same. This is to say that Socrates and the Republic name 'the same entity *in two different modes of being*': they are, if you like, the truth of Athens: Socrates is, for us, the only one in all Athens who educates and the Republic is the city where this education is the education of all. The course of our analysis will necessarily show that the Republic (of the *Republic*) to which Socrates qua participant *belongs* is therefore (a) *for someone*; (b) *in itself*; (c) *in relation to others*. In fact, more reductively, and in line with Scolnicov's claim, we would say that 'in itself' under the Form of justice it is 'for all'. Socrates, *knowing nothing* (of what this state knows), *not teaching* and *not being paid*, gives what he has freely and to all. In the guise of the subjective figure of the 'subjective complex' immanent to the corpus, Socrates 'works for *nothing*'.

Given that the event/encounter establishes the exceptional nature of his work, Socrates can only work for the impossibility of a sophistic education. This is nothing to sophistry. Under the rules of Plato's subtle dialectic to 'work for nothing', which *is* the work of love, is in fact to work for that which *is* everything. In the city of the Republic therefore *all* work to make the lack of a non-sophistic education *unknown*. That is to say, everyone, 'doing the work best suited to them', *despite* what work they do, does 'Socratic work'. Or again, to put it in the terms of Plato's doctrine of fair shares, that 'friends have all things in common' is articulated through the work of love. This 'egalitarian statement', whose name is 'justice', cuts through the statist or empiricist framework that Socrates gives to his ideal city.[6]

THE LOVE OF FORM

This framework is Plato's much criticised division of the ideal state into immutable classes with a fixed division of labour. Given that our emphasis is on the affirmative force of a Platonic education, we have little room here for a thorough critique of these criticisms.[7] Nevertheless, in terms of our ethic of 'working through' a short excursus is in order especially as it allows us sketch the trajectory inherent to the generic – between the local and the universal. It is interesting to note that it is not necessarily the division itself that is most often criticised; after all, this could hardly offend the sensibilities of the liberal-democrat, that most common of objectors, whose *raison d'être* is the presumption of meritocracy. What is most criticised is the declaration that *confines* one to the work prescribed for one's particular class: that each inhabitant of the ideal city stick to and pursue the work best suited to them. We should note in passing that the citizens of the Republic are not born into this confinement but throughout the years of their youth they are tested as to their *apparent* suitability to this is or that type of work. The Olympic standards of Gold, Silver and Bronze attributed to mark this typology of labour are results, eminently revisable, and not matters of heredity. This is clearly an argument of Form. For Plato, the irrefutable argument for the justice of this typology boils down to saying that this work, whatever the work is, is what we are calling the 'work of love'. In essence, if one does work *not their own*, work they are *demonstrably* unsuited to, they show that they do not do the work of love. Despite what they might profess, they work in support of *other* interests. Of course, this is the essence of Plato's refutation of the sophist: they, by demonstration, are not lovers of wisdom because at every turn they betray their infidelity to its proper Form.[8] The consequences of this refutation are extensive insofar as this is what the *Republic* will be: a city that realises as itself the very consequences of this refutation. We would claim that what is common to all in this 'stratified' Republic – stratified in the sense that there is a variety of work as there is a variety of workers, but only one ideal-form of this work, as such – is that by keeping to *one's own work* one participates in the exemplary practice of non-sophistry. This is the collective production of justice, of that which *is* for all and, as such, is the *work* of love.

For our liberal critic (Vlastos, Rorty, for example), the work of love apparently infringes on the rights of the liberal-democrat, the good 'Athenian' citizen, – so well defined by Anytus, friend of the Athenian bourgeoisie (Ap. 24a), those exemplary educators to all Athens and beyond (Men. 92e) – to pronounce on anything at all from the sophisticated vantage of their particular expertise, whatever it may be. After all, one's right to promotion is at stake. In this, as we have noted, our liberal, despite being a self-professed 'Socratic', sides with the sophistic democracy. Plato was well aware of this 'debater's ruse' and, as we have shown, the conceit it hides is the target of all Socratic enquiries. What is truly at stake in such objections –

sometimes admitted, sometimes not – is the very existence of the Ideal city and of truth itself. What irks the debater in Plato is that reason alone demands that one must decide for the truth of such a place. *The risk of reason is the lack of consensus*. This is a price too high for some and so truth itself is accused of being unreasonable – just like it was for Protagoras's monkey (Tht. 161c). Quite simply, if one does not *decide* for truth, which is far from *knowing* the truth, one remains safely, comfortably and shamelessly a sophist.

There is another objection to the division of classes: that which demands that the concept of class ceases to exist, at least insofar as it has a determining character for those who inhabit the state. One of the things we hope to have shown (and in this chapter reiterate) is that Plato's axiomatic conception of justice, which amounts to nothing more than prescribing 'case by case, situation by situation the *impossibility of non-egalitarian statements*' (M, 112) subordinates this empirical division to a fundamental equality. Plato's entire effort is to preclude as determinative the lack of non-sophistry. As we have seen, this is not a matter of knowledge – representative stratification – but of truth – indifferent to stratifications. What is common or generic to all in the Republic, manifest in the distributive lack of privilege, is, as we said, that everyone works *for* nothing. 'The generic is *egalitarian*, and every subject, ultimately, is ordained to equality' (BE, 408–9/ 447). Unlike other states, the Republic is not a 'state' but the subjective exposure of its lack. It is not founded on the 'prohibition on un-binding' but is instead a labour of love, supplement to the lack of *rapport*.[9] The Republic is realised as a counter-state: or, as we say, an 'ideal non-state'.

Plato's equation: the addition of the generic and the ideal name

In order to grasp this conception of the Republic as an ideal non-state or even 'counter-state', Plato's 'city in words' will be understood to be the *generic extension* of the Athenian situation. It is the 'generic' *truth* of Athens – a truth pursued relentlessly by those rare figures that enter into the practice of non-sophistry – *added* to Athens itself. In other words, the Republic (and the *Republic*) provides the gathering place of all that is expressible in the contention of a 'post-Socratic' education by truths. This can be expressed as 'what *constitutes* the Republic *is* an education by truths' and what the Republic verifies precisely is that such an education *will have* existed in the

Athens of the dialogues. The circularity of this definition is interrupted when we realise that in Athens the sign of this education was not the Republic, the site of verification, but Socrates, the site of its (existing) inexistence, and that in the *Republic* the Republic presents as itself all the matter that this sign signifies. In other words, the Republic includes Socrates just as Socrates includes all that is non-sophistic in Athens.

All the difficulties of this chapter are exposed in this concept of 'addition': an addition that for Plato is constituted by the most minimal of differences possible (R. 473b). As such, a good part of our argument is concerned with the *thought-idea* of the Republic rather than the dialogue itself. What we mean is that by examining the Republic under condition of Badiou's concept of the generic, a concept as fundamental to his project as is the Republic to Plato's, we see, as we have already suggested, that the Republic is always already present in the dialogues. Once we establish the full extent of what Socrates names we will see that Plato's equation is rather simple: Athens plus Socrates equals the Republic. The whole difficulty of this equation, which is intuitively straightforward for anyone familiar with the dialogues, is that Socrates, the gadfly of Athens, the figure who will not leave the confines of the city, does not in effect *belong* to Athens but to the Republic alone, a city which exists nowhere and is as such nothing. Yet, as Plato notes, the city is not-impossible and for the subject, worth working for. The question is, 'by what "ontological argument" shall we pass from the concept to existence?' (BE, 372/409).

THE ANALYTIC OF THE GENERIC

In terms of tracing this change – from the *concept* of a non-sophistic education to the *existence* of an education by truths – within the context of Badiou's categories we can reduce the task to this succinct equation: 'what is forced in the situation is veridical in the generic extension'. This equation prescribes a general set of tasks: first, three general definitions concerning the generic – the generic set, forcing and the generic extension.

The analytic of the generic, with which Badiou concludes *Being and Event*, even though its *procedure* as such has constituted the entire Meditation which is *Being and Event*, is, as Barker, Hallward and Feltham all note, the most complex of what is already a difficult work of philosophy.[10] Our aim in providing the general definition is twofold. We want to identify the crucial moment of this transformation, whose subtle dialectic we have sketched above, *and* (the second aspect to the general task) within this moment we will identify or in fact re-identify several component parts: conditions, statements and names. The latter are critical insofar as we have to demonstrate the force of the generic within the Platonic corpus. We have to render these Badiouean abstractions *real* and so, to quote Desanti, 'let us agree to leave the technicalities aside, not least because Badiou's book is entirely self-sufficient in this regard' (TA, 63).

We have already given innumerable indications concerning the names which pertain to the generic even before we have given their proper articulation. Within a philosophy conditioned by the 'thought of the generic' such retroactive analysis is unavoidable. We have said that the 'generic set' or 'that which is indiscernible to the Athenian state of the situation' is made up of everything that in some aspect of its being escapes sophistic determination. We have said that the 'generic extension' is what Socrates refers to in the *Phaedo* as the 'world to come' and what Plato formalises as the Republic of the *Republic.* This extension has been visibly anticipated throughout the dialogues insofar as it is the thought of such a world that animates Socratic enquiry. As argued, Plato begins the *Republic* with an explicit and post-Parmenidean illustration of the arrival of this new idea into the non-ideal city. Socrates' encounter with the 'genealogy of sophistry', oligarch, timocrat and tyrant, whose very gathering in a single place indicates that we are within a democracy – a constitution in which all constitutions flourish 'equally' – initiates the '*forcing* in discourse' of this idea into this very city. Forcing therefore indicates, as Badiou says, the 'law of the subject'. The 'subject' works in the here and now *as if* the world to come was here and now. That is to say, his work is conditioned on the one hand by the event at its site and on the other by the world to come, the animating idea (of justice in this case), which, as fidelity to the event at its site demonstrates, is in fact here and now. The difficulty which forcing indicates is that it is only with regard to the world to come that justice, what *is* here and now, will be known to have been true. In terms of knowledge, the truth of Athens is therefore suspended in the future anterior. In other words the subject is an 'immanent' forcing of the truth of Athens – that it knows nothing of the lack of a non-sophistic education – such that in the ideal city nothing will be known of the lack of a non-sophistic education. If this is indeed veridical in the Republic, our generic extension, then it will have been true in Athens. The subject therefore forces – or is the force of – that equation. In a real and effective sense the event returns, via the force of the subject, *to the situation* in the form of the generic extension. This is the importance of the Republic for the Platonic corpus and for the education by truths of which it is the foundational expression.

The generic set

We have encountered the generic set under these terms: it is the set of all those connected for a fidelity to the name of the event. This is the set indicated by the subject as the matter of its enquiries. It is worthwhile completing this definition. The generic set is simply the truth of the situation. It is conceived as 'set' because like any element of a situation it is a multiple. Unlike any other element, however, the multiple of truth cannot be discerned by the knowledge of the situation. Ontologically speaking then a truth *exists* in a situation but as *nothing* of this truth can be known 'it retains nothing expressible of the situation' (BE, xiii), its existence as such can only be conceived as an exception to this situation. This is to say, that as no 'state' predicate can circumscribe this set, no property of the encyclopaedia can discern its constitution, this truth qua multiple is a 'generic' or 'indiscernible' set (BE, 327/361). This set, therefore, concerns every inhabitant of the situation insofar as it is made up of 'a little bit of everything' (BE, 371/407). It is 'inclusive – given any property, some [but not all] of its elements possess it – and yet indiscernible – no property serves to classify the whole'.[11] In Badiou's words this set 'detains in its multiple-being all the common traits of the collective in question: in this sense, it is the truth of the collective's being' (BE, 17/23–4). The generic set is a set of those parts of the situation that have no part in the state. The generic set does not therefore belong to the situation but is a part of it. In this sense it is excrescent, excrescent *with* the situation's being. We hesitate to put it this way but as the state is itself excrescent in regard to its situation the generic set is *like a state* within the state. The generic set is something like the local articulation of the universal prescription of itself. Badiou often cites the *Internationale* in just this context. What makes this more than a slogan is that the movement it prescribes has ontological support. The being of the statement from 'almost nothing' to 'almost everything' is *consistent*. For Badiou, the mathematical concept of the generic provides the ontological consistency to the real – or true – process of structural change. However, given that the generic set is pregnant – to use the midwife metaphor – with the truth and not a wind-egg, and given that the state knows nothing of truth, this counter-state delivered by the *subject* (those who enquire) will be '*unlike* any other state', as Socrates notes: so much so that the very *constitution* of the state is at stake. If we take a step back we can recall that the generic is the formal articulation of the event. That is to say, the concept of the generic set is, ontologically speaking, what an event is for a 'historical situation'. The event, as we have seen, is made up of all the elements of its site – and these are not presented in this situation – and itself. It is the set of itself so to speak given that no property of the current state of the situation can properly represent it within its regime of ordered parts. This is what it means to be generic: that *new sets* may be engendered on the basis of this 'set of conditions' (TA, 65).

Extrapolating from Cohen, Badiou argues that as such a 'set' is indiscernible by reference to the current knowledge of its state, its existence is undecidable. As we have seen in relation to the event, it must be decided and as a consequence its indiscernibility must (come to) be affirmed. If the event is decided its multiple is too, insofar as it is conceived. Through enquiry the subject practises this affirmation. Enquiry by enquiry it 'fills' the generic set with 'indiscernible elements'. These elements are tested for their connection to the event, which is to say for their active capacity to lack a sophistic education. It all comes down to *association*, for it is not so much that individual elements of the generic set cannot be discerned by a property of the sophistic state – every inhabitant of Athens is somehow touched by sophistry let's say – it is rather that *recollected* as such, gathered into a set of itself, its existence is determined only by the fact that it is made up of elements *connected to the event* – associated with Socrates, in other words. To be connected to the event means nothing to the sophistic state. Such a set of elements is nothing. The event is not an element of the state and as such engenders that which to the state is not. It is for *this* nothing, for the *love* of this nothing, that our subject works. Badiou argues that this set, despite it being with-out knowledge, by this very capacity offers information to the subject. Having decided that such a set exists, this very decision tells the subject something. It tells the subject that there is the set of that which is not the state. The subject certainly knows the state. Our subject knows that the state is sophistic. Recall Socrates in the *Phaedo*, 'the wise and disciplined soul follows its guide *and* is not ignorant of its surroundings' (Phd. 108a, emphasis added). It is a matter, then, on the basis of this decision in regard to a non-sophistic (non-constructible) set of establishing non-sophistry, the truth of Athens as conceived, as knowledge. A fundamental condition of this generic set therefore is that it doesn't know sophistry. This is its 'concept'.

In line with Badiou's adaptation of Cohen, we can say that the generic set yields this conditional information about itself: that whatever it is, it is the affirmative reversal of sophistry. This is to say that the subject can think or conceive of this *operative* reversal, while the reversal itself must be established. It is this condition which forces a statement of the situation. It is in the generic extension, the established *place* of the displacement of sophistry, that the truth of this statement will be verified. We should note, however, that the Republic is no *synthesis* as such. The animating logic is rather that which Badiou identifies in his interpretation of Saint Paul: it is the logic of the 'immanent-exception-to' or of 'not . . . but'. For Badiou, the act of saying *No* is fundamental in the face of a sophistic state of the situation.

However, this *No* to what has been, is constituted entirely by a *Yes* to that which, to the state, is not. Saint Paul's initial interventional gesture of *No* is immediately supplemented by a conditional, *But*, Badiou says (SP, 63). Paul says *No* to the persistence of what has been. But what has supplemented his saying *No* is the event – the resurrection. This *No* effectively appears *within* Paul's decision to declare *for* this event. He does so on the basis of the new, so far entirely fictional situation to come. Between the declaration and the 'world to come' as Paul well attests, is the time of the event, the new present. He says *No* to persevering in this state wherein the resurrection is nothing and *Yes* to that which is (will have been) the situation in which this inexistence finds its proper presentation. In saying *Yes* to what will have been the truth of the situation Paul refuses both poles of the sophistic discourse – its teachings of worldly wisdom, of interest in the state of the situation on the one hand and the equally sophistic gesture of the cynic. The event, to which Paul decides to subject himself, provides the world to come with the possibility of an 'other' education. One consequence of this orientation is that the Republic, as the world to come, is not a closed set. It is not the end of an education by truths but its sole point of beginning. We will return to this.

The function of the generic extension

Let's leave forcing aside for the minute and skip to the generic extension. In terms of an equation we have already noted that the generic extension is the original situation *plus* the generic set. Or the original situation with the truth of this situation added to it. Or the Republic is Athens with Socrates added to it. Immediately we know that this last addition is the reverse of the sophistic achievement. What we will do here is describe its function.

We have already noted that the dialogues, as a series of enquiries, anticipate the ideal city in which sophistry is assigned its proper place. There are many statements to this effect. In the *Apology* Socrates agrees with his accusers that he is a stranger to the language of the present state. He cannot take part in its politics. In the *Gorgias* his argument with Callicles over the proper conception of justice provokes Callicles to say, 'by the gods Socrates . . . if you are in earnest, and these things you're saying are really true, won't this human life of ours be turned upside down, and won't everything we do evidently be the opposite of what we should do' (Grg. 481c). Socrates' reply, worth noting, is a satire, a mixture of sarcasm and seriousness. First, he makes fun by noting Callicles' inability to contradict either of his lovers: a boy named Demos and the polis of the same name. Socrates points out that in order to 'stay on side' with both, Callicles will say whatever is necessary. This is to say, he is rhetorician, a 'cook' – despite his protestations to the contrary. In turn, Socrates' lovers are Alcibiades and philosophy. Philosophy, by contrast and regardless of whom it addresses, always says the same thing (unlike Alcibiades, Socrates notes). Socrates' fidelity to the demands of the love of wisdom is *invariant* despite how out of tune it puts him with his lover Alcibiades. In this context Alcibiades is exemplary of a city in which all the best virtues have gone astray by want of an education *without interest* (Grg. 481d–482c).[12] Ironically, Callicles then accuses Socrates of 'playing to the crowd' – ironic, because in our sense he *is*. Again, in *Euthydemus*, Socrates is forced to wonder at a polis so constituted that, despite not caring whether a fellow is clever or not, it becomes extremely 'disturbed the moment [it] suspect[s] he is giving his *ability* to others'. Its people 'get angry', he says, 'whether out of jealousy . . . or . . . some other reason' (Euthphr. 3cd). He goes on to remark that the Athenians must think him 'too kindly' in his imparting of wisdom in the sense of his giving it too freely: '. . . I pour out all I have to everyone and not merely without pay – nay, rather glad to offer something if it would induce someone to hear me' (Euthphr. 3cd).

It is this typically ironic recital of his singularity in regard to the normative determination of the Athenian state that is telling. As we have seen, the central and abiding reason for Socrates' exclusion from the statist consideration of what it is to educate is that he is a figure without 'interest'. Enquiry certainly 'knows' what is *of interest* in this sense. Every enquiry proceeds *through* the state. But between those who might hear Socrates and those who will not is the conviction that sophistry, interest in interests, is not all. What is lamented here by Socrates is that the work of love, the desire for that which you need but do not have (Smp. 201b), has no currency in such a state. We should recall that the work of love, which is to say the 'truth of love', is the only work Socrates admits to knowing anything about and this precisely because, as both the *Symposium* and *Phaedrus* remind us, it is unknown and comes, if it does, of a 'sudden' (Smp. 199ab and cf. Ap. 17a). In the *Crito*, as we have consistently noted, Socrates speaks past the representatives of the polis and directly to the justice of its constitution. He will not retreat from the justice of the constitution, from what he *loves*, by running away into exile. On the contrary, he seeks to fulfil it by staying in Athens which *for him*, and perhaps for him alone, is the *place* of the Republic.[13]

We could multiply these examples but the point to be taken from them all is that each in its own way evokes that which is lacking in the present state. In Badiou's conception the generic extension is the place (the 'thought-place' to be more accurate) by which such statements as Socrates makes above are *shown* to *have been* true.[14] However, while it is possible to resurrect from the dialogues every such statement – this because the *corpus* can be defined 'historically' as a subject of the Socratic encounter and as such is finite (there are only so many words that belong to the Platonic corpus) – it is not possible to resurrect every statement that might be true of the encounter between Socrates and the sophistic state. This procedure has by no means been exhausted despite the century or so of rumours to the contrary.

Statement

To that end we must find a statement, veridical in the Republic of the *Republic*, that is true of the sophistic situation of Athens and that stands, moreover, as the referent of all possible statements that would be true in light of this statement. Such a statement must be recognisable to the sophistic situation but the truth of that statement, such that it is forced by that which conditions it, is not. The role of the generic extension is essentially twofold. As hypothesised, assumed to be all that it can be, it gives the subjective procedure a certain currency. (In passing we can note here that *forcing* gives the subject something to hang on to, it reaffirms the ethic that subtends his activities – to keep going, to never give up on that thought which is the desire for the end of the state.) Secondly, the extension *is*. This is to say that, if the 'generic set' (truth) *is* added to the original (Athenian) situation then the generic extension (Republic) not only *will have been* the thought of *what is* in the Athenian situation but *will be-come* the being of this very thought. The event, through the work of the subject, returns the situation to its being. This is Badiou's reworking of the Parmenidean maxim, which he so likes to quote: 'the same indeed is at once to think and to be'.[15] The question therefore is, 'what is the statement that fulfils this equation?' As we have argued throughout, the *capacity* for non-sophistry is *generic* to the Athenian situation. That is to say, every inhabitant of Athens belongs – through being separated from representation in its very being – to that which is not sophistry. Yet being represented as such, each element nevertheless suffers from the sophistic conceit that non-sophistry cannot be: there cannot be the *lack of a non-sophistic education*. We have argued that this lack is constitutive of this state. In other words *what prohibits the unbinding of this state is the lack of a non-sophistic education* (BE, 109/125). This, then, is a statement common to all inhabitants of Athens. But it must, in Badiou's words, 'undergo the trial of its subtraction' (TW, 103), or again, it must be 'made manifest' (HB, 14).

Condition

For Plato, Socrates names the very insistence of this lack as something for all. The site of this disjunction between the capacity that *insists* and the sophistic demand that this lack be nothing is education. Education is the site of Plato's minimal difference, the site of the smallest change possible that manifests the Republic from the *situation* of Athens. We can see, then, that this statement is *conditioned* by a certain capacity at the same time as it denotes the form of elemental inclusion. While every Athenian *shares* this capacity only one is *known* for or by this 'abnormal' capacity. As we have argued, his insistence (which for sophistry in-exists) is the singular (at first) mark of the immanent universality of this capacity. For Plato, the problem of Athens is the *reverse* and so in the Republic *there cannot be the lack of a non-sophistic education*. It is essential to Badiou's concept of the generic or 'indiscernible' that this *statement* 'there cannot be the lack of a non-sophistic education' is known to both the sophistic state and the generic extension of the Athenian situation. Plato's entire effort is to manifest *there* this 'what cannot be, for all'.

We have now two things: firstly, a *condition* drawn from the decision in regard to the generic. A condition of the generic is to 'know nothing' of sophistry. It is important to note that this condition denotes a concept of order such that it contains within it a set of conditions in turn (BE, 362/399). Suffice for us to reiterate that this condition 'to know nothing of sophistry' includes within it all non-sophistic conditions, some statements of which we noted above. It just so happens that in the dialogues every element of non-sophistry can be included within this condition. As Badiou says, this condition is 'richer in sense' than the others. In the dialogues, this condition is fundamentally Socratic and *there* he signifies the most sustained effort to not know what sophistry knows as knowledge and by this re-collect all these non-sophistic parts. As such it is reasonable, given the situation presented to us in the dialogues, to work with this condition (of all conditions) so long as we know what it is 'conditioned by'. The latter is the capacity intrinsic to all for non-sophistry, what Plato calls the equal capacity for reason.

Secondly, we have a statement intrinsically attached to this condition yet which is recognised by the state. However, as we noted, what the state does not know is the force of the attachment that links the subjective procedure to the evental site. For the sophists, nothing belongs to nothing. There are no 'non-constructible sets' for sophistry and as such nothing can be implicated by these non-sets in turn. The intrinsic attachment which the thought of the generic allows can be said like this: 'what is not known' is 'the lack of a non-sophistic education'. If *this* condition forces *this* statement, then in the 'world turned upside down', this statement will be veridical such that what is not known (in the Republic) is the lack of a non-sophistic education. These poet/sophists Plato says, those who tell us that Homer is the 'educator to all Hellas' who should be studied as a guide for life, 'deserve to be listened to politely' but the poetry of the 'honeyed muse' or the 'lyric verse' must, the argument requires, be banished from the *commonwealth*. Such is our '*apology*', he continues, and if we are *convicted* for being too harsh we will remind these devotees of Homer that there is a 'longstanding quarrel between poetry and philosophy'[16] (sophistry and non-sophistry): a quarrel that can only be displaced if poetry recant from its attachment to 'pleasure and imitation'. If it does so it will be welcomed back into the city, 'being as we are conscious of its charms' (cf. HB, 17). However, as things stand, it would be unholy to betray what is true (R. 606a–607d). This passage from Book X is justly famous and is one way or another always cited as the culmination of Plato's efforts to expel poetry from the city. However, two things in passing: (a) What Plato cannot allow is that the poet-sophist has the educational effect he does; alter this effect, interrupt this effect, counter this effect and the poets will 'farewell'; (b) Book X is not the point of expulsion but the climax to the demonstration of the truth of this assignation. Essentially, from the point at which Thrasymachus is seen to blush, the poet/sophists *will have been* assigned to the place proper to them.[17]

Forcing

Now that we have our *condition* and our *statement* we are in a position to discuss *forcing*. Forcing concerns the production of *new* knowledge. Therefore we know already that this concerns the work of the subject. If it concerns the work of the subject we know that it concerns the generic set and by definition the generic extension. But forcing denotes a particular aspect of the subjective complex. Crucially, the concept of forcing was invented by Cohen to establish the existence of generic or non-constructible sets. Summarising Badiou's summary, this invention enabled him to prove that Gödel's proof that all axiomatised mathematical systems fail by their own resources to establish their own consistency was itself 'incomplete'. Cohen proved that along with the axiom of choice (AC), the continuum hypothesis (CH) was neither consistent nor inconsistent with the ZF axioms of set theory and so was undecidable from within the set theoretic situation.[18] Basically, Cohen constructed a '*fundamental quasi-complete situation*', a 'ground model' (BE, 356/392) of set theory, consistent with the theory itself (that is to say that the elements presented in the original situation are entirely compatible with those in the ground model: they correspond one-to-one) in which his hypothesis about the independence of CH and AC from the axioms of set theory 'would be correct'. From this hypothetical model wherein his hypothesis was 'already' veridical or correct he was able to project back into set theory a point at which set theory lacked the means for accounting or discerning the truth of the Continuum (and AC) either way. The means for doing this depended on establishing a form of nomination which allowed Cohen to talk about the elements of this non-constructible thus unknowable set, before *knowing* them. In short, the referent for this name (a name including within it conditions (terms) and statements that are part of the original set), which counts out the elements that belong to the 'generic set' without knowing them, is contained in the supposed or quasi-complete 'generic extension'. Admitted into the generic set under condition of the name are elements whose inclusion in the generic set is only properly established with reference to the future anterior. The most we can say about these elements is that their belonging to the generic set will have been true.

In essence, forcing names a point in a situation where the situation's inconsistency will have been exposed. If the 'ground model' corresponds to the original set (if the Republic corresponds to Athens – the Republic includes all the elements belonging to Athens) then whatever can be known about the ground model can only be known as such on the basis of those elements that belong to the original set or situation. Whatever subsets were formed or known in the extension had *to be* in the original situation. However, in that situation or by the resources of knowledge current to that situation they remain indiscernible or generic (BE, 355–71/391–408).

Two statements on forcing

We need to cut through this formality and subtract what is essential to our reading of the corpus. To do so, we will elaborate two statements on forcing. We begin with:

> (a) Forcing is the point at which a truth, although incomplete, authorises anticipations of knowledge concerning not what is but *what will have been if truth attains completion*. (TW, 127)

Essentially, given that the subject works in the situation it cannot know the final form of the work it does. As we noted, it does have some information given that, in connecting elements to the event, thus constructing a generic multiple, it knows that any such element will have the condition of being unknown to the state. One can then imagine that if such a set were complete, a set of all the elements that were unknown to the state or that 'didn't know the state', then a particular statement could be made of this original situation that would in fact be correct. The statement is correct rather than true because what is true is the condition which forces this statement. This statement, made about the situation from within the situation, is a knowable statement as such but its truth remains subtracted from this knowledge. That is to say, what the statement refers to is something unknowable *in* the state but on the basis of it being veridical in the generic extension it can be thought. Socrates' claim, referring to a generalised sophistry, that he is 'neither wise with their wisdom nor stupid with their stupidities' is a prime example of such a statement (Ap. 22e).

Badiou summarises the parameters of the forcing procedure in the following manner, which will be our second statement:

> (b) *If* such and such an element [condition] *will have been* in the supposedly complete generic subset, *then* such and such a statement, rationally connectible to the element in question, is, or rather will have been correct. (TW, 128)

The subjective process picks out an element of the situation. It is assumed that this element is a part of the generic set, which is to say it is *conditioned* by being an element of this set, or again, that insofar as it is an element of this set, it is particular in some way. As we noted above, this element, picked out by the subject to be connected to the generic set, is conditioned by its lack of state knowledge. That is to say, what makes an element an element of this set is this condition – that it *knows* nothing. Let's put it this way, all the elements of the generic set are such that by their very belonging to this set they 'know nothing' of the sophistic state. The condition of these elements is their indiscernibility to the state. So, such an element will have been an element of the generic set. What is described here is essentially the procedure of enquiry undertaken as a fidelity. As with the definition above of the generic set, we are returned to aspects of the truth process we have encountered under different names and with different relations. The real difference now is that we are dealing with the knowledge of these processes: that is, how they can figure as something *for* the subject in the sense that they are not merely obscure or obtuse 'correct' opinions. In establishing the veracity of the procedure by recourse to the generic extension, an extension wholly consistent with the elementary material of the situation (and thus with the subject), the fidelity, belief or confidence of the subject cannot be reduced to one opinion among many. It can indeed be treated as such (by the state) but in fact, as we often see, the excessive treatment meted out to such 'opinions' signifies there is something anomalous at work. Via the anticipations a forcing allows to the subject, what is at stake ultimately is to make the generic set, the set of that which is not sophistry, belong to the Athenian situation – note: *not to be included by*. To make this set belong means that the situation must change. If the truth is added to Athens, Athens is then known as the Republic. Our formula, *what is forced in the situation is veridical in the generic extension*, refers to exactly this. To put it another way, the situation is returned to its very 'constitution' for in Badiou's words:

> [This] hypothesis consists in saying that one can only *render justice* to injustice from the angle of the event and intervention. There is thus no need to be horrified by an un-binding of being, because it is in the undecidable occurrence of a supernumerary non-being that every truth procedure originates, including that of a truth whose stakes would be that very un-binding. (BE, 284–5/314–15)

Keeping in mind our survey of Cohen's discovery, let's make a general summary of terms. When speaking of the point of forcing two things matter: a condition and a statement. It is a *condition* that *forces a statement*. The statement, *so conditioned*, will be veridical in the generic extension and, as such, will be a verifiable statement of the truth of the (Athenian) situation. What we looked for in the dialogues was a condition that we could demonstrate *as a* condition *and* a statement of this condition such that if expressed exposed the truth of which this condition is a condition.

Names, stratification – richer in sense

Cohen's method relies on a certain manipulation of names. In effect, what happens in a forcing is 'to name the thing which it is impossible to discern' (BE, 376/413 and cf. R. 499a). This has two essential parts: the first is the 'constitution' of a name; the second, the stratification of names. We noted above that a condition marks a set of conditions. It is, in the order of sense, the richest condition. Our condition is 'to know nothing of sophistry'. This condition is coupled to a statement: in our case, 'the lack of a non-sophistic education'. Following Cohen, Badiou gives the following definition of a name: 'a name is a multiple whose elements are pairs of names and conditions. That is: if u_1 is a name, $(\alpha \in u_1) \rightarrow (\alpha = <u_2,\pi>)$, where u_2 is a name, and π a condition' (BE, 376/413). This 'name' u_2 is what we have called a statement. In Meditation 34 on the theory of the subject, Badiou reverts to this metaontological terminology. The premise is the same: the statement/name designates in the situation and with its resources that which is an element of the generic extension (BE, 376/413). It is an element of the generic extension to not know sophistry. Following this logic we need to assign a name to this combination of condition and statement. Quite obviously it is Socrates. This is where stratification matters. As Badiou notes, one could object that this definition is circular: 'I define a name by supposing that I know what a name is' (BE, 376/413).[19] However, if one assigns to the names a nominal rank, an order based on the minimal conditions that satisfy a particular name, starting with the Ø, the name that 'conditions nothing', and π as this indeterminate (nothing) condition, it is possible to construct sets of names and conditions that 'outrank' this name. In essence, the minimal pair denoting the most elementary of names {Ø, π} is assigned the rank of 0.

> If μ is a name (simplifying matters a little): μ is of the nominal rank $0 \leftrightarrow [(\gamma \in \mu) \rightarrow \gamma = \langle \emptyset, \pi \rangle]$.

The upshot is that, given a minimal definition, it is possible to build a series of names upon it such that each succeeding name will include that which it succeeds. This logic follows the principles of 'ordinality'. The way to test this is to start with a name of a particular nominal rank. It will consist of a condition and another name. This name must already be defined if the successor name is. Suggestively, Badiou notes that the circularity is broken when one 'redescend[s] in this manner until we reach the names of the nominal rank *0*, which are themselves explicitly defined (a set of pairs of the type $\langle \emptyset, \pi \rangle$)'. Further – and this is all we need:

> The names are deployed starting from the rank *0* via successive constructions which engage nothing apart from the material defined in the previous steps. As such, a name of the rank *1* will be composed from pairs consisting of names of the rank *0* and conditions. But the pairs of the rank *0* are defined. Therefore, an element of a name of the rank *1* is also defined; it solely contains pairs of the type $\langle\langle \emptyset, \pi_1 \rangle, \pi_2 \rangle$, and so on. (BE, 377/414)

Simply, out of all the *teachers* at a school one will be the *Principal*. The name Principal already includes *within* it what it names; both what the name *teacher* names – all the conditions and statements that can be generated as belonging to that name *teacher* – and the name *teacher* itself. Therefore in Athens there will be a condition that forces a statement and it is possible to conceive of this forcing under a single name. This name will itself be included, though in no sense diminished in regard to what it names by another name – a higher name, a name whose reach is 'richer' still, more prescriptive, more universal.

The law of the subject

This order *will* work (and therefore *has* worked) for us in two instances: firstly, we will say that the name *Socrates* consists of the condition to not know sophistry and the statement it forces concerning the lack of a non-sophistic education. Further, this allows us to say that as this condition forces this statement it is Socrates who names this point in the Athenian situation. This is nothing other than what we have said all along. As the name of the event at the point of the intervention, he articulates the subjective procedure which the corpus enumerates – point by point. The capacity that the generic set of conditions marks 'to not know' sophistry is *the* Socratic condition of Athens. This is to say, it is Athens' unknown capacity. Nominally, this condition is the condition of all enquiries and materially, the set of its results. The resulting recollection authorises the statement on its result – the lack of a non-sophistic education. For the sophistic state there cannot be the lack of a non-sophistic education and in the context of this prohibition it is a statement of the state. As we know, the ontology of sophistry does not allow for the existence of nothing. Plato's does. This lack is: it is not, not. Therefore this statement, as an expression of that which is nothing to sophistic Athens is a statement concerning its very being. Such a statement forced by its condition realises itself only in the future anterior – in our case, the Republic. For as we have said, here alone will the combination of the condition and the statement constitute the form of a new knowledge. The shorthand for this, throughout the dialogues is the Platonic name of exile: Socrates (stranger, visitor, Athenian stranger). If the true condition of Athens is Socratic, the Republic is its forced result. In terms of our stratification of names the Republic will name or include Socrates *and* the set of conditions that Socrates names. The Republic names, then, the thought-place where one 'does not know the lack of a non-sophistic education'. From the beginning, from the *Apology* let's say, this has been the singularity of Socrates – the only non-sophist, the only non-teacher/educator in all Athens. The trajectory Plato has followed is from this singular insistence marked by death for the state, to the universal Republic where that very state is displaced by the forced existence of what it lacked.

That Socrates has been marked by death for the state is the direct result of his evoking 'the law of the subject'. Whereas the fidelity that constitutes the subject as a practice is not visible except as its result, the *law* of the subject is known to the state. The state does not register the subject per se but the 'gadfly' that it is in its act: that which exposes the state to its fundamental irrationality, its excess, its conceit. The subject is the point through or by which the true condition of Athens is forced into the situation as the founding declaration of its new knowledge. 'This testifies,' Badiou notes, 'as to how an enunciated veridicality can be called knowledge, but knowledge *in truth*' (TW, 128). It is therefore not Socrates that interests the state but that of which he is the name or, very ironically, *the law*. He is the figure whose sole reason for being is the manifestation of this non-state form as the real and extensive result of his subjective practice.

THE LAW OF THE SUBJECT *REDUX* OR 'MANIFESTO OF EDUCATIONISM'

We now want to take up Plato's injunction to look forward and back at once in order to illustrate finally how our preceding work is explicitly linked to its formalisation as the Republic. We will see the 'immanent' link between the subtractive effects and their realisation in the generic extension or, in other words, how the work of subtraction is always already that which is added to Athens. Let's put it this way: the Republic is the forced result of all that Socrates anticipates throughout the dialogues, and Socrates is the immanent term which names that which can only be verified as such under the name of the Republic. The question is of the equivalence between these names. It is wholly a Platonic question – one which the *Republic* addresses when it discerns the reciprocity between the constitution of the individual and that of the state. Again, we note that 'the *participating* and the *participated in* are not, in the last analysis, essentially different from each other, but are [*generically*] the same entity *in two different modes of being*'.

State

We established the distinction between the Athenian situation and the state of this situation. For Plato, the state of the Athenian situation was sophistic. Under the injunction of what we called the Protagorean ethic 'Of all things the measure is Man, of the things that are, that they are and of the things that are not, that they are not' sophistry set up its (well-paid) school. We determined that this ethic was one that supported an understanding of knowledge based in interest. Plato characterises the sophist as a merchant peddler in goods who doesn't distinguish between his produce but hopes to sell them on the premise that they are all equally beneficial (or not). The extent of this logic is articulated by Anytus in the *Meno* and Meletus in the *Apology* when they claim that any Athenian citizen, being by definition a good man, is therefore an educator to the youth of Athens. A virtuous circle of transmission is thereby established wherein interest is the object of reflection proper to any 'educated' subject and 'to know' is to be properly instructed in an interest in interest. For Plato, such an exchange of interests was anathema: (a) because it guaranteed the false division of the state into classes predicated on particularities that had utility but no truth; (b) because there is absolutely no equation between education and money, truth and profit. For Plato, these teachings were predicated on an excessive conceit regarding what constitutes knowledge. Ultimately, what we were able to show was that the measure of sophistic conceit was unknown to sophistry and that in fact its conceit was at its limit in presuming that what it knew was what there was to know. This excess became 'visible' when sophistry singled out Socrates as the only non-educator in all Athens. If Socrates was a non-educator, then there *existed in Athens the limit point of a sophistic education* – for had he been a proper educator he would be a good citizen of Athens who, for Plato, despite the claims of Anytus and Callicles to the contrary, so long as they remained within the encyclopaedia of conceit, were nothing but 'sophists' anyway. If the present state of society is sophistic, as Plato affirms in the *Republic* (492a–d), and thus to be educated therein is to have a sophistic education, then to not be an educator is to not be a sophist. Socrates marks the limit of sophistry – the singular or local point of its *reverse*. Whatever it is that Socrates does, and the state knows he does something, it is not a state education. Of course, if the state is sophistic this means that it doesn't know what it professes to know. It is not only ignorant in regard to what it knows – a problem that can be fixed – but conceited in regard to this ignorance – a problem that must be forced because it knows nothing of its lack of knowledge. Instead, it is in its interest that what it doesn't know *must not be*. Thus is Socrates' fate sealed. However, in this context Socrates is the index of that which inexists for sophistry. He is not, as Plato makes clear, the sum of non-sophistry. Socrates functions as the negative term of a sophistic education such that he signifies that what *exists* in this situation indiscernibly so is the 'lack of a non-sophistic education'. Socrates exemplifies what is not sophistry and as such he names what insists in Athens 'the lack of a non-sophistic education'. Its existence is in excess of the knowledge of this state – it occupies the immeasurable space between Athens qua situation of presented multiples without discernment and the state which presumes to know the multiple form of all Athens. The name Socrates (and thus the statements that belong to him alone) has no referent in the Athenian state. It marks only what is indiscernible there. In this way we can see that the *Apology* is already in dialogue with the Republic for this indiscernible condition of Athens will recur as such in the (Socratic) Republic of the *Republic*.

Site

For Badiou, any 'historical situation' – such as the Athens of the dialogues – will present an element none of whose elements will be presented in turn. This is a singular or abnormal multiple. It harbours within it the 'peril of the void' (BE, 98/115), the very threat to the state which the state qua inclusion or representation exists to preclude. For the state, this abnormal element, which we know of as the site, has nothing further to present and as such what belongs to it will be included as 'nothing'. This is to say that, what is of the education-site is nothing to the state. It is axiomatic for sophistry that what is not known *is* nothing: to 'express the inexpressible' is the height of irrationality and impiety. This is not to suggest that Socrates expresses the inexpressible per se. What the site marks is the inexpressible *existing* 'gap' between the situation and its state. On this gap turns the difference between the sophistic state and the ideal city. As Plato insists, education decides the correct trajectory. This gap therefore is the problem of the state, for it shows that what the state knows is not all. It is an encyclopaedia devoid of that which it professes most. Socrates marks the real existence of this gap – whose name is the site – between what is presented and what is represented in the sophistic discourse of what presents. It is the very existence of an education which is not sophistic that determines that education be understood as a site. Plato seeks the proper form for its expression.

Event/Intervention

It is over education that sophistry and its model repeatedly clash. The importance of this encounter is twofold: following the axiom of the void, what is unpresented for a situation is a part of every element of that situation. In other words, the site presents the (as yet uncollected – so indiscernible) set of that which is nothing to sophistry.

Education, as the name of the site, invokes this commonality. Each element of Athens, beneath the force of representation and as such despite it, shares in the lack of a non-sophistic education. Every one shares the capacity for reason. Recall that Plato's definition of justice is that 'friends have all things in common'. The 'work of love', the 'doctrine of fair shares', is 'for all'. Note that this is not an ascription but the designation of how this 'lack of a non-sophistic education' will subjectively appear. If education is the lack of sophistry, then, as the site it is what remains unpresented in Athens as common to all. In our case education, marking the point at which the state is minimally disassociated from what it represents, is the fundamental constituent of the procedure of thinking into being a new situation, a situation other than that which is subject to the sophistic encyclopaedia. Education is therefore the point of minimal difference that separates the knowledge of sophistry from the *immanent* yet indiscernible 'world to come', whose inconceivable name is the Republic. To intervene at this point and to decide for that which is not sophistry is to begin the procedure of elaborating, on the basis of 'nothing', an education 'for all' – what Plato refers to as the only education worthy of the name. We can see that as Plato, dialogue by dialogue, articulates this minimal distinction between sophistry and non-sophistry to be at the heart of all enquiries, he is anticipating the place wherein the full capacity of the latter will be find its veridical expression. The very *Idea* of the Republic, void yet conceived *as such* (which is to say immanent to the name 'Socrates'), animates the very procedure which will constitute its discursive form.

Fidelity

In common with all dialogues, the *Republic* begins with an encounter. These staged encounters manifest the Ideal and so *Real* encounter between the 'exemplary figure of thought' and the 'exemplary figures of interest' – non-sophist and sophist. This event, in Badiou's words, is the index of the void of the (Athenian) situation for which this event is an *event*. What the event opens up to the situation is what the situation has hitherto recognised as nothing: the *indiscernible* or the *generic*. The event exposes the very form (whose constitution is hitherto lacking) *for* the constitution of the 'thought-institution' named the Republic. Although these encounters *take place*, their evental status depends on the decision which decides on the basis of a pure undecidability that what happened by chance belongs to that situation. This decision marks the intervention of the subject instituted as such by this very decision. When Plato decides that the encounter between the sophistic state and the singular non-sophist is an event he authorises against the state the legitimacy of the illegal name Socrates. The trial of Socrates as recounted in the *Apology* – the only 'public dialogue' – criminalised this name in direct reference to the education of youth. Plato in turn reaffirms the immanent conjunction between the education of the youth and the name Socrates. Such an affirmation is without support and is subtracted from the state for which Socrates and, crucially, that which he indicates as existing therein must be seen to be qua education as nothing at all. In other words, there is no knowledge in the Athenian sophistic state of Socrates as educator. Socrates, quite obviously is *without* the encyclo-*paideia*. Given that Socrates is never an educator 'after their [sophists] pattern' he then names for Plato the very encounter between sophistic 'teachings' and that which is not sophistry. Recall, he is not the encounter itself. This illegal *name* is, however, present at each such encounter and all enquiry takes place with reference to this name – even if this name is substituted with the more generic term 'Stranger'. Even if the Platonic corpus is the subject-body which sustains (beyond the individual lifetime of *Platocrates*) the truth of the Socratic encounter within the unfolding drama of the dialogues themselves, the name Socrates articulates the manifest-appearing of the invariant couple event/subject. He does not unify these but articulates their conjunction. In the dialogues, Socrates *names* the living body of enquiry even as he is the dead figure that necessitates the Platonic corpus which gives body to his now absent praxis. Socrates is a name which serves the dialogues in three ways:

1. It marks the encounter between sophistry and non-sophistry over education.
2. It stands as the name of that education which is not sophistic, which is nothing other than the indiscernible capacity shared by every inhabitant of the Athenian situation.
3. In naming what is not sophistry he names within this situation the possible 'impossibility' of the world to come. *Socrates is the present name in Athens of the 'Republic'* – an unknown name.

On the very premise, established by sophistry itself, of Socrates' constitutional singularity, Plato establishes the Republic, whose singular universality is such that it is the only state worthy of the name (R. 422e), just as Socrates is the only non-sophist of Athens. The constituents of the Republic have a twofold provenance. On the one hand any element of the Athenian state, any inhabitant is already capable of being connected for a fidelity to the name of the event and thus being *recollected* subject to enquiry, such that they will have formed a properly constituted generic part of Athens: a part whose veracity depends on the situation to come. This 'already capable' refers to their shared but indiscernible connection to that which is nothing to sophistry. But as Plato makes plain, and as Badiou confirms, if not by the same means, this capacity must be acted upon – both from without and from within. Precisely because this shared capacity is nothing to the sophistic state it is by no means obvious that this capacity either exists or is of any value at all. The state puts this manifest capacity in the shape of Socrates on trial, showing precisely that it is worse than worthless (as Callicles notes) and is in fact traitorous, and that being as it is fundamentally irrational and incommensurable with the proper discourse of the state it must therefore 'not be'. The show trial of the *Apology* makes it universally known that such a thing as a 'non-sophistic education', the 'law of the subject', makes no sense to the state. It is the mark of something 'foreign at work'. Plato must then produce this inexistent capacity. He must follow the Socratic interruptive injunction – know thyself as the truth of all (Ap. 23b, Tht. 151e and L. 713e) – and open the situation to enquiry – sophist by sophist, youth by youth, demagogue by demagogue – in order to establish subtractively the 'generic set' made from all those elements connected to it on the basis of their non-sophistic capacity for an education by truths. Each element that presents itself on the basis of this shared condition undergoes 'the trial of its subtraction' from the knowledge of sophistry. Socrates, as *the midwife of knowing nothing that sophistry knows*, stands to orient all enquiries under the injunction peculiar to him but not his alone. This knowing nothing is not knowledge of what nothing *is* (and this is why, despite Plato's attempts, a curriculum is not what is at stake here). Rather, it is an axiomatic statement that (the) nothing *is*. It is a declared conviction that concretises the break with all sophistic predication, with all forms of sophistic argument, logic or teaching. It asserts the real separation between the world of sophistry *as it is* and the 'world to come' on whose basis all Socratic enquiries take place. Subject to enquiry, under the injunction that one does not know what sophistry knows – which ultimately is to declare oneself not to be a citizen of this state and thus to suffer the consequences that ensue – the inhabitants of Athens are tested for their fidelity to the break with sophistry. We have seen that across the dialogues they are a rare few who decide for (the non-knowledge of) the 'world to come'. However, given that all share the capacity for reason equally, the universal address of non-sophistry virtually includes all inhabitants despite their conviction. It is simply a fact of existence that nothing compels an inhabitant of sophistic Athens to subject themselves to the type of enquiry which results in them declaring themselves partisans of that which is properly indiscernible. Indeed, everything consequent on submitting to the determinant of the encyclopaedia, wealth, the privileges of citizenship, interests, honour, and the virtue that accompanies them, suggests it is realistic to disavow the Socratic injunction, to deny the extension of the event, to refuse all enquiry into the constitution of the situation and to consider one's education as conditional on this very state. It is obvious that even as this attitude of submission is anathema to Plato's good state, where, as we see, all these disavowed practices are put into practice to think the very constitution of the good state, there nevertheless remains in the Republic a majority of citizens whose fidelity is partial. Nevertheless, for Plato, there is one proviso for this state which cuts across all particularities, all claims to interest and judgment, and that is what is good (or true) of the good state is only that which is good for all. As Badiou provocatively puts it, 'the individual, in truth, is nothing' (TC, 101/144, trans. modified). In light of Plato's insistence that friends have all things in common, such a statement is provocative only if one remains intuitively sophistic. The coercion at stake in the Republic is the extreme obverse of that which we see in the State. Badiou notes that in the State, 'this coercion consists in not being held to be someone who belongs to society, but as someone who is *included* within society' (BE, 107/124). In the *Republic*, despite one's identification as man, woman, guardian, artisan or philosopher, despite one's reflexive inclusion, that is to say, *what* work one does or how one *participates*, each one belongs to the truth that animates such identifications. This inversion, coupled with Plato's own comment on the matter (R. 422e, above) authorises us to nominate the Republic as the 'ideal non-state'. For Plato, then, the *Idea* displaces the representative state insofar as it secures the egalitarian 'consistency' already guaranteed by presentation (BE, 105/122). The free citizen of the Republic therefore is subject to the truth of the idea and not to the state. This immanent and absolute separation between the Idea and the state is Plato's 'Socratic invention' which a history of 'political-philosophy' has forgotten to notice.

Subject

Our insistent point is that Plato and Socrates form something of an 'originary Two'. In Badiou's schema it is love which forms the supplemental basis for any Two. At the point of an encounter, each declares as for the other. Under this condition, verifying the truth of this declaration will form the work of the Two. Clearly, Plato declares himself for Socrates and Socrates, in both the *Apology* and the *Phaedo*, declares himself for such (becoming) 'philosophical' associates. We have covered enough ground and demonstrated the links between the event and the series of subjective enquiries or dialogues to show this. We have even demonstrated how the Republic is the institution constituted entirely on the thought and practice of the figure of Socrates and, as such, on the work of love. In other words, Plato, on the basis of the non-relation this work of love sustains, invents a Socratic city, the kind where such a figure could very well take part in the politics that go on there. As we suggested, Socrates is not simply the name for the Republic *in* Athens but is more the mark of the Republic in exile within Athens. If Plato can add Socrates to Athens then what he achieves is the Republic. This was his goal all along. As we noted, each enquiry is a retrial – not of Socrates but of sophistic Athens. In the *Apology*, Plato's Socrates gives the jury instruction in what is proper to judgment. A jury 'does not sit to dispense justice as a favour, but to decide where justice lies' (Ap. 35c–e). Obviously sophistry, inherently inconsistent in judgments as Socrates here explicitly notes, is incapable of finding justice but the decision as to 'where justice lies' is exactly what is at stake in the *Republic*. The verdict for Plato is that without Socrates Athens is sophistic and it is only *with* Socrates that it has the chance to force the re-collection of the capacity immanent to it for a non-sophistic education. The Republic is the subjective result of Plato's fidelity to Socrates. This fidelity is not to the death of Socrates. The guilty verdict and the sentence of execution do not constitute an event for Plato. It is the life of Socrates, the figure who day after day intervenes in the smooth running of the sophistic polis and forces therein Athens to know itself as the place that knows nothing of the lack of a sophistic education, which Plato decides for and configures anew (L. VII. 341c). The truth of non-sophistry becomes the constitutional discourse of the ideal city – built by Plato's fidelity to Socrates, the singular, insistent, immanent and anticipatory figure it evokes. The Republic *is* Socrates as universal singularity. Thanks to the establishment of *his* (non-sophistic) pattern Socrates is seen in retrospect in all his consistency and coherence. His animating ethic is that the subjective process of recollection carried out with confidence is open to all. Every soul contains the basis of truth as its generic capacity. What is needed for this truth to come to knowledge is the encounter with the orientation of thought that can generate its recollection. To associate with Socrates is to participate in a forcing of new knowledge or the forcing of *the lack of a non-sophistic education.* As the presumed truth of the Athenian situation, the supposed mark of the generic capacity, the Republic is proposed as that which truly institutes the thought of all. This is the true radicality of the Socratic figure as exemplary figure of thought. What we see here is that Plato has truly altered the encyclopaedia. The killing of this figure of incommensurable equality who introduces not only the incommensurable act – *to* know what one didn't *know* (corruption) – but the very concept of incommensurability as a fundamental trope of every intervention (impiety) is the sophistic response.

Generic

That the Republic *exists* is the very idea of the subjective procedure; that it insists is the result of forcing the truth of this idea into the situation as the condition of its thought. The *knowledge* of this truth must be forced into existence by the subject. All that the subject has to hang on to, so to speak, is the belief that it can be forced, such is why this Socratic procedure is fragile, limited and under attack. It is why we have aporia, the failure of validation at a point in the process, and it is why each dialogue restarts the procedure as an instance of what it is to continue. To continue is to pursue with courage what we don't know, knowing only that we can come to know. The Republic names all this which Socrates names. The displacement effected in the procedures of the generic – event, intervention, operator of fidelity, enquiry – and by the law of forcing if achieved, show that that which is not in the new situation was already lost to the original situation. 'No information can be extracted from the [indiscernible] set α which was not already present in *M* [the fundamental (*sophistic*) situation]' (BE, 416–17/455–6). Affirmation and not destruction is the accomplishment of a truth procedure and thus an education by truths is conditioned not just by the poem but is equally conditioned by the demands of the matheme, the work of love and the politics of fair shares. The only education is that which addresses the generic 'capacity for reason' whose disavowal is the constitutive condition of the sophistic state. Surely the formalisation of this address is Plato's singular and decisive in(ter)vention. What this Socratic taking place makes manifest is simply that the sophist cannot educate, that what one receives in exchange for one's 'callous cash payment' is not an education but a calculated return on one's investment and a stake in the regime predicated on the conceited yet powerful knowledge of what – at all costs – must *not* be. In the Republic – the decided place of philosophy, constituted by a thoughtful, subjective transformation – a place where sophistry cannot be *for all*, it cannot be simply because it never was an 'education by truths'.

Notes

1. Kahn's proposal is read all the dialogues – and in particular all the early ones – as the 'work of an author whose world-view is defined by the *Phaedo* and *Republic*' (Charles H. Kahn, 'Response to Christopher Rowe').
2. G. R. F. Ferrari, 'Editor's Introduction', *The Cambridge Companion to Plato's Republic*, pp. xv–xxvi.
3. Scolnicov, 'Two faces of Platonic knowledge', p. 7. Not incidentally, Scolnicov makes the point that such an understanding distances Plato further from Aristotle's 'historically challenged' (Kahn, 'Response to Christopher Rowe', p. 1) 'misrepresentation' of the Forms. Scolnicov notes that Aristotle misses Plato's indistinction between 'being essentially and being accidentally', and further that Aristotle's own theory of substances makes the acceptance of the former impossible (pp. 6–7).
4. Scolnicov, 'Two faces of Platonic knowledge', pp. 8–9, emphasis added.
5. Cf. 'All things are symbolical; and what we call results are beginnings' (Ralph Waldo Emerson, 'Plato: or the philosopher', *Representative Men: The Complete Prose Works of Ralph Waldo Emerson*, p. 177).
6. Cf. IT (72), E (61) and R. (444a).
7. Jacques Rancière offers the most interesting series of objections to Plato's 'distribution of sense' precisely because he begins from a position of axiomatic equality. To do justice to Rancière's critique is beyond the scope of this work. We do hope to address it elsewhere. See, for example, *The Philosopher and His Poor*.
8. See R. (495c–496a) for a portrait of such a betrayal.
9. This is not a case of mixing psychoanalysis and politics but of realising the *form* of their composition.
10. See Peter Hallward, *Badiou: A Subject to Truth*, pp. 131–9; Oliver Feltham, *Alain Badiou: Live Theory*, pp. 108–13; Jason Barker, *Alain*

Badiou: A Critical Introduction, pp. 107–10. See also François Wahl, 'The Subtractive' (C, esp. xxxvii–xliv); B. Madison-Mount, 'The Cantorian revolution', pp. 41–91; Zachary Luke Fraser, 'The category of formalisation: from epistemological break to truth procedure' in CM (xii–lxi) and 'The law of the subject: Alain Badiou, Luitzen Brouwer and the Kripkean analyses of forcing and the Heyting calculus', in *The Praxis of Alain Badiou*, pp. 23–70, and finally, Jean-Toussaint Desanti, 'Some remarks on the intrinsic ontology of Alain Badiou', in Peter Hallward (ed.), *Think Again: Alain Badiou and the Future of Philosophy*, 59–66 (hereafter TA). Importantly, see also Feltham's unpublished PhD thesis, 'As Fire Burns', esp. Ch. V, Sections III and IV, pp. 170–84.

11. Feltham, *Live Theory*, p. 109.
12. Cf. the last exchange of the *Alcibiades*: 'Alcibiades – Strange but true; and henceforward I shall begin to think about justice. Socrates – And I hope that you will persist; although I have fears, not because I doubt you; but I see the power of the state, which may be too much for both of us' (Alc. 135e). The Platonic provenance of this dialogue is in dispute. However, this final exchange is certainly within that 'provenance'. Cf. the *Symposium* where a drunk Alcibiades, about to recite an encomium to Socrates, says that he will speak only the truth. Socrates quips that he would love to hear the truth from Alcibiades.
13. 'Socrates entered the prison and took away all ignominy from the place, which could not be a prison whilst he was there' (Emerson, 'Plato: or, the philosopher', in *Representative Men*, p. 178).
14. See Scolnicov, 'Two faces of Platonic knowledge', pp. 1–9, on the distinction between 'to see' and 'to show'.
15. We follow Louise Burchill's translation of Badiou's *Deleuze*. For an explanation of Badiou's usage see Louise Burchill's note (D, 137), fn.1 to Chapter 7. Badiou's citations: TW (177), C (87), BE (38/39), for example. Given its context in the 'Proem' Badiou's use is not without irony as Parmenides has just declared that to go down the path of discerning that which is nothing 'is a path wholly inscrutable for you could not know what is not (for it is not to be accomplished) nor could you point it out.' See Patricia Curd, 'Parmenides and after: unity and plurality', in Mary Louise Gill and Pierre Pellegrin (eds), *A Companion to Ancient Philosophy*, p. 37. Ray Brassier, in 'Presentation as anti-phenomenon in Alain Badiou's *Being and Event*', understands Badiou's invoking of Parmenides' maxim as meaning 'thinking and being are both nothing' (63). Thus there is no identity between them and this lack of predication is the point of the same. For Brassier, this results in an impossibility to distinguish 'between discourse and world, thought and reality, logical consequences and material causes' (63).
16. See HB (17) and C (74). For an exegeses of this ancient quarrel

which draws conclusions similar to Badiou see Charles L. Griswold Jr, 'Plato's metaphilosophy: why Plato wrote dialogues', *Platonic Writings, Platonic Readings*, pp. 143–67.

17. At 443bc Socrates tells Glaucon that if, as they have discovered, justice is every part doing its proper work then 'the dream we had has been completely fulfilled – our suspicion that, with the help of some god, we had hit upon the origin and pattern of justice right at the beginning in founding our city.' One should compare Thrasymachus' blush with that of Hippocrates in the *Protagoras*. When Socrates asks Hippocrates what he will become if Protagoras trains him Plato says, he 'blushed at this – there was already a streak of sunlight – to betray him . . .' Hippocrates blushes because he realises that under Protagoras' tutelage he would become a sophist. The beauty of the image is that Hippocrates is having a reflective and conscious moment as betrayed in his blush. This blush is illuminated by the sun. The whole image returns us to the Cave analogy, to the very heart of Plato's concept of education. Hippocrates stands on the threshold but he has not yet been turned to the 'sun' (Prt. 312a). In contrast, Thrasymachus blushes because he cannot account for his conceit. No light shines on him.
18. Desanti notes that at the end of Cohen's book *Set Theory and the Continuum Hypothesis*, Cohen states that in his eyes the CH 'is obviously false'. The continuum is 'so incredibly rich', he says, 'there is no reason why it should simply be equivalent to M_1 [extension]' (TA, 66).
19. Recall Geach's claim above against Plato's 'what is X?'

Epilogue

Plato's singular difficulty in and by the constitution of the *Republic* is in maintaining this subversive and revolutionary 'education of the educators' within the configuration of the new form of the state. This difficulty results in two things: Plato attempts to design a curricular structure for maintaining this education, both in the constitution of the Republic and in that of his 'academy', and in so doing he makes a particular form of representation 'not appear'. As different as they are, both Vlastos and Badiou object to these final prescriptions. For Plato, the ideal-city can admit no alteration to its constitution. For Vlastos, this is the essence of Plato's mathematical tyranny that would see Socrates, the wily debater, man of the market, playfully seeking out the non-wisdom in any and every profession of wisdom, would be inadmissible in such a state. He would go the way of the sophist and the Republic would do over what Athens already did. In a strange reversal of fortunes the Republic *imitates* Athens while Socrates is subject to the flux of being sophistic and non sophistic by turns. Referring to the *Laws*, Badiou supposes the Athenian Stranger is something like an agent of the state whose pronouncements against 'Socratic' corruption in favour of 'the implacable fixity of criminal laws', is a sign of Plato's 'giving way on his desire', giving up on *polemos* (C, 64 and 75). These criminal laws, Badiou claims, are exactly those which saw Socrates fall foul of Athens – laws against impiety and the corruption which is its effect. Badiou argues there is a tension inherent in the 'philosophical act' or the setting up the philosophical apparatus of thought. Because philosophy thinks truths, it is tempted to think that it alone knows the Truth. This move is from the 'divided subject' of truths – the founding declaration of philosophy that *there are truths* and the invention of the discursive apparatus of their capture and transmission – to Sovereign. This turn, in Book X of the *Laws*, for Badiou, is of a piece with the tense (and somewhat ambiguous) proscription of the sophist in the *Republic*. Plato succumbs to the tendency to know the All of truth Badiou says – truth as presence.

This is not the place to argue this case in detail (we have already argued against the substance of the charge above) but suffice to say that the argument of the *Laws* is directed explicitly against the sophistic tendency which dissembles in support of whatever contemporary interests are at stake, and the summary prescriptions against impiety and corruption are entirely consistent with Socrates' public position in the *Apology*, to wit 'the gods exist, they are concerned with us, and they are absolutely above being corrupted into flouting justice' (L. 907b). The position of Socrates in the *Apology*, and of Plato across the entire corpus, is that in regard to all these things it is only Socrates, the *figure of Socrates*, who would speak the truth (Ap. 17a). Moreover, this being the case, sophistic Athens merely imitated piety and so was the epitome of corruption and the flouting of justice as prescribed by the gods. There is no contradiction between what Plato says in Book X of the *Laws* concerning the maintenance of the ideal Republic and what Socrates says concerning its indiscernibility in the *Apology*. These 'criminal laws', as Badiou calls them, are the rational result of a thinking directed towards ensuring the continued failure of the corruptions of sophistry. Quite simply, and this is the *reversal* staged by Plato, to corrupt the corrupt is the work of reason, while to corrupt the work of reason is corrupt. What is incommensurable to the Good is never good. Was Socrates, the name of the Republic in Athens, ever incommensurable to the good? The force of Plato's position here, and this is the anxiety it delivers, is to reveal any dissent as sophistic relativism. 'You, [Callicles], for all your cleverness, have failed to grasp the truth; you have not observed how great a part geometric equality plays in heaven and earth, and because you neglect the study of geometry you preach the doctrine of unfair shares' (Grg. 508a).

For Plato, sophistry remains over as the constant and internal limit to the constitution of the good state and, as such, Plato subscribes to Badiou's ethic for philosophy, which is to preserve the polemic with sophistry. At the very end of the *Laws*, for example, the Athenian offers to take up the discussion of education one more time precisely because it is the central site for all that occurs and reoccurs in the constitution of the *subjective* and thus ideal non-state. The thinking of an education by truths has not come to an end. The central question for Plato is not 'why was Socrates killed?' as Badiou contends (C, 64); rather, Plato's entire thought is directed to answering the question 'how is Socrates to live?' To think with Plato is to think through this same question.

The problem of education, education against, opposed to or, finally, *despite* sophistry, remains. It does so precisely because the ideal non-state is 'to come'. If it is to come then it will have been forced through the determinations of the state and against its constant return. This is entirely consistent with the 2,500-year history of a post-Platonic education. While sophistry may have been discursively assigned its place in the *Republic* the sophists never left the historical city whose impossibility was Plato's generic idea. Education understood as only *by truths* over and over again has had to force its way back into and through the knowledge of the city for which it was nothing. We see this effort in the work of Saint Paul, Augustine, Descartes, Spinoza, Hobbes, Marx and Lacan, to name only a few. This effort remains again today, still to come. That the contemporary university and its attendants use the name 'Academy' means next to nothing with respect to Plato's intentions but it does signal a certain weight of anxiety. In the *Sophist*, Plato showed us that the teacher for money, the merchant professor of 'the false conceit of wisdom', took its name from the indiscernible figure of wisdom. This imitator was ever anxious about what he knew, which is to say what he lacked, even as he professed to know it. His entire legitimacy therefore was dependent on the maintenance of a consensus concerning this lack (of a non-sophistic education).

Badiou claims that whenever a consensus is pronounced philosophy becomes suspicious. To be undemocratic today, Badiou claims, is deemed pathological and is as such forbidden (M, 78). The same consensus surrounds education. Everyone knows the refrain: there is no need to repeat the endless platitudes concerning the goods of education nor further elaborate the terror of the endless policy documents which propose reform after reform, modification after modification, in the service of the state and thus in the foreclosure of change, and in which almost everyone colludes precisely because the authority of democratic opinion demands that you do. It seems almost churlish (and in Plato's sense quite useless) to note that almost no one ever asks 'what is education?' (This is because everyone already knows exactly what it is.) As we have seen, this question 'punches a hole in such knowledge'. For sophistry, there can be no hole. This consensus must be constantly investigated. Plato's work was extensive, paradigmatic *and* preliminary. The idea of an education by truths is always yet to come. At the same time it is always already *there*. This is the immanent dialectic of participation, the ideal realisation or subjective manifestation of that which is not *known*. Thanks to Plato, this is always what education refers too – the subjective declaration *for* truths and the work of establishing their existence *there* where the event reveals them to be – and never to the sophistic state. This suggests to us that there is the possibility for the extension of a project such as this to other thinkers and to other 'states'. This work merely begins such an enquiry. What we are proposing could provisionally be understood as a 'genealogy of education', one that stakes its existence on the Platonic declaration that the '*only* education is an *education by truths*'. This genealogy would be punctuated by discontinuities insofar as the manifest instances of an education by truths would be realised in association with a disparate, yet coherent set of proper names. We named some figures above. Each of these, as disparate as they appear one to another, could be seen to intervene, to resume and to re-form the trajectory Plato established as that of an education by truths – from the encounter with the state at a site to the thought extension of its consequences. To take up this Platonic work of deciding the 'forms of change', which we hope to have begun, is to enquire once again into 'how Socrates can live'. Plato's Socrates will have then made us say 'far more than ever was in [us]' (Tht. 210b).

Bibliography

Ahbel-Rappe, Sara and Kamtekar, Rachana (eds), *A Companion to Socrates*. Malden: Blackwell, 2006.

Althusser, Louis, 'Ideology and the state', in *Lenin and Philosophy and Other Essays*, trans. Ben Brewster. New York: Monthly Review Press, 2001.

—*For Marx*, trans. Ben Brewster. London: Verso, 2005.

—*Lenin and Philosophy and Other Essays*, trans. Ben Brewster. New York: Monthly Review Press, 2001.

—*Philosophy of the Encounter: Later Writings, 1978–87*, ed. François Matheron and Oliver Corpet, trans. G. M. Goshgarian. London: Verso, 2006.

Aristophanes, *Lysistrata/The Archarnians/The Clouds*, trans. Alan H. Sommerstein. Harmondsworth: Penguin Books, 1973.

Aristotle, *Nicomachean Ethics*, trans. D. P. Chase. Mineola, NY: Dover, 1998.

—*On the Heavens*, trans. J. L. Stocks. eBooks@Adelaide, 2004.

—*The Complete Works of Aristotle*, ed. and trans. Jonathon Barnes, Bollingen Series. Princeton: Princeton University Press, 1985.

—*The Politics*, trans. T. A. Sinclair. Harmondsworth: Penguin Books, 1962.

Armitage, John, 'From discourse networks to cultural mathematics: an interview with Friedrich A. Kittler', *Theory Cuture Society*, vol. 23, no. 17, 2006.

Badiou, Alain, 'A musical variant of the metaphysics of the subject', trans. Justin Clemens, *Parrhesia*, no. 2, 2007, pp. 29–36.

—'Afterword: some replies to a demanding friend', in *Think Again: Alain Badiou and the Future of Philosophy*, ed. Peter Hallward. London: Continuum, 2004, pp. 232–7.

—'An interview with Alain Badiou: after the event: rationality and the politics of invention', conducted by 'Radical Politics', *Prelom*, no. 8, Fall, 2006.

—'Anxiety', trans. Barbara P. Faulks, *Lacanian Ink*, no. 26, 2006, pp. 70–1.

—'Beyond formalisation: an interview', trans. Bruno Bosteels and Alberto Toscano, *Angelaki: Journal of the Theoretical Humanities*, vol. 8, no. 2, 2003, pp. 111–36.

—'Fifteen theses on contemporary art', *Lacanian Ink*, vol. 23, 2004, pp. 103–19.

—'Figures of subjective destiny: on Samuel Beckett', *Lacan.com*, 2008, http://www.lacan.com/article/?page_id=21.

—'Gilles Deleuze, the fold: Leibniz and the baroque', in Constantin Boundas and Dorethea Olkowski (eds), *Deleuze and Theatre of Philosophy*, trans. Thelma Sowley. New York: Columbia, 1994, pp. 51–69.

—'Is there a theory of the subject in Georges Canguilhem?', trans. Graham Burchell, *Economy and Society*, vol. 27, no. 2/3, 1998, pp. 225–33.

—'La scène du Deux', *De L'amour*, ed. L'Ecole de la Cause Freudienne. Paris: Flammarion, 1999, pp. 177–90.

—'La subversion infinitesimal,' *Cahiers pour l'analyse*, No. 9, Summer. Paris: Seuil, 1968.
—'Lacan and the pre-Socratics', in Slavoj Žižek (ed.), *Lacan: The Silent Partners*. London: Verso, 2006, pp. 7–16.
—'Logic of the site', trans. Steve Corcoran with Bruno Bosteels, *Diacritics*, vol. 33, no. 3–4, pp. 141–50.
—'Metaphysics and the critique of metaphysics', trans. Alberto Toscano, *Pli: Warwick Journal of Philosophy*, no. 10, 2000, pp. 174–90.
—'Of an obscure disaster', trans. Barbara P. Faulks, *Lacanian Ink*, no. 22, 2004, pp. 58–99
—'Of life as a name of being, or, Deleuze's vitalist ontology', trans. Alberto Toscano, *Pli: Warwick Journal of Philosophy*, no. 10, 2000, pp. 191–9.
—'On a finally objectless subject', in Eduardo Cadava, Peter Connor and Jean-Luc Nancy (eds),*Who Comes After the Subject*, trans. Bruce Fink. New York: Routledge, pp. 24–32.
—'Philosophy and politics', trans. Thelma Sowley, *Radical Philosophy*, 1999, pp. 29–32.
—'Philosophy as biography', *The Symptom*, no. 9, 2008, http://www.lacan.com/symptom9_articles/badiou19.html.
—'Philosophy, sciences, mathematics: interview with Alain Badiou', *Collapse*, vol. 1, 2006, pp. 11–26.
—'Plato, our dear Plato!', trans. Alberto Toscano, *Angelaki*, vol. 2, no. 3, 2006, pp. 39–41.
—'Pour aujourd'hui: Platon!', Séminaire d'Alain Badiou, 2007–2008, http://www.entretemps.asso.fr/Badiou/07-08.htm.
—'The adventure of French philosophy', *New Left Review*, no. 35, 2005, pp. 67–77.
—'The communist hypothesis', *New Left Review*, 49, 2008, pp. 29–42.
—'The ethic of truths: construction and potency', trans. Selma Sowley, *Pli: Warwick Journal of Philosophy*, no. 12, 2001, pp. 245–55.
—'The event in Deleuze', trans. Jon Roffe, *Parrhesia*, no. 2, 2007, pp. 37–44.
—'The factory as event site', trans. Alberto Toscano, *Prelom*, no. 8, 2006, pp. 172–6.
—'The flux and the party: in the margins of Anti-Oedipus', trans. Laura Balladur and Simon Krysl, *Polygraph*, nos. 15–16, 2004, pp. 75–92.
—'The formulas of l'étourdit', *Lacanian Ink*, vol. 27, 2006, pp. 80–95.
—'The political as a procedure of truth', trans. Barbara P. Faulks, *Lacanian Ink*, no. 19, 2001, pp. 71–81.
—'The question of democracy: Analía Hounie interviews Alain Badiou', *Lacanian Ink*, vol. 28, 2006, pp. 54–9.
—'Towards a new concept of existence', *Lacanian Ink*, vol. 29, 2007, pp. 63–72.
—'What is a philosophical institution? Or: address, transmission, inscription', trans. A. J. Bartlett, in Paul Ashton, A. J. Bartlett and Justin Clemens (eds), *The Praxis of Alain Badiou*. Melbourne: re.press, 2007.
—'What is love?', trans. Justin Clemens, *Umbr(a)*, vol. 1, 1996, pp. 37–53.
—'Who is Nietzsche?', trans. Alberto Toscano, *Pli: Warwick Journal of Philosophy*, no. 11, 2001, pp. 1–10.
—*Being and Event*, trans. Oliver Feltham. London: Continuum, 2005.
—*Briefings on Existence: A Short Treatise on Transitory Ontology*, trans. Norman Maderasz. Albany, NY: SUNY, 2006.

—*Conditions*. Paris: Éditions du Seuil, 1992.
—*Conditions*, trans. Steve Corcoron. London: Continuum, 2008.
—*Court traité d'ontologie transitoire*. Paris: Seuil, 1998.
—*Deleuze: The Clamor of Being*, trans. Louise Burchill. Minneapolis: University of Minnesota Press, 2000.
—*Ethics: An Essay on the Understanding of Evil*, trans. Peter Hallward. London: Continuum, 2001.
—*Handbook of Inaesthetics*, trans. Alberto Toscano. Stanford: Stanford University Press, 2005.
—*Infinite Thought: Truth and the Return to Philosophy*, ed. and trans. Justin Clemens and Oliver Feltham. London: Continuum, 2003.
—*L'Etre et l'événement*. Paris: Seuil, 1988.
—*Le Concept de modèle*. Paris: Maespro, 1969.
—*Logics of Worlds*, trans. Alberto Toscano. London: Continuum, 2009.
—*Logiques des mondes: l'être et l'événement, 2*. Paris: Seuil, 2006.
—*Manifeste pour la philosophie*. Paris: Seuil, 1989.
—*Manifesto for Philosophy*, trans. Norman Maderasz. Albany, NY: SUNY Press, 1999.
—*Metapolitics*, trans. Jason Barker. London: Verso, 2005.
—*Number and Numbers*, trans. Robin Mackay. Cambridge: Polity Press, 2008.
—*On Beckett*, ed. and trans. Alberto Toscano and Nina Power. Manchester: Clinamen, 2003.
—*Petit manuel d'inesthétique*. Paris: Seuil, 1998.
—*Petit panthéon portatif*. Paris: La fabrique éditions, 2008.
—*Polemics*, ed. and trans. Steve Corcoran. London: Verso, 2006.
—*Rhapsodie pour le théâtre*. Paris: Le Spectateur français, 1990.
—*Saint Paul: The Foundation of Universalism*, trans. Ray Brassier. Stanford: Stanford University Press, 2003.
—*The Concept of Model: An Introduction to the Materialist Epistemology of Mathematics*, ed. and trans. Zachary Luke Frazer and Tzuchien Tho. Melbourne: re.press, 2007.
—*Theoretical Writings*, ed. and trans. Alberto Toscano and Ray Brassier. London: Continuum, 2004.
—*Théorie du sujet*. Paris: Seuil, 1982.
—*Theory of the Subject*, trans. Bruno Bosteels. London: Continuum, 2009.
—and Bosteels, Bruno, 'Can change be thought: a dialogue with Alain Badiou', *Alain Badiou: Philosophy and Its Conditions*, ed. Gabriel Riera. Albany, NY: SUNY Press, pp. 237–61.
—and Hallward, Peter, 'Politics and philosophy: an interview with Alain Badiou', *Angelaki*, vol. 3, no. 3, 1998, pp. 113–33.
—and Sedofsky, Lauren, 'Being by numbers', *Artforum*, October 1994, http://www.encyclopedia.com/doc/1G1-16315394.html.
—and Sedofsky, Lauren, 'Matters of appearance: an interview with Alain Badiou', *Artforum*, vol. 45, no. 3, 2006, pp. 246–53/322.
—, Fraser, Zachery Luke and Tho, Tzuchien, 'An interview with Alain Badiou: the concept of model forty years later', in *The Concept of Model*, trans. Zachery Luke Fraser and Tzuchien Tho, Melbourne: re.press, 2007, pp. 79–106.
Balibar, Etienne, 'The history of truth: Alain Badiou in French philosophy', *Radical Philosophy*, vol. 115, 2002, pp. 16–28.

Barker, Jason, *Alain Badiou: A Critical Introduction*. London: Pluto Press, 2002.
Barnes, Jonathon (ed.), *Early Greek Philosophy*. London: Penguin, 2001.
Barthes, Roland, *Sade, Fourier, Loyola*, trans. Richard Miller. Baltimore: Johns Hopkins University Press, 1997.
Bartlett, A. J., 'Conditional notes on a New *Republic*', in Paul Ashton, A. J. Bartlett and Justin Clemens (eds), *The Praxis of Alain Badiou*. Melbourne: re.press, 2006, pp. 210–42.
—'The pedagogical theme: Alain Badiou and an eventless education', *anti-Thesis*, vol. 16, 'The Event', 2006, pp. 129–47.
—and Clemens, Justin (ed.), *Badiou: Key Concepts*. London: Acumen, 2010.
Benardete, Seth, *Socrates' Second Sailing: On Plato's Republic*. Chicago: University of Chicago Press, 1989.
Benson, Hugh H. (ed.), *A Companion to Plato*. Oxford: Blackwell, 2006.
Bloom, Alan, 'Preface to the second edition', *The Republic of Plato*. New York: Basic Books, 1991, pp. vii–x.
Bosteels, Bruno, 'Alain Badiou's theory of the subject: the recommencement of dialectical materialism? (Part I)', *Pli: Warwick Journal of Philosophy*, no. 12, 2001, pp. 200–29.
—'Alain Badiou's theory of the subject: the recommencement of dialectical materialism? (Part II)', *Pli: Warwick Journal of Philosophy*, no. 13, 2002, pp. 173–208.
—'Can change be thought? A dialogue with Alain Badiou', in Gabriel Riera (ed.), *Alain Badiou: Philosophy and Its Conditions*. Albany, NY: SUNY, 2005, pp. 237–61.
Bostock, David, 'The soul and immortality in the Phaedo', *Plato 2, Ethics Politics, Religion and the Soul*, ed. Gail Fine. Oxford: Oxford University Press, 1999, pp. 404–24.
Bowe, Geoff, 'The case against teaching for pay', in Patricia O'Grady (ed.), *The Sophists: An Introduction*. London: Duckworth, 2008, pp. 226–40.
Boyd, William, *The History of Western Education*, 8th edn. London: Adam & Charles Black, 1966.
Brassier, Ray, 'Aleatory rationalism, post-face to Alain Badiou's *Theoretical Writings*'. Unpublished manuscript, 2004.
—'Enigma of realism', *Collapse: Journal of Philosophical Research and Development*, vol. II, March 2007, pp. 15–24.
—'Presentation as anti-phenomenon in Alain Badiou's *Being and Event*', *Continental Philosophy Review*, vol. 39, no. 1, March 2006, pp. 59–77.
—Badiou's materialist epistemology of mathematics', *Angelaki: Journal of Theoretical Humanities*, vol. 10, no. 2, 2005, pp. 135–50.
—*Nihil Unbound*. London: Continuum, 2008.
Brecht, Bertoldt, 'Socrates wounded', in Frederick R. Karl and Leo Hamalian (eds), *The Existential Imagination*. London: Pan Books, 1973, pp. 132–44.
Brickhouse, Thomas, C. and Smith, Nicholas, D., *Routledge Philosophy Guidebook to Plato and the Trial of Socrates*. New York: Routledge, 2004.
—*The Philosophy of Socrates*. Boulder: Westview Press, 1999.
Brunschwig, Jacques and Lloyd, Geoffrey E. R., *Greek Thought: A Guide to Classical Knowledge*, ed. with the collaboration of Pierre Pellegrin. Cambridge, MA: Belknap Press of Harvard University Press, 2000.
Burnyeat, M. F., 'Utopia and fantasy: the practicability of Plato's ideally just city', in

Gail Fine (ed.), *Plato 2, Ethics Politics, Religion and the Soul*. Oxford: Oxford University Press, 1999, pp. 297–308.

Bury, J. B. and Meiggs, Russell, *The History of Greece to the Death of Alexander the Great*. London: Macmillan, 1975.

Cassin, Barbara, 'From organism to picnic: which consensus for which city?', *Angelaki*, vol. 11, no. 3, December 2006, pp. 21–38.

—'Who's afraid of the sophists? Against ethical correctness', trans. Charles T. Wolfe, *Hypatia*, vol. 15, no. 4, Fall, 2000, pp. 102–20.

—*L'effet sophistique*. Paris: Gallimard, 1995.

Chiesa, Lorenzo, 'Le resort de l'amour: Lacan's theory of love in his reading of Plato's Symposium', *Angelaki*, vol. II, no. 3, December, 2006, pp. 61–80.

Clay, Diskin, *Platonic Questions: Dialogues with the Silent Philosopher*. University Park: Pennsylvania State University Press, 2000.

Clemens, Justin, 'Doubles of nothing: the problem of binding truth to being in the work of Alain Badiou', *Filozofski Vestnik*, vol. 26, no. 2, 2005, pp. 21–35.

—'Had we but worlds enough, and time, this absolute, philosopher . . .', *Cosmos and History*, vol. 1, no. 1–2, 2006, pp. 277–310.

—'Letters as the condition of conditions for Alain Badiou', *Communication and Cognition*, vol. 36, no. 1–2, 2003, pp. 73–102.

—'Platonic meditations', *Pli: Warwick Journal of Philosophy*, vol. 11, 2001, pp. 200–29.

—*The Romanticism of Contemporary Theory: Institution, Aesthetics, Nihilism*. Aldershot: Ashgate, 2003.

Cohen, I. Bernard, *Revolutions in Science*. Cambridge, MA: Belknap Press, 1985.

Cohen, Paul J., *Set Theory and the Continuum Hypothesis*. New York: W. A. Benjamin, 1966.

Cornford, F. M., 'Mathematics and the dialectic in the Republic VI–VII (I)', *Mind*, New Series, vol. 41, no. 161, January 1932, pp. 37–52.

—'Mathematics and the dialectic in the Republic VI–VII (II)', *Mind*, New Series, vol. 41, no. 162, April 1932, pp. 173–90.

—*From Religion to Philosophy: A Study in the Origins of Western Speculation*. New York: Harper & Row, 1957.

—*Principium Sapientiae: The Origins of Greek Philosophical Thought*. Cambridge: Cambridge University Press, 1952.

Dancy, R. M., *Plato's Introduction of Forms*. Cambridge: Cambridge University Press, 2004.

Dauben, Joseph W., 'Georg Cantor and the battle for transfinite set theory', *Proceedings of the 9th ACMS Conference*. Westmont College, Santa Barbara, CA, 2004, pp. 1–22.

Daubier, Jean, *History of the Chinese Cultural Revolution*, trans. Richard Sever. New York: Vintage Books, 1974.

De Romilly, Jacqueline, *The Great Sophists of Periclean Athens*, trans. Janet Lloyd. Oxford: Clarendon Press, 1992.

Deleuze, Gilles, *Difference and Repetition*, trans. Paul Patton. London: Continuum, 2004.

—*The Logic of Sense*, trans. Mark Lester and Charles Stivale. New York: Columbia University Press, 1990.

Derrida, Jacques, 'Plato's pharmacy', in *A Derrida Reader: Between the Blinds*, ed. and trans. Peggy Kamuf. New York: Harvester Wheatsheaf, 1991.

—*Dissemination*, trans. Barbara Johnson. London: Continuum, 2004.
—*Eyes of the University: Right to Philosophy 2*, trans. Jan Plug et al. Stanford: Stanford University Press, 2004.
—*The Post Card: From Socrates to Freud*, trans. Alan Bass. Chicago: University of Chicago Press, 1987
—*Who's Afraid of Philosophy: Right to Philosophy 1*, trans. Jan Plug. Stanford: Stanford University Press, 2002.
Desanti, Jean-Toussaint, 'Some remarks on the intrinsic ontology of Alain Badiou', in Peter Hallward (ed.), *Think Again: Alain Badiou and the Future of Philosophy*. London: Continuum Books, 2004, pp. 59–66.
Descartes, René, 'Meditations on first philosophy', in *The Philosophical Works of Descartes: Volume I*, ed. and trans. Elizabeth S. Haldane and G. R. T. Ross. Cambridge: Cambridge University Press, 1969, pp. 131–99.
Dewey, John, *Democracy and Education*. New York: Free Press, 1966.
Dolar, Mladen, *A Voice and Nothing More*. Cambridge, MA: MIT Press, 2006.
During, Elie, 'How much truth can art bear? On Badiou's "Inaesthetics"', *Polygraph*, vol. 17, 2005, pp. 143–55.
Ehrenberg, Victor, *From Solon to Socrates*. London: Methuen, 1968.
Eiland, Howard, 'The pedagogy of shadow: Heidegger and Plato', *boundary 2*, vol. 16, no. 2/3, Winter–Spring 1989, pp. 13–39.
Emerson, Ralph Waldo, *Representative Men: The Complete Prose Works of Ralph Waldo Emerson*. London: Ward, Lock & Co., 1900.
Empiricus, Sextus, *Against the Logicians*, ed. and trans. Richard Bett. Cambridge: Cambridge University Press, 2005.
Feltham, Oliver, 'And being and event and . . .: philosophy and its nominations', *Polygraph*, vol. 17, 2005, pp. 27–40.
—'As Fire Burns'. Unpublished PhD thesis, Deakin University, Melbourne, 2000.
—'Singularity happening in politics: the Aboriginal Tent Embassy, Canberra 1972', *Communication and Cognition*, vol. 37, no. 3–4, 2004, pp. 225–45.
—*Alain Badiou: Live Theory*. London: Continuum, 2008.
Ferguson, John (ed. and partially trans.), *Socrates: A Source Book*. London: Macmillan for the Open University Press, 1970.
Ferrari, G. R. F., 'Editor's introduction', G. R. F. Ferrari (ed.), *The Cambridge Companion to Plato's Republic*. Cambridge: Cambridge University Press, 2007, pp. xv–xxvi.
Fine, Gail (ed.), *Plato 1, Metaphysics and Epistemology*. Oxford: Oxford University Press, 1999.
—*Plato 2, Ethics, Politics, Religion, and the Soul*. Oxford: Oxford University Press, 1999.
Fink, Bruce, *The Lacanian Subject: Between Language and Jouissance*. Princeton: Princeton University Press.
Fontenrose, Joseph, *The Delphic Oracle: Its Responses and Operations with a Catalogue of Reasons*. Berkeley: University of California Press, 1978.
Fraser, Zachary, 'The law of the subject: Alain Badiou, Luitzen Brouwer and the Kripkean analyses of forcing and the Heyting calculus', *Cosmos and History*, vol. 1, no. 1–2, 2006, pp. 94–133.
—'This Infinite, Unanimous Dissonance: A Study in Mathematical Existentialism, Through the Work of Jean-Paul Sartre and Alain Badiou'. Unpublished master's thesis, 2008.

Geach, P. T., 'Plato's *Euthyphro*: an analysis and commentary', *The Monist*, no. 50, 1966, pp. 369–82.

—*Logic Matters*. Berkeley: University of California Press, 1972.

Gill, Mary Louise and Pellegrin, Pierre (eds), *A Companion to Ancient Philosophy*. Malden: Blackwell, 2006.

Gillespie, Sam, *The Mathematics of Novelty: Badiou's Minimalist Metaphysics*. Melbourne: re.press, 2008.

Gramsci, Antonio, *Selections from the Prison Notebooks*, trans. Quentin Hoare and Geoffrey Nowell-Smith. New York: International Publishers, 1971.

Grigg, Russell, 'Lacan and Badiou: logic of the pas-tout', *Filozofski Vestnik*, vol. 26, no. 2, 2005, pp. 53–66.

Griswold, Charles L. Jr, 'Plato's metaphilosophy: why Plato wrote dialogues', in Charles L. Griswold, Jr (ed.), *Platonic Writings, Platonic Readings*. New York: Routledge, 1988, pp. 143–67.

Grote, George, *Plato, and the Other Companions of Sokrates*. Bristol: Thoemmes Press, 1992.

Gulley, Norman, *Plato's Theory of Knowledge*. London: Methuen, 1962.

Guthrie, W. K. C., *History of Greek Philosophy*, Vol. 3. Cambridge: Cambridge University Press, 1969.

—*Socrates and Plato*. Brisbane: University of Queensland Press, 1958.

Hallward, Peter, *Badiou: A Subject to Truth*. Minneapolis: University of Minnesota Press, 2003.

—(ed.), *Think Again: Alain Badiou and the Future of Philosophy*. London: Continuum, 2004.

Havelock, Eric, *Preface to Plato*. Oxford: Blackwell, 1963.

Hegel, G. W. F., *Lectures on the History of Philosophy, Vol. 2*, trans. E. S. Haldane and Frances H. Simson. Lincoln, NE: University of Nebraska Press, 1995.

Heidegger, Martin, *Pathmarks*, ed. and trans. William McNeill. Cambridge: Cambridge University Press, 1998.

—*Plato's Sophist*, trans. Richard Rojcewicz and André Schuwer. Bloomington: Indiana University Press, 1997.

Heijenoort, Jean van (ed.), *From Frege to Gödel: A Source Book in Mathematical Logic, 1879–1931*. Cambridge, MA: Harvard University Press, 1967.

Heraclitus, *The Fragments of the Work of Heraclitus of Ephesus On Nature*, trans. G. T. W. Patrick from the Greek text of I. Bywater. Chicago: Argonaut, 1969.

Homer, *The Iliad*, trans. E. V. Rieu. London: Penguin Books, 1966.

—*The Odyssey*, trans. E. V. Rieu. Baltimore: Penguin Books, 1946.

Irwin, Terence, *Classical Thought*. Oxford: Oxford University Press, 1989.

—*Plato's Moral Theory: The Early and Middle Dialogues*. Oxford: Clarendon Press, 1977.

Isocrates, 'Against the Sophists', 1, in *Isocrates: On the Peace. Areopagiticus. Against the Sophists. Antidosis. Panathenaicus*, trans. George Norlin. Loeb Classical Library, 1929.

Kahn, Charles, H., 'Response to Christopher Rowe', *Journal of the International Plato Society*, http://www.nd.edu/~plato/plato2issue/kahn.htm.

—*Plato and the Socratic Dialogue: The Philosophical Use of a Literary Form*. Cambridge: Cambridge University Press, 1996.

Kant, Immanuel, *Education*, trans. Annette Churton. Ann Arbor: University of Michigan Press, 1960.

Kerferd, G. B., *The Sophistic Movement*. Cambridge: Cambridge University Press, 1981.
Kierkegaard, Søren, *Concluding Unscientific Postscript*, trans. David F. Swenson and Walter Lowrie. Princeton: Princeton University Press, 1968.
—*The Concept of Irony: With Constant Reference to Socrates*, trans. Lee M. Capel. New York: Octagon Books, 1983.
Kittler, Friedrich, 'Number and numeral', *Theory, Culture and Society*, vol. 23, nos. 7–8, 2006, pp. 54–61.
Klein, Jacob, *Greek Mathematical Thought and the Origin of Algebra*, trans. Eva Brann. Cambridge, MA: MIT Press, 1968.
Kofman, Sarah, *Socrates, Fictions of a Philosopher*, trans. Catherine Porter. London: Athlone Press, 1998.
Kraut, Richard, 'The examined life', in Sara Ahbel-Rappe and Rachana Kamtekar (eds), *A Companion to Socrates*. Malden: Blackwell, 2006, pp. 228–42.
Lacan, Jacques, *Ecrits: The First Complete Edition in English*, trans. Bruce Fink with Heloise Fink and Russell Grigg. New York: W. W. Norton, 2006.
—Seminar XXIII, 1975–6, ed. Jacques-Alain Miller, trans. from the *texte établi* by Luke Thurston, *Ornicar?*, 1976–7, pp. 6–11.
—*The Seminar of Jacques Lacan, Book I: Freud's Papers on Technique 1953–1954*, ed. Jacques-Alain Miller, trans. John Forrester. New York: Norton, 1991.
—*The Seminar of Jacques Lacan, Book VII: The Ethics of Psychoanalysis, 1959–1960*, ed. Jacques-Alain Miller, trans. Dennis Porter. New York: Norton, 1992.
—*The Seminar of Jacques Lacan, Book XVII: The Other Side of Psychoanalysis*, ed. Jacques-Alain Miller, trans. Russell Grigg. New York: Norton, 2007.
—*The Seminar of Jacques Lacan, Book XX: On Feminine Sexuality, The Limits of Love and Knowledge, 1972–1973*, ed. Jacques-Alain Miller, trans. Bruce Fink. New York: Norton, 1999.
Laertius, Diogenes, *Lives of Eminent Philosophers*, trans. R. D. Hicks. London: Heinemann, 1925.
Lazarus, Sylvain, 'A propos de la politique et la terreur', in *La République et la Terreur*, sous la direction de Catherine Kintzler et de Hadi Rizk. Paris: Éditions Kimé, 1995.
—*L'Anthropologie du nom*. Paris: Seuil, 1996.
Leibniz, G. W., *Selections*, ed. Philip P. Wiener. New York: Charles Scribner's Sons, 1951.
Lenin, V. I., *On the Intelligentsia*. Moscow: Progress Publishers, 1983.
Ling, Alex, 'Can Cinema Be Thought?: Alain Badiou and the Artistic Condition', in Paul Ashton, A. J. Bartlett and Justin Clemens (eds), *The Praxis of Alain Badiou*. Melbourne: re.press, 2006, pp. 291–305.
—*Badiou and Cinema*. Edinburgh: Edinburgh University Press, 2010.
Lodge, R. C., *Plato's Theory of Education*. New York: Harcourt, Brace & Co., 1947.
Lucretius, *The Nature of the Universe*, trans. R. E. Latham. Harmondsworth: Penguin Books, 1951.
Lyotard, Jean-François, *Libidinal Economy*, trans. Iain Hamilton Grant. Bloomington: Indiana University Press, 1993.
—*The Postmodern Condition: A Report on Knowledge*, trans. Geoff Bennington and Brian Massumi. Minneapolis: University of Minnesota Press, 1984.

McCoy, Marina, *Plato on the Rhetoric of Philosophers and Sophists*, Cambridge: Cambridge University Press, 2008.
McKim, Richard, 'Shame and truth in *Plato's Gorgias*', in Charles L. Griswold Jr (ed.), *Platonic Writings, Platonic Readings*. New York: Routledge, 1988.
Madison-Mount, B., 'The Cantorian revolution', *Polygraph*, no. 17, 2005, ed. Mathew Wilkens, pp. 41–91.
Marx, Karl, *The Class Struggles in France (1848–50)*. New York: International Publishers, 1964.
—and Engels, Friedrich, *Manifesto of the Communist Party*. Moscow: Foreign Languages, 1959.
Meillassoux, Quentin, 'Potentiality and virtuality', *Collapse: Journal of Philosophical Research and Development*, vol. II, March 2007, pp. 55–81.
—*After Finitude: An Essay on the Necessity of Contingency*, trans. Ray Brassier. London: Continuum, 2008.
Miller, Jacques-Alain, 'On shame', in Russell Grigg and Justin Clemens (eds), *Jacques Lacan and the Other Side of Psychoanalysis*. Durham, NC and London: Duke University Press, 2006, pp. 11–28.
—'Philosophy <> psychoanalysis', trans. Justin Clemens. Melbourne: unpublished, 2008.
Montiglio, Silvia, 'Wandering philosophers in classical Greece', *Journal of Hellenic Studies*, vol. 120, 2000, pp. 86–105.
Morrison, Donald, A., 'The utopian character of Plato's ideal city', in G. R. F. Ferrari (ed.), *The Cambridge Companion to Plato's Republic*. Cambridge: Cambridge University Press, 2007, pp. 236–51.
Nails, Debra, 'The trial and death of Socrates', in Sara Ahbel-Rappe and Rachana Kamtekar (eds), *A Companion to Socrates*. Malden: Blackwell, 2006, pp. 5–20.
—*Agora, Academy, and the Conduct of Philosophy*. Dordrecht: Kluwer Academic, 1995.
—*The People of Plato: A Prosopography of Plato and other Socratics*. Indianapolis, IN: Hackett, 2002.
Navia, Luis E., *Classical Cynicism: A Critical Study*. Westport, CT: Greenwood Press, 1996.
Nehamas, Alexander, 'Plato on the imperfection of the sensible world', in Gail Fine (ed.), *Plato 1, Metaphysics and Epistemology*. Oxford: Oxford University Press, 1999, pp. 171–90.
—*The Virtues of Authenticity*. Princeton: Princeton University Press, 1999.
Nettleship, R. L., *The Theory of Education in Plato's Republic*. London: Oxford University Press, 1935.
Nietzsche, Friedrich, 'Schopenhauer as educator', *Untimely Meditations*, ed. Daniel Breazeale, trans. R. J. Hollingdale. Cambridge: Cambridge University Press, 1997, pp. 125–94.
—*Beyond Good and Evil*, trans. R. J. Hollingdale. Harmondsworth: Penguin, 1973.
—*On the Future of Our Educational Institutions*, trans. Michael W. Grenke. South Bend, IN: St Augustine's Press, 2004, Lecture III, pp. 175–6.
—*Thus Spoke Zarathustra*, trans. Walter Kaufmann. Harmondsworth: Penguin Books, 1966.
O'Grady, Patricia (ed.), *The Sophists: An Introduction*. London: Duckworth, 2008.
Pascal, Blaise, *Pensées*, trans. A. J. Krailsheimer. Harmondsworth: Penguin, 1966.

Peters, F. E., *Greek Philosophical Terms: A Historical Lexicon*. New York: New York University Press, 1967.
Plato, *Complete Works*, ed. John M. Cooper and associate ed. D. S. Hutchinson. Indianapolis, IN: Hackett, 1997.
—*Apology*, trans. G. M. A. Grube, pp. 17–36.
—*Charmides*, trans. Rosamond Kent Sprague, pp. 639–63.
—*Cratylus*, trans. pp. 101–56.
—*Critias*, trans. Diskin Clay, pp. 1292–306.
—*Crito*, trans. G. M. A. Grube, 37–48.
—*Euthydemus*, trans. Rosamond Kent Sprague, pp. 708–45.
—*Euthyphro*, trans. G. M. A. Grube, pp. 1–16.
—*Gorgias*, trans. Donald J. Zuel, pp. 791–869.
—*Greater Hippias*, trans. Paul Woodruff, pp. 898–921.
—*Ion*, trans. Paul Woodruff, pp. 937–49.
—*Laches*, trans. Rosamond Kent Sprague, pp. 664–86.
—*Laws*, trans. Trevor J. Saunders, pp. 1318–616.
—*Lesser Hippias*, trans. Nicholas D. Smith, pp. 922–36.
—*Letters*, Glenn R. Morrow, pp. 1634–76.
—*Lysis*, trans. Stanley Lombardo, 687–707.
—*Menexenus*, trans. Paul Ryan, pp. 950–64.
—*Meno*, trans. G. M. A. Grube, pp. 870–97.
—*Parmenides*, trans. Mary Louise Gill and Paul Ryan, pp. 359–97.
—*Phaedo*, trans. G. M. A. Grube, pp. 49–100.
—*Phaedrus*, trans. Alexander Nehamas and Paul Woodruff, pp. 506–56.
—*Philebus*, trans. Dorothea Frede, pp. 398–456.
—*Protagoras*, trans. Stanley Lombardo and Karen Bell, pp. 746–90.
—*Republic*, trans. G. M. A. Grube, rev. C. D. C. Reeve, pp. 971–1223.
—*Sophist*, trans. Nicholas P. White, pp. 235–93.
—*Statesman*, trans. C. J. Rowe, pp. 294–358.
—*Symposium*, trans. Alexander Nehamas and Paul Woodruff, pp. 457–505.
—*Theaetetus*, trans. M. J. Levett, rev. Myles Burnyeat, pp. 157–234.
—*Timaeus*, trans. Donald J. Zeyl, pp. 1224–91.
—*Apology*, trans. Hugh Tredennick, in *The Last Days of Socrates*. Harmondsworth: Penguin, 1954.
—*Cratylus*, trans. H. N. Fowler, in *Plato: with an English Translation*, Vol. IV, trans. Harold North Fowler, W. R. M. Lamb, R. G. Bury and Paul Shorey. Cambridge, MA: Harvard University Press, 1914–39.
—*Euthyphro*, trans. Lane Cooper, in *Plato: The Collected Dialogues*, ed. Edith Hamilton and Huntington Cairns, Bollingen Series LXXI. Princeton: Princeton University Press, 1961.
—*Gorgias*, trans. W. Hamilton. Harmondsworth: Penguin Books, 1960.
—*Laws*, trans. Trevor J. Saunders. London: Penguin, 2004.
—*Parmenides*, in *Plato and Parmenides: Parmenides' Way of Truth and Plato's Parmenides*, trans. with running commentary, Francis MacDonald Cornford. London: Routledge & Kegan Paul, 1939.
—*Plato's Cosmology: The Timaeus of Plato*, trans. with running commentary, Francis MacDonald Cornford. London: Routledge & Kegan Paul, 1948.
—*Plato's Parmenides*, trans. S. Scolnicov. Berkeley: University of California Press, 2003.

—*Plato's Theory of Knowledge: The Theaetetus and the Sophist*, trans. with running commentary by Francis MacDonald Cornford. Mineola, NY: Dover, 2003.
—*Protagoras and Meno*, trans. W. K. C. Guthrie. London: Penguin, 1956.
—*The Republic*, trans. Paul Shorey, in *Plato: The Collected Dialogues*, ed. Edith Hamilton and Huntington Cairns, Bollingen Series LXXI. Princeton: Princeton University Press, 1961.
—*The Republic*, trans. Desmond Lee. London: Penguin Classics, 1974.
—*The Republic of Plato*, trans. Alan Bloom. New York: Basic Books, 1991.
—*The Republic of Plato*, trans. with running commentary, Francis MacDonald Cornford. New York: Oxford University Press, 1945.
—*The Symposium*, trans. Christopher Gill. London: Penguin Classics, 1999.
Plutarch, *The Rise and Fall of Athens*, trans. Ian Scott-Kilvert. Baltimore: Penguin, 1960.
Queensland Department of Education and Training, 'New Basics Research Program', http://education.qld.gov.au/corproate/newbasics, 2010.
Rancière, Jacques, 'Aesthetics, inaesthetics, anti-aesthetics', in Peter Hallward (ed.), *Think Again: Alain Badiou and the Future of Philosophy*. London: Continuum, 2004, pp. 218–31.
—*Disagreement: Politics and Philosophy*, trans. Julie Rose. Minneapolis: University of Minnesota Press, 1999.
—*On the Shores of Politics*, trans. Liz Heron. London: Verso, 2007.
—*The Ignorant Schoolmaster: Five Lessons in Intellectual Emancipation*, trans. Kristin Ross. Stanford: Stanford University Press, 1991.
—*The Philosopher and His Poor*, trans. John Dury, Corrinne Oster and Andrew Parker. Durham, NC and London: Duke University Press, 2003.
Rankin, H. D., *Sophists, Socratics and Cynics*. London: Croom-Helm, 1983.
Reeve, C. D. C., 'A study in violets: Alcibiades in the Symposium', in J. H. Lesher, Debra Nails and Frisbee C. C. Sheffield (eds), *Plato's Symposium: Issues in Interpretation and Reception*. Cambridge, MA: Harvard University Press, 2006, pp. 124–46.
Rorty, Amélie Oksenberg (ed.), *Philosophers on Education: New Historical Perspectives*. London: Routledge, 1998.
Rorty, Richard, *Contingency, Irony, and Solidarity*. Cambridge: Cambridge University Press, 1989.
—*Philosophy and the Mirror of Nature*. Princeton: Princeton University Press, 1979.
Rosen, Stanley, *Plato's Symposium*. New Haven, CT: Yale University Press, 1968.
Rosivach, Vincent J., 'Some Athenian pre-suppositions about the poor', *Greece and Rome*, 2nd Series, vol. 38, no. 2, October 1991, pp. 189–98.
Ross, Kristin, *May '68 and Its Afterlives*. Chicago: University of Chicago Press, 2002.
—*The Emergence of Social Space : Rimbaud and the Paris Commune*. Minneapolis: University of Minnesota Press, 1988.
Rousseau, J.-J., *The Social Contract and Discourses*, trans. G. D. H. Cole. London: Dent, 1966.
Rowe, Christopher, 'Socrates in Plato's Dialogues', in Sara Ahbel-Rappe and Rachana Kamtekar (eds), *A Companion to Socrates*. Malden: Blackwell, 2006, pp. 159–70.

Safoun, Moustapha, *Why Are The Arabs Not Free – The Politics of Writing*. Malden: Blackwell, 2007.

Saint Augustine, *City of God*, trans. Henry Bettenson. London: Penguin Classics, 2003.

Sallis, John, *Being and Logos: Reading the Platonic Dialogues*. Bloomington: Indiana University Press, 1996.

Saltman, Kenneth J. and Gabbard, David A. (eds), *Education as Enforcement: The Militarization and Corporatization of Schools*. New York: RoutledgeFalmer, 2003.

Saunders, A. N. W. (ed. and trans.), *Greek Political Oratory*. Harmondsworth: Penguin Books, 1970.

Schleiermacher, Friedrich, *Schleiermacher's Introduction to the Dialogues of Plato*, trans. William Dobson. London: Pitt Press, 1836.

Scolnicov, Samuel, 'Two faces of Platonic knowledge', *Journal of International Plato Studies*, no. 4, http://www.nd.edu/~plato/plato4issue/Scolnicov.pdf.

—*Plato's Metaphysics of Education*. London: Routledge, 1988.

Scott, Dominic, 'Platonic recollection', in Gail Fine (ed.), *Plato 1, Metaphysics and Epistemology*. Oxford: Oxford University Press, 1999, pp. 93–124.

Sellars, John, 'The problem of Socrates: review of Sarah Kofman', *Socrates: Fictions of* a *Philosopher*', *Pli: Warwick Journal of Philosophy*, vol. 10, 2000, pp. 267–75.

Shorey, Paul, *What Plato Said*. Chicago: University of Chicago Press, 1933.

Strauss, Leo, *The Argument and the Action of Plato's Laws*. Chicago: University of Chicago Press, 1975.

Szabó, Árpád, *The Beginnings of Greek Mathematics*, trans. A. M. Ungar. Dordrecht: Reidel, 1978.

Tarrant, Harold, *Plato's Earliest Interpreters*. London: Duckworth, 2000.

Taylor, C. C. W., 'Plato's totalitarianism', in Gail Fine (ed.), *Plato 2, Ethics Politics, Religion and the Soul*. Oxford: Oxford University Press, 1999, pp. 280–96.

—(ed. and trans), *The Atomists, Leucippus and Democritus: Fragments*. Toronto: University of Toronto Press, 1999.

—*Socrates*. New York: Oxford University Press, 1998.

Thucydides, *History of the Peloponnesian War*, trans. Rex Warner. Harmondsworth: Penguin Books, 1972; trans. Charles Foster Smith. London: Heinemann, Books I–VIII, LXXXIV.

Tiles, Mary, *The Philosophy of Set Theory: An Historical Introduction to Cantor's Paradise*. New York: Dover, 1989.

Toscano, Alberto, 'Communism as separation', in Peter Hallward (ed.), *Think Again: Alain Badiou and the Future of Philosophy*. London: Continuum Books, 2004, pp. 138–49.

Tse-Tung, Mao, *Combat Liberalism*. Peking: Foreign Languages Press, 1954.

—*Oppose Book Worship*. Peking: Foreign Languages Press, 1930.

Untersteiner, Mario, *The Sophists*, trans. Kathleen Freeman. Oxford: Basil Blackwell, 1954.

Urmson, J. O., *The Greek Philosophical Vocabulary*. London: Duckworth, 1990.

Vlastos, Gregory, 'Epilogue: Socrates and Vietnam', in Miles Burnyeat (ed.), *Socratic Studies*. New York: Cambridge University Press, 1994, pp. 127–33.

—'Socrates' disavowal of knowledge', in Gail Fine (ed.), *Plato 1, Metaphysics and Epistemology*. Oxford: Oxford University Press, 1999, pp. 64–92.

—'The historical Socrates and Athenian democracy', in Myles Burnyeat (ed.), *Socratic Studies*. New York: Cambridge University Press, 1994.
—'The Socratic elenchus', in Gail Fine (ed.), *Plato 1, Metaphysics and Epistemology*. Oxford: Oxford University Press, 1999, pp. 36–63.
—*Exegesis and Argument: Studies in Greek Philosophy Presented to Gregory Vlastos*, ed. E. N. Lee, A. P. D. Mourelatos and R. M. Rorty. New York: Humanities Press, 1973.
—*Plato: A Collection of Critical Essays*. Garden City, NY: Anchor Books, 1971.
—*Socrates, Ironist and Moral Philosopher*. Ithaca, NY: Cornell University Press, 1991.
—*Studies in Greek philosophy*, ed. Daniel W. Graham. Princeton: Princeton University Press, 1995.
—(ed.), *The Philosophy of Socrates*. Garden City, NY: Anchor Books, 1971.
—(ed.), *The Philosophy of Socrates*. Notre Dame, IN: University of Notre Dame Press, 1980.
Wahl, François, 'Le soustractif', in Alain Badiou, *Conditions*. Paris: Seuil, 1991.
Waterfield, Robin, *The First Philosophers: The Pre-Socratics and the Sophists*. Oxford: Oxford University Press, 2000.
Woodruff, Paul, 'Socrates amongst the Sophists,' in Sara Ahbel-Rappe and Rachana Kamtekar (eds), *A Companion to Socrates*. Malden: Blackwell, 2006, pp. 36–47.
White, Michael J., 'Plato and mathematics', in Hugh Benson (ed.), *A Companion to Plato*. Malden: Blackwell, 2006.
Whitehead, A. N., *Process and Reality*. New York: Free Press, 1979, p. 30.
—*The Aims of Education and Other Essays*. London: Williams & Norgate, 1929.
Xenophon, *Memoirs of Socrates & The Symposium (The Dinner Party)*, trans. Hugh Tredennick. Harmondsworth: Penguin, 1970.
—*The Anabasis of Cyrus/Xenophon*, trans. and annotated Wayne Ambler. New York: Cornell University Press, 2008.
—*The Shorter Socratic Writings: Apology of Socrates to the Jury, Oeconomicus, and Symposium*, trans. Robert C. Bartlett. New York: Cornell University Press, 1996.
Zilioli, Ugo, *Protagoras and the Challenge of Relativism: Plato's Subtlest Enemy*. Aldershot: Ashgate, 2007.
Žižek, Slavoj, 'From purification to subtraction: Badiou and the Real', in Peter Hallward (ed.), *Think Again: Alain Badiou and the Future of Philosophy*. London: Continuum, 2004, pp. 165–81.
—(ed.), *Lacan: The Silent Partners*. London: Verso, 2006.
—*The Ticklish Subject: The Absent Centre of Political Ontology*. London: Polity Press, 1999.
Zuckert, Catherine H., *Postmodern Platos*. Chicago: University of Chicago Press, 1996.
Zupančič, Alenka, 'Enthusiasm, anxiety and the event', *Parallax*, vol. 11, no. 4, 2005, pp. 31–45.

Index